Weapons and Tactics

HASTINGS TO BERLIN

JAC WELLER

Weapons and Tactics

HASTINGS TO BERLIN

WITH NINE MAPS AND FORTY-EIGHT PAGES OF PLATES

NICHOLAS VANE
LONDON

First published by
NICHOLAS VANE (Publishers) LIMITED
194–200 Bishopsgate, London, EC2
1966

Printed in England by
ADLARD AND SON LIMITED
London and Dorking

DEDICATION

To the Soldiers of the Free World and the U.S. Marines

Contents

Illustrations

A German crew with their Model 1908 Maxim MMG
German Maxim Model 1908 MMG with crew in gas masks
British soldiers with a tank, field guns, SMLE rifles and Lewis
  ARs
An Italian soldier in the trenches with a periscope-sighting rifle
The three main allied MMGs of World War I

BETWEEN PAGES 72 AND 73

A British ·303 water-cooled Vickers MMG
The Meuse-Argonne offensive
The Springfield Model 1903 calibre ·30-'06 rifle and bayonet
Outpost sentries in the Forest of Paroy, World War I
French rifle-armed infantry mingling with British MMG crews
US artillerymen about to fire one of the primitive mortars
  widely used in 1918
A US soldier firing his BAR in combat in the Philippines in 1945
US Marines at Iwo Jima

BETWEEN PAGES 88 AND 89

A German soldier in Russia camouflaged so as to blend in with
  the snow
German MG 34 and crew in Russia
A German MG 34 with biopod mount on a sled firing from a
  drum magazine
A water-cooled Maxim Model 1908-15 MMG reactivated for
  AA defence in the Pas de Calais area in France, 1943
A German 8-cm. mortar crew in a defensive position
German infantry with their auxiliary transport, a one-mule cart
German troops practising for the proposed invasion of England
  during the summer of 1940
A German mobile AT gun crew with the reducing bore 28-20-
  mm. high-velocity weapon that was of considerable value
  early in World War II
German soldiers handling a captured Model 1910 Russian
  Maxim MMG on an estuary next to the Black Sea

BETWEEN PAGES 104 AND 105

Light AT rifles of Germany and Britain
The famous German MG 42 with bipod mount
The equally famous US BAR

A US Army 75-mm. RR team in action

Weapons used to a considerable extent by US Army and USMC in the Korean conflict

A Marine Corps flame-thrower in action against an enemy pill-box in Korea

A USMC 75-mm. RR team in a road-block position in Korea

British and Swiss revolvers

The British BREN AR and Sten SMG, the German Model 1898-37 rifle and MP44 assault rifle

BETWEEN PAGES 120 AND 121

The new US 90-mm. RR

A modification of the US M14 fully-automatic rifle

A simple Viet Cong single-shot smoothbore weapon of village manufacture

US M60 GPMG

The Stoner 63 rifle

French infantry rifle Model 1949-56 and the AT rifle grenade

Norwegian rifle company weapons

Spanish CETME assault rifle being fired from the shoulder

The Netherlands AR-10 assault rifle being fired from a prone position with bipod mounts

A British infantryman firing an ENERGA AT rifle grenade from the SLR

A British soldier firing the new GPMG from a bipod mount AR fashion

The unique British 2-in. mortar being fired in the open

BETWEEN PAGES 136 AND 137

The Danish Madsen AR and crew with a tripod mount to convert it to an MMG

The Danish 81-mm. mortar crew firing on manoeuvres

Danish jeep-mounted 106 RRs and crews in a typical setting

The jeep-mounted 106-mm. RR and Spanish soldiers

Turkish soldiers and their bolt-action Mauser rifles

A Belgian soldier with a FALO rifle, bipod attached

A French soldier firing an AT grenade from the Model 1949-56 French service rifle

A FALO team firing from the prone position

The compact Turkish service pistol
A Turkish soldier and his Hotchkiss Squad AR
This Turkish soldier has a US model 1919A6 MMG
Turkish soldiers with a Cal ·50 MMG

BETWEEN PAGES 152 AND 153

A small task force of eight US Marines going ashore
US soldier in a one-man flying machine
US Marines leaving a helicopter fast during manoeuvres in
    North Carolina
US MG equipment transported by helicopters
A Greek MMG team with the Model 1919A4 weapon
Training in the Greek army with the 57-mm. RR
A Canadian regimental serjeant major with the A2E3 SMG
A Canadian crew fires an 81-mm. mortar
A Canadian rifle squad in front of their APC

BETWEEN PAGES 168 AND 169

A British Vickers ·303 MMG and crew
British demonstration team with an RR of large size
The modern West German AT weapon
A West German G3 rifle being fired off-hand
A West German soldier and the Uzi SMG
Greek infantry armed predominantly with British weapons
Five Italian soldiers armed with SMGs, a BAR and M1s
The Spanish ALFA Model 1955 MMG
The new French Model 1952 GPMG in two separate versions
A special night-illuminating device mounted on a US Model
    1919 A4 MMG

BETWEEN PAGES 184 AND 185

French rifle instruction with the Model 1949-56
Netherlands rifle training with instructor and two recruits
A Canadian APC which is actually a converted tank
The US M60 tank and M113APC
The US M113 APC
The author firing the Russian Models 1943 PPS SMG, the DP
    AR or LMG and the SK3 carbine
Three semi-military or military shotguns
Weapons captured from the Viet Cong

Illustrations

A Norwegian soldier and the folding stock Schmeisser (MP40) SMG

The present family of US NATO round small arms

Irish soldiers with the new 84-mm. Carl Gustav light RR; the Carl Gustav SMG; an FLR; and a ·303 BREN

A West German customs guard within touching distance of the wall between East and West Berlin

Two US Model M48A2 tanks with bulldozer attachments at Checkpoint Charlie

US Army adviser oversees weapons inspection carried on by a Vietnamese and infantryman

Vietnamese soldiers crossing a stream

Maps

Abbreviations

AA—Anti-aircraft
AMMO—Ammunition
APC—Armoured personnel
  carrier
AR—Automatic rifle
AT—Anti-tank
BAR—Browning automatic
  rifle
CO—Commanding officer
CP—Command post
EM—Enlisted men
FN—Fabrique Nationale
  d'Armes de Guerre
FO—Forward observer
GL—Grenade launcher
GPMG—General purpose
  machine-gun
HE—High explosive
HMG—Heavy machine-gun
HQ—Headquarters
H.W.—Heavy weapons
LMG—Light machine-gun

MG—Machine-gun
MLR—Main line of
  resistance
MMG—Medium machine-
  gun
MP—Machine pistol (German
  terminology for SMG)
NCO—Non-commissioned
  officer
PIAT—Projector infantry
  anti-tank
RL—Rocket launcher
ROK—Republic of Korea
RR—Recoilless rifle
SMG—Sub-machine-gun
TO & E—Table of
  organization and equipment
WW I—World War I
  (1914–18)
WW II—World War II
  (1939–45)

Preface

SOLDIERS have asked me about a single source of information about military arms and their use, a book on weapons and tactics. A work of this type, which describes not only what has happened in the past but what is taking place today, has not been available. There are excellent books on weapons both old and new. There are also many works devoted to strategy, grand tactics and military history. So far as I know, however, there has been nothing which deals briefly with these and also with how weapons will be used tomorrow at squad, platoon and company level. I have tried to fill this gap.

My study and writing of military history has left me with a strong conviction of the value of the individual soldier and his personal arms. Wars in final analysis are usually won or lost in the lower echelons. Great commanders, strong generous nations, and fine ordnance and supply systems can all give soldiers advantages over their enemies, but if the officers and men who are actually face to face with their opponents don't use what they have properly and courageously, the whole team will lose disastrously. One soldier with his personal weapon is the basic substance from which all victories have been and will be made. There are indications that nuclear arms have not changed war fundamentally in this regard, so long as belligerents want to win, rather than exterminate each other.

We all realize the complexity of modern science, technology and industry. Even arms that are carried by one man, or small infantry teams, are more varied today than ever before. In my travels, which have exceeded 150,000 miles in the past eight years, I have noticed changes everywhere, or at least the desire for them. Every NATO and BLOC army is better equipped right now than ever before. They are all thinking about and planning for better weapons in the immediate future. Even some small and militarily unimportant neutrals seem to be concerned with their personal arms and how they can be improved; new weapons and tactics are and will be of great importance. But science is not going to change combat at squad and platoon level as much as it will higher up. In the foreseeable future, men with rifles will have advantages over all other types of military force.

Even though the primary purpose of this book is to tell about the weapons of today, one cannot understand them completely without a basic knowledge of those of the past. Weapons and tactics have evolved; they have rarely been suddenly invented. The principle that war does not change is open to question, but there are many similarities between the present and the past.

A lot of people have made this book possible. I am particularly indebted to the editors of American and British publications who have taken scores of articles about this general subject, particularly Colonel Leo A. Codd of *Ordnance*, Walter J. Howe of *The American Rifleman*, Lt Col Thomas N. Greene and Lt Col W. L. Traynor of the *Marine Corps Gazette*, and Lt Col W. H. Zierdt, Jr of *Armor*. I am also grateful to many U.S. Army officers in the various Public Information offices and on MAAG duty with the armies of our allies, particularly Lt Col. James W. Campbell, Lt Col Stan L. McClellan, Maj. Robert B. Nelson, and Lt Col Charles W. Burtyk, Jr, to mention only four out of several dozen. I have also received kind and courteous hospitality from many soldiers in the armies of the Free World. It seems unfair to single out a few, but I must mention Maj. H. Thwaites and Capt. Gwynne L. Davies of Great Britain, Lt Col C. De Ruiter of the Netherlands, and Capt. P. Hviid-Nielsen of Denmark.

On a slightly different level, I have received so much assistance from Col Burling Jarrett at the Aberdeen Proving Ground, William C. Davis at the Frankford Arsenal, M. R. Laloux and his wonderful organization at FN near Liege in Belgium, and Walter Lamp of Heckler and Koch in Oberndorf in West Germany. Gerald C. Stowe of the West Point Museum has been extremely helpful.

The U.S. Army has been most kind and considerate. I recall particularly General Bruce C. Clark when he was U.S. 7th Army Commander at Stuttgart and several highly efficient infantry experts at Fort Benning in Georgia. I must also thank soldiers at both Fort Knox (Armor) and Fort Bragg (Airborne and Special Forces). All these men, and many more, have been patient with my requests and have given more than I asked in information and in time.

Preface

The U.S. Marine Corps, from general officers to drill instructors, has treated me with uniform kindness and consideration at Quantico, Lejeune, Parris Island and Washington. Without the encouragement that I have received from the Marines, a civilian like myself might not have the courage to tackle the writing of a book in this field. I cannot refrain from mentioning particularly Maj. Gen. A. L. Bowser and Brig. Gen. L. W. Walt. They gave me a boost in morale when I needed it most. I also want to express my appreciation for special favours to Col Charles H. Brush, Jr, Col Walter R. Walsh, Lt Col Robert M. Calland, Maj. Edward F. Musgrove and the people at USMC Division of Information in Washington.

I must apologize for many abbreviations, but have added a key to them. This book has been written with a maximum number of words constantly in mind made necessary by rising publishing costs against a final reasonable retail price.

As always, my writing has depended on the loyal and faithful performance of difficult writing duties by my small staff headed by my wife. They have found scores of elusive books, transcribed from damaged audograph records, deciphered my notes, and kept dozens of pounds of written material and pamphlets so that they could find anything I wanted quickly with only my imperfect descriptions. My wife has travelled most of the miles with me, made dozens of appointments long beforehand and kept them in order by telephone and by other means in spite of language differences, adverse weather and unusual living conditions. We have kept to tight schedule day after day for long periods because of her efforts in areas where general efficiency has been low and mix-ups monumental.

JAC WELLER

Princeton, New Jersey
20 January 1965

I

Before Hastings

MAN was inferior to many beasts in strength, speed and physical equipment. Primitive men probably fought with their hands, feet and teeth, but dominated other species only after they began to use weapons. Our ancestors of the middle Pleistocene, roughly 250,000 years ago, were already fashioning and carrying crude arms which they used in combat with beasts and other men.

All civilizations have depended upon prowess in war; until recently, this was the ability to handle comparatively simple weapons. Professor Yadin's researches in the Near East indicate some organization and co-operative tactics among fighting men at Jericho as far back as 7,000 B.C. Not much is known about weapons and tactics, however, before the Chariot Period which extends roughly from about 3000 B.C. to the eve of the Greco–Persian wars about 500 B.C. Even this 2,500-year era is mostly conjecture. Chariots were not always employed, nor always decisive when they were; to us their use indicates comparative military efficiency. Infantry was important throughout, but soldiers were probably not mounted on horses before 1000 B.C.

The two basic types of weapons are those used for striking, shock weapons, and those which are thrown, missile weapons. Both types evolved before any form of writing. When primitive man hit an enemy or a potential supply of fresh meat with a club, he was employing shock of the simplest type. Clubs were more effective when sharp pieces of stone were added axe-style. Wooden spears for thrusting, with points hardened in fire or having sharp stone heads, were also shock weapons. Axes, thrusting spears and various primitive types of swords were greatly improved when metal replaced stone. This change began to take place in the eastern Mediterranean area long before the beginning of true history. Iron was probably employed experimentally as far back as 2000 B.C., but some of the Persians in Darius's army had wooden spears with points hardened in fire 1,500 years later.

When one of our early ancestors picked up a stone and flung it in anger, fear or for personal gain, he was using the simplest of missiles. Throwing spears or javelins were more effective, but greater distances could be achieved with the sling and the bow which were also evolved before the earliest type of writing.

Weapons have always been important, but the way in which men have used them, tactics, have often been more decisive. The earliest tactical advantage in shock warfare was probably a combined charge made by several men in a compact group against their enemies. Men moving together were able to exert a total force made up of several components. First, there was their capability to do damage with their shock weapons. Second, there was the total momentum of the group in motion. Finally, there was the psychological shock caused by the sight and sound of their charge.

Simple missile tactics work in much the same way. When one man throws something, it is easy to avoid. But when a number of men co-operate in discharging a shower of missiles, they gain an additional tactical value. Further, a combination of shock and missile tactics into an integrated team effort enhances considerably their weapons power. Chariots often provided such a combination. Momentum could be supported by shock weapons such as lances and missile power from arrows. Towards the end of the Chariot Period, some commanders combined chariots with infantry and cavalry.

Both shock and missile weapons could be defeated by armour. Shields, helmets and various types of mail shirts were in limited use before the Trojan War. This defensive protection not only increased the efficiency of each man who had it, but also that of a group of men co-operating with each other. Men in armour could exert more shock and discharge more missiles.

Our earliest military historians (Herodotus and Xenophon mainly) tell us something of the weapons and tactics which the Greeks and Persians used in their wars. We know the Greeks won because they had better infantry and usually fought where the Persian cavalry was at a disadvantage. No chariots were used in Europe, even though Alexander had to face them 150 years later in Mesopotamia. Before discussing details, a few words should be said about the extent of our knowledge of military organization and small unit tactics in Classical times and later.

We know a great deal about strategy, grand tactics and weapons, but far less of how men actually fought. Philosophy, drama, rhetoric and even a good deal of political and social history survive, but details of organization are seldom clear, often subject to question, and sometimes missing entirely. In the Roman period, Livy, Tacitus, and even Caesar are disappointing. The oft-quoted Vegetius is of far less value in regard to organization and weapons employment than is generally supposed. Polybius wrote about weapons and tactics, but these particular works have been lost.

Modern research and common sense, particularly that of the great German historian Hans Delbruck, has revealed many errors in what was believed even 100 years ago. Our detailed knowledge of what actually took place in battles before Hastings (A.D. 1066) is far from complete. We know what contemporary historians thought we would want to know; we frequently have a clear big picture including overall formations and major dissimilarities in weapons and ways of using them. But we lack details of exactly how men stood, marched and fought. The Norman conquest of Britain can be taken as an arbitrary beginning of our relatively more accurate knowledge of tactics.

THE FIRST AGE OF THE FOOT SOLDIER

The Greek soldiers who beat the Persians at Marathon (491 B.C.) and Plataea (479 B.C.) fought on foot. They had better offensive weapons, better armour and better combat mobility and control than their enemies. Each man was free and of considerable economic stature. He furnished his own equipment and had for offensive action a strong thrusting spear and a short sword. He had also a complicated helmet which protected not only his head but also his neck and face, a corselet which protected his body from shoulders down to mid thigh, and a large shield. Bronze was more important than iron in these arms, but the actual shape, means of fabrication and extent of other materials, such as wood in the shield and spear and leather in the corselet, are unknown.

The power of the Greek heavy infantry lay in shock weapons; the spear was seldom thrown. They were formidable because of the individual physical condition of the hoplites, their courage, their discipline and the fact that they had done sufficient manoeuvring together to form and hold a united phalanx. They won their victories over the Persians by being able to maintain efficiency in mass, presumably eight ranks deep by several hundred files long. The Greeks could not only receive an attack in this formation, but also attack in it. This was not as easy as it may seem. Many soldiers alive today remember how hard it was to get even a war strength company to advance in line. It can be done without gaps and crowding, but requires a lot of practice with rigid control of integral parts. The early Greeks must have had subordinate units which corresponded to modern sections, platoons and companies. They managed to control in battle solid formations which were sometimes as large as modern divisions.

As the Greek city states became larger, wealthier and evolved a science of war based on their almost continual fighting one against the other and against barbarians, their basic formation shifted away from a single heavy phalanx with flanks protected by terrain or light troops. Athens, in particular, developed missile infantry and flexible co-operation between different forces. Epaminondas of Thebes beat the traditional Spartan heavy-line formation by using a column at Leuctra (371 B.C.). He weakened his centre and right so as to augment greatly his left, which may have manoeuvred semi-independently and was certainly partially shielded. It probably advanced in step with the individual soldiers in such close proximity that they may have exerted shock through hydrostatic pressure as well as by momentum and weapons. The Theban column smashed the Spartan line. The column would have been at a disadvantage against missile weapons, but Spartan armies neglected these. This manoeuvre has been called the first instance of an oblique order.

Philip and Alexander of Macedon carried heavy infantry arrayed in column to the very limit. Macedonian phalanxes were practically unbeatable so long as they retained their formation. Their main weapon was a pike more than twenty feet long. We don't know the precise array which they used, but they probably often formed a hollow square. We can be sure that they were not packed together as the Thebans had been; there was some free space around each man so that the pikes could be levelled in various ways. Through long training, the Macedonian phalanx was able to act to some extent offensively, but was of real value to Alexander because it gave him an unbeatable base for manoeuvre of other arms.

Alexander defeated more numerous hostile armies with relatively few casualties of his own because he and his father had also developed cavalry, artillery and light infantry. He was the first Greek to get real offensive power from light troops in loose formations. He was also the first great captain to utilize to the full the shock power of heavy cavalry which charged in formation at considerable speed with lances. The Macedonian heavy cavalry was almost surely composed of large men protected by armour on large horses.

Alexander's army, which was victorious from west of the Nile to east of the Indus, must have had an organization and supply system of a high order. Subordinate officers were all well trained and veterans of years of successful war. Most of the soldiers in the important units were professionals. We have no TO&Es for this army, but can be certain that an efficient system for control and manoeuvre existed. Alexander won by strategic audacity and offensive tactics based on sound teamwork between his various arms. He frequently did the unexpected, but always took advantage of his invulnerable infantry phalanx and the great shock power of his heavy cavalry. His light troops were good at reconnaissance and at fixing the enemy before the main attack; they also formed a connecting link between the heavy cavalry and the pikemen. Missile weapons were used mainly by these light forces; Alexander's battles were won by shock.

Rome dominated the known world mainly because of her legions. These varied over the 800 years of their existence, but retained a basic similarity. The early legions to about 400 B.C. were line phalanxes like those of Greece, but by degrees became more and more flexible. Perhaps no formation has ever had as great a capability for combat manoeuvre. An early legion was normally arrayed in open order in three lines of ten maniples each. Each maniple and its constituent centuries could move independently, or in concert with others in accordance with orders from higher authority. The manipular legion could take advantage of terrain and enemy weaknesses as they developed, but it may have been a trifle too flexible and open. Marius reorganized the legion about 104 B.C. into ten cohorts each of the three maniples. Cohorts became the basic element of manoeuvre thereafter, although each could undoubtedly perform internal convolutions by maniples and centuries.

The weapons of the legion are said to have remained fairly constant from beginning to end. At the time of maximum power, each legionary was a heavy infantryman, even though not always large physically. His offensive arms were the same as those of the Greek heavy infantry, a spear and sword, but they were used differently. The Roman spear, the pilum, was predominantly for missile use. It was heavy, but could be thrown accurately for a short distance and had tremendous power. Its long slender steel head would penetrate any armour, even two shields. Romans could destroy the front rank of any phalanx with a volley of pila; after these were thrown, legionaries fought with their short swords.

The defensive arms of the legions were of great importance. Minor changes were made in protective armour from time to time, but it always included a metal helmet, a corselet of leather and metal and a large wood and metal shield. The half-cylindrical shields gave great protection and made the short thrusting swords formidable. The legions frequently had organic cavalry in small quantity and also artillery; they always had some light infantry and were good at fortifications. But their greatness lay in their heavy professional infantry.

The manipular legion took full advantage of the open spaces in its lines; the Marian legion emphasized the integrity of the cohorts which were normally placed four in the first line, three in the second and three in the third. But this arrangement was often changed by great commanders. Caesar once used all ten cohorts of each of his available legions in a single line, but employed four lines in Africa against cavalry. A legion could be used as a close column of cohorts, but seldom was. The greatness of these forces lay in the effectiveness of their weapons and their ability to perform any and all evolutions quickly and efficiently even in combat.

We know that Roman heavy infantry was not packed together,

but arrayed with sufficient room between each man so that he could throw his pilum and take advantage of his skill and training as a swordsman. The actual formations assumed, however, are subject to question—scholars argue violently over this—but probably the basic unit was always the century. A formed century appears to have been either two or three ranks deep; a maniple could have its two centuries in line or in column. A cohort could have formed a fighting column thirty to fifty files wide and twelve or eighteen ranks deep, but a far wider and shallower order was probably normal. A veteran legion could take a dozen different formations in as many minutes; each would have had tactical advantages and disadvantages.

Hannibal was the most successful enemy of the Romans; at Cannae he hemmed in the legions by a combination of a refused centre and cavalry charges from the flanks. The individual soldiers were crowded together so that they could not manoeuvre nor finally even use their weapons in the normal way. Individual maniples were slaughtered with their pila still unthrown.

The legions also had trouble on level plains in the East when opposed to light cavalry that would not close, but showered them with arrows and javelins from a range greater than that of the pilum. Crassus in 53 B.C. and Valerian in A.D. 260 were victims of these tactics; their legions were destroyed. But others took their places and at least restored the Roman boundaries.

There was more to the Roman system of war than the legion and its auxiliaries; road systems, military intelligence, and almost modern logistic support contributed heavily to Roman victoriest But the entire magnificent structure of Roman civilization ultimately depended upon the fighting power of their heavy infantry. In spite of temporary lapses, the legions were able to beat all shock and missile weapons used both separately and in combination by infantry, horse cavalry and even elephant units until late in the fourth century.

THE FIRST CAVALRY SUPREMACY

Alexander had both heavy and light horsemen; the early legions had small organic units of cavalry (300). Even though the Roman infantry maintained its effectiveness over all types of enemies, cavalry gradually gained stature during the Empire. As mentioned, missile horsemen occasionally beat the legions in the East, but a

Battle of Hastings, from the Bayeux tapestry

Mid 13th-century. A great deal of mail, but only a little plate; the helmet shown at the bottom has a visor. The general shape and type of the axe resembles that used by the huscarles at Hastings

This photograph of the ruins of Battle Abbey shows (through the opening in the wall) the steepest grade up which the Normans and their allies had to advance. Harold's actual position may have been a few yards to the right rear of the abbey ruins

The curvature of the tongue of land behind the Saxon position at Hastings. The windmill on the skyline is the probable position of the last effective resistance of the Saxon army, the so-called Malfosse

A view of the battlefield of Crécy showing the area across which the French cavalry attacked. This photograph was taken just in front of the traditional position of the windmill occupied by Edward III

A view of the slope up which the French attacked at Crécy: The village is beyond the trees, top left, and the mound on the skyline is all that remains of the windmill

JOHN DUKE OF SOMERSET.
A.D. 1444

This 15th-century halberd is slightly
shorter and more elaborate than most

KNIGHT ARMED À LA HAUTE BARDE.
A.D. 1425

Jousting armour

The way that crossbows were often
used in sieges

Two professional soldiers of the German
type; the weapon in the hand of the
dismounted man is the type of wheel-
lock pistol used by the reiters

A CROSS-BOW-MAN AND HIS PAVISER.
A.D. 1468

more significant Roman defeat came in the Balkans. Men who grew up on the banks of the lower Danube and in the Ukraine learned to ride almost as soon as they began to walk. The Goths who inhabited this area evolved a way of fighting that was similar to that of Alexander's heavy cavalry.

A Gothic army of about 45,000 men defeated a Roman army of similar strength at Adrianople (A.D. 378). The barbarian horsemen fought mainly with heavy lances and long straight swords; their flank attack crushed the Roman cavalry auxiliaries and forced the legions together as Hannibal had done at Cannae. The Emperor Valens, all the Roman general officers, most of the centurions and 35,000 soldiers were killed.

The result of this battle changed war; heavy cavalry employing shock became the principal force even in Roman armies. The Eastern Empire went on for more than 1,000 years and beat the barbarians with their own tactics carefully improved. Belisarius and Narses even reconquered part of North Africa and most of Italy for Justinian in the sixth century, mainly because of fine professional heavy cavalry which was provided with defensive armour for both men and horses. But these mounted soldiers had missile weapons also. Both horses and men were sufficiently well trained to fire volleys of arrows from short, strong bows while mounted, but stationary. Missiles softened up enemy formations of either heavy cavalry or infantry before Byzantine heavy horse archers put away their bows and charged with shock weapons.

The decline in military power of the Western Empire allowed invasions of Gaul, Spain, Italy, the Western Balkans and even North Africa by a variety of enemies. The Goths, Visagoths, Vandals, Lombards, Franks, and others who came originally to pillage, finally took over what had once been Roman territory. The military strength of all these new nations was principally in heavy cavalry. After the decline of the Roman legions, barbarian horsemen could defeat West European infantry of any existing type when numbers were even.

The new shock cavalry was challenged, however, by Attila the Hun and his light missile cavalry of Asiatic origin in A.D. 451. The Huns used virtually the same weapons and tactics which the Parthians had employed against the Romans in Mesopotamia. They refused to close as long as their enemies were fresh and in good order, and relied mainly on missiles which were either hand-thrown darts, or arrows from bows. They were masters of apparent disorderly flight, but could turn on blown heavy horsemen strung out in pursuit, or in terrain difficulties, with lances and swords. Attila was beaten at Chalons, but the Saracens used much the same weapons and tactics to conquer most of Spain by the middle of the eighth century.

These early Mohammedans swept into Southern France, but the Franks under Charles Martel met them in a battle between Tours and Poitiers in A.D. 732. The Frankish army appears to have fought entirely dismounted, although for normal action against European foes they were still following, to some extent at least, the Adrianople pattern of combat.

Martel must have known the Saracens and their tactics well. He appears to have formed his men in a chequered arrangement of squares with those soldiers best protected by armour in the front ranks. In addition to the normal pike and sword, the Franks had both a throwing axe similar to a heavy American Indian tomahawk and a strong javelin. The battle began with a shower of Saracen arrows and darts at medium range, to which the Franks could make no effective reply. Some Saracen light units penetrated between the Frankish squares, however, and found themselves exposed to Frankish missiles which could penetrate the best Saracen armour. The Saracen cavalry could not break the infantry squares, but did incur missile and shock weapon casualties.

Martel was virtually surrounded, but confident in his array, the courage and stamina of his soldiers, and a character weakness of his enemies. These followers of the Prophet courted death in battle; the Franks were willing to help them towards Paradise. When the Saracen missile assaults failed, the Mohammedans charged home with lance and scimitar. Martel's foremost men were more powerful, equally well disciplined, and better protected both by their own partial armour and shields and by the pikes of men to their rear. The Frankish infantry held; heavy swords and axes killed horses and riders.

In a long day of fighting, the Saracen army finally destroyed itself. The Mohammedan power which had moved thousands of miles from central Arabia conquering all in its path was finally decisively defeated. The Franks became the dominant force in

Western Europe; Charlemagne, the grandson of Martel, was later to improve their organization, training and logistics and to extend the borders of his kingdom from the Ebro in Spain to the North Sea and the middle Danube; he held most of the Italian peninsula also.

The Frankish armies of the ninth century (death of Charlemagne A.D. 814) were composed of both cavalry and infantry; both were protected by armour made of iron and hardened leather. The heavy armoured cavalry began to dominate infantry after the conquest of Lombardy in North Italy, but good infantry was still necessary because of two powerful external military pressures.

Western Europe was ravaged in the ninth century by the Magyars, the descendants of Attila's Huns. These people were still mainly mounted bowmen; they fought with the tactics of their ancestors. The Franks beat the Magyars by refusing their stratagems, using heavy infantry as a base for short, controlled charges by shock cavalry, and producing nearly arrow-proof armour for everyone. The heavy Frankish horsemen could always scatter the Magyars on an open battlefield; if pursuit was not carried too far, at least a partial victory was assured. The descendants of the Huns are said to have lost 20,000 men killed at Augsburg (A.D. 953).

The other reason for the retention of infantry was the sudden eruption of the Vikings from Scandinavia which created confusion throughout Europe, even as far south and east as Gibraltar and the Caucasus. These sea rovers fought on shore as infantry; when cornered, they took a defensive formation called a shield wall in a place inaccessible to formed cavalry. These raids were so profitable that hundreds of ships and thousands of men were soon engaged in them. Plunder could be obtained only at greater distances from the coast and navigable rivers, so the Vikings seized horses and moved fast and far away from where they left their ships. But they fought on foot and could normally be defeated only by similar tactics.

In the century before Hastings, the Viking raids developed in an unusual way. Because these forces were seaborne, defeating even a large raid did not greatly diminish the chances of future invasions. But the Vikings themselves produced, in part at least, protection against further incursions. Instead of continuing to return to their homes, later Norsemen sometimes settled permanently in territory they overran, or had given to them. Portions of both England and France were colonized in this way. Both the Normans and the Saxons who fought each other at Hastings were in part the descendants of the Vikings, but they had adopted some of the weapons and tactics of the places where they settled.

II

Hastings

T HE Battle of Hastings may be taken as the beginning of
our detailed knowledge of weapons and tactics. We have
several descriptions of the fighting, some surviving
weapons, and the Bayeux Tapestry. We don't know all that
we would like to know about Hastings; our knowledge of many
battles which were fought later is even more fragmentary. But
after Hastings we usually have a solid foundation for conjectures,
while some of the battles discussed in the preceding chapter are
hardly more than names.

Edward the Confessor was the last but one of the Saxon kings.
He appears to have been an albino and was certainly deeply
religious, but was not vigorous in body or mind. His brother-in-
law, Harold Godwinson, had been the acting head of his government for several years. At Edward's death on 5 January 1066,
Harold was proclaimed king in London, although he had less
than a perfect claim to the throne. He took over, however, with
strength, skill and considerable political ability. He recognized
the importance of defeating, probably in battle, his two major
rivals. One was his own elder brother, Tostig, who appears to
have been the choice of Edward's widow; Harald Hardrada of
Norway was Tostig's friend and ally. Harold Godwinson's
other rival was William the Bastard, Duke of Normandy, a
blood relative of Edward; William and his friends claimed that
the Confessor had designated the Norman as his successor.

Harold consolidated his hold on the country during the spring
and prepared for the coming struggle with his brother and
William. The power of the Anglo-Saxon army lay in professional
soldiers, known as huscarles, provided with armour and numerous
weapons. These men were supported in time of war by the county

militia or fyrds. Modern research indicates that there were two of these; the select fyrd was composed of trained soldiers fairly well armed and organized. The great fyrd included almost all males of military age; their arms and training appear to have been primitive.

The huscarles were first-rate in discipline, training, skill with their weapons, individual prowess and equipment, and occupied an independent socio-economic position. They travelled on horses, but fought on foot. They wore helmets, mail shirts (byrnies), and usually some other armour. They carried large kite-shaped shields made of linden wood reinforced with an iron rim, and used spears, swords and especially a heavy axe with a four-foot haft. The spears could be thrown, but had no great range. Some swords were of the long Scandinavian type for cutting; others were short thrusting weapons of the Saxon pattern. The axe was unusual and extremely effective. Even though most soldiers who wielded one needed both hands and had to leave their shields stuck in the ground, a single blow could kill a horse instantly.

Missile weapons in the Anglo-Saxon army, in addition to the spears already mentioned, were limited; real javelins were known, but apparently not popular. Archery was understood and used for sport, but not to any considerable extent for war. A kind of tomahawk, the Frankish throwing axe, was fairly common, but difficult to retrieve. The best English missile of this period appears to have been a heavy, long-handled stone hammer which was thrown in the manner of the modern field event.

We must not forget an important part of Harold's force, even though it did not fight at Hastings. King Alfred had started the British navy more than a century before. The new king took pains during the spring to have it in the best shape possible. Since his enemies had to come by sea, it was possible that they could be defeated before they landed. If Harold's navy had intercepted William, there would probably have been no invasion. The Anglo-Saxon navy appears to have been strong enough to have beaten the Norman easily, if it could have caught him afloat.

The Vikings who settled in the part of France that later became Normandy had an astonishing ability to adapt themselves to new and more efficient weapons and tactics. These sea rovers, raiders of Europe in the ninth and tenth centuries, had at first only crude helmets, rough iron offensive weapons and little armour. Within a few years, however, they were able to capture fine helmets, mail and a large assortment of offensive arms; their smiths, soon learning their trade, may have been the first to surface carburized iron. The Norman knights had the finest arms available at the time; their armour was similar to that of Harold's huscarles, but probably more protective and of better quality on the average. For offence, the favourite Norman weapon appears to have been the long Scandinavian cutting sword used throughout Western Europe for several centuries. The thrusting spear or lance was also carried, but the battle-axe in Normandy was a much smaller weapon and of little importance. The fighting bishops and priests used maces so as to avoid the intentional shedding of blood.

The real difference between the Norman and Saxon armies lay in their use of horses and their specialization in weapons. The Normans placed great reliance on Frankish-style heavy shock cavalry. William is said to have had great skill in the type of mounted personal combat which reached its height in tournaments several decades later. Norman knights and squires habitually fought mounted. The Normans also took advantage of light missile infantry. The Vikings who settled in western France continued to use bows and arrows and adopted the crossbow to a limited extent. The Norman bow was similar to those used aboard Viking ships for centuries, not the powerful British longbow of the fourteenth century. The crossbow was either a survival or a re-creation of a weapon used by the Romans. Between the armoured knights, and the light infantry archers, William's army contained a considerable body of men who could fight either mounted or on foot and were protected by fairly adequate armour. More of these presently.

HAROLD'S YORKSHIRE CAMPAIGN

After Harold had established himself firmly on the English throne, William of Normandy and Tostig Godwinson made common cause against him. The outlawed son of Earl Godwin was to raid, or threaten to raid, the English coast. He landed on the Isle of Wight in May, moved east along the southern coast, and remained for some time at Sandwich. He threatened other points and caused Harold to call out his militia. Finally, Tostig joined Harald Hardrada and a force from Norway, sailed into the Humber, and began land operations in earnest. They beat the Yorkshire earls and their retainers and militia, and were on the point of receiving the capitulation of York when Harold of England arrived from London on 24 September. His force had covered 200 miles in nine days along the old Roman road. He must have brought with him mainly his small professional army, all of whom probably travelled mounted. But they were on foot the next day when they beat the invaders decisively at Stamford Bridge. Both Tostig and Hardrada were killed; only about a tenth of the invading force managed to get back to their ships.

We don't know precisely what happened at Stamford Bridge, but can piece together some details. At the beginning of the battle, Harold Godwinson's force had to capture a bridge and cross a small stream. Once across, they attacked Tostig's and Hardrada's probably 360-degree shield-wall with missiles. Skilled men among the huscarles threw the great stone hammers so that they fell at a steep angle spinning into the enemy mass. A volley of these must have been most disorganizing. Once the Norwegians were shaken by the missile attack, Harold's men fought them hand-to-hand using predominantly their great, long-handled axes. They won because they were the more skilful fighters, more efficiently organized and better directed.

Tostig Godwinson, even though he lost his army and his life, had done William's work well. William's descent upon the south coast had caused Harold to call out his select fyrd too soon and to begin the naval patrol of the Channel too early. Harold knew of the force that William was raising and concentrating near the mouth of the Somme, but by September the British vessels had to come round into the Thames to be refitted and resupplied. William appears to have heard of this and the absence of Harold's army from London on the Yorkshire expedition; many friendly Normans had settled in England before 1066. The Conqueror took advantage of a favourable wind to cross in twenty-four hours. He and his entire force landed at Pevensey on 28 September.

The Normans and their allies—adventurers from all over Western Europe took part—established a fortified camp near Hastings to protect their ships and began systematically to ravage the surrounding country. Buildings were burned and livestock killed; men and old women were cut down and left where they fell, but young women and children were taken back to the camp as slaves. William knew Harold personally; he wanted the last Saxon king to come down and fight an open battle near the coast quickly and was taking the steps necessary to force him to do it.

Harold heard of William's invasion soon after his victory at Stamford Bridge; his army again covered the distance from York to London in nine days. If Harold had waited two or three weeks his army could have been twice the size of William's, but he could not bear to have his country treated so harshly. He left London on 11 October and marched sixty miles in forty-eight hours to the vicinity of the modern village of Battle.

Early on the morning of the fourteenth, Harold took up a position just south of the great forest of Andrewswald on both sides of the old road from Hastings to London. The actual area occupied can be determined precisely. William's Battle Abbey was built here shortly after the conflict; the high altar was precisely where Harold's two banners stood. Unfortunately, the passage of nearly 900 years has changed the surface of the earth; we do not know how the countryside looked in 1066. Eminent authorities do not agree about this, nor as to the exact British formation. Harold's army may have taken advantage of some weatherworn trenches dug by an earlier English army under Alfred, but there was no time to construct any new works.

The original configuration of the land has also been questioned; the brooks in the area may have been larger then and bordered by swamp. But none of this is really important. There was, and is, a fairly steep hill then joined to the forest behind it by a tongue of high land. The Saxon army appears to have formed on the morning of 14 October 1066 in one continuous line of considerable thickness all the way across the south face of this hill and to some extent refused its flanks. Harold's line was probably about 800 yards long with some light troops posted behind the marshy land on either flank. Sir Charles Oman and historians of his era believed Harold's line to be practically U-shaped, but Belloc, Fuller and other recent researchers suggest a shorter, straighter formation.

Harold probably had between 7,000 and 8,000 men of all types, but his huscarles numbered less than 2,000. These men had marched from London to York, fought a bloody but decisive battle, returned to London and come down to Battle all within a single month. They cannot have been in the best physical condition. The Yorkshire campaign must have been even harder on the select fyrd who were probably not mounted. Virtually none of them who went to Stamford Bridge could have been at Hastings, but their places were taken by men from the great fyrd from the south-eastern counties.

The composition of the English line is also subject to question, but we may safely conclude that Harold's armoured huscarles all fought on foot and formed the first two ranks of his phalanx. Their large kite-shaped shields were in front of them, probably fixed in the ground to form the shield-wall so often mentioned. These front-rank men relied on their great axes, spears, swords and minor missile weapons. Behind the professional soldiers, there were men of the fyrds, less completely armed and armoured. The awe-inspiring stone hammers were thrown from the rear over the Anglo-Saxon formation by men of unusual strength. The skill and training required indicates that they were huscarles. When their missiles were exhausted, they probably returned to their places in the front ranks.

William the Norman received intelligence of the approach of the Saxon army on the night of the thirteenth. He appears to have had his army stand to arms inside his fortified camp at Hastings, perhaps on receipt of intelligence that Harold was planning a night attack. It is unlikely, however, that the English had any such plan; they were too tired. William moved along the old Hastings-to-London road soon after dawn and deployed north-east of Telham Hill about nine o'clock. The appearance of Harold's army bore out intelligence already received; it was not of great strength. William's force was probably nearly equal in total numbers and superior in fully armed professional soldiers. If he could beat Harold in battle, the rest of the conquest of Britain would be easy. He decided to attack.

Although accounts are conflicting in some details, the Norman army was certainly divided into three portions, or battles, which advanced abreast so that all three would make contact together. This involved some complication in timing because the right, or eastern, battle deployed on both sides of the road, while the centre and left had to move successively more to the west before forming their combat array. The centre battle was under William personally and contained most of the Normans in his army. The left was predominantly Breton, and the right had Flemings and French perhaps under Robert of Beaumont and the Norman,

Battle of Hastings: 14th. October 1066

Each huscarle occupied an area about 40 in. wide by 36 in. deep. These men used spears, swords and axes as primary weapons, and could interchange them as needed. To receive cavalry a line of spears could probably project beyond the shield wall while axes were immediately available. The shield wall may have been two shields in thickness through-out most of its length.

NOTE. The Hastings to London road is shown much as it is today. Some authorities believe that at the time of the battle it ran straight over the hill close to Harold's position.

Details of Harold's Formation :

- — · — · — · — · —   area used by hammer men
- — — — — — —   area of incompletely armed Infantry with archers in front
- ↓ ↓ ↓ ↓ ↓   Huscarles armed with spears
- ↓ ↓ ↓ ↓ ↓   Huscarles armed with axes
- ⊗⊗⊗⊗   Shield wall

N

500 Yards

Thick Woods

area where Saxons tied their horses

LONDON to LONDON

ENGLISH ARMY

HAROLD'S Standard

last counter attack

small stream

marshy area

see above for details

marshy area

poor ground

part of Harold's army pursues against orders

Archers

Armoured Infantry

Armoured Cavalry

FLEMISH & FRENCH
Eustace of Boulogne

Battle of Montgomery
Battle of Roger of Gomery

William's flank attack

William's Norman Battle

predominantly Breton Battle
(commander not now definite)

HASTINGS to LONDON Road

Telham Hill & Hastings

small stream

Roger of Montgomery. There appears to have been some marshy ground between the centre and left battles.

Each of these divisions was composed of three separate formations, one behind the other. In front, there were archers in open order. Initially about 100 yards behind them, there were phalanxes of heavily armed, armoured men-at-arms, probably six ranks deep. These men might have fought mounted, if enough horses could have been carried across the Channel for their use. The third element of each battle was composed of knights who did have horses and fought mounted; these were probably divided into several squadrons within each unit.

The armies which now faced each other were similar in many respects. Both wore the same sort of armour, which was mostly of the interlocking link type chain mail over heavy leather or quilted cloth garments that were necessary to absorb the shock of blows, even though the iron links prevented penetration. All shields, even those used by the Norman leaders, were still made mostly of wood. Helmets were open save for nose-protectors; most men had large areas of arm and leg unprotected by armour. The long straight swords and fairly light lances were the same on both sides.

Another similarity of these two armies was in their commanders; both Harold and William were able professional soldiers as well as politicians. Each was a large strong man physically, an expert with his personal arms, and knew a great deal about war. They understood the strengths and weaknesses of their own forces, and the weapons and tactics of their opponents. Harold was almost certainly planning an immobile defence similar to that used by Charles Martel against the mounted Saracens at Tours. He realized, however, that William's archers and armoured infantry presented additional problems. He hoped to counter these by forming a continuous line behind his shield-wall instead of a chessboard formation of squares. He also planned to use more missiles.

William knew about the long English battle-axe and the strength, valour and discipline of Harold's huscarles. He realized that these men could present a line of shields, spear-points and axes which could stop any cavalry charge, but he hoped to win by shaking the opposing phalanx with arrows, disorganizing the front ranks of huscarles by some combat with similar Norman heavy infantry, and then routing the English with a shock charge by his cavalry. It would appear that the Conqueror was initially over-confident and hoped to win too cheaply, but his caution since landing in Britain more than two weeks before belies this.

As soon as William had formed his three battles, all moved almost due north against Harold's position. His archers opened fire from skirmish order, but did little damage. They were firing uphill against men protected by shields, helmets and mail shirts. The arrows and bolts that missed them flew harmlessly over the rest.

William's heavy infantry now advanced to the attack, perhaps partially protected by a barrage of arrows, but finally masking this supporting fire. At a range of about seventy-five feet, Harold's missile men went into action. A few archers fired from between the huscarles and over the shield-wall; javelins were thrown hard and straight. But the great stone hammers were by far the most effective; they came mysteriously over the English line in high arcs, slowly spinning as they fell. They probably caused only a few casualties but disrupted the Norman armoured infantry at a critical time. Suddenly, there was hand-to-hand fighting all along the line. In places, William's men had advanced to the shield-wall. Elsewhere, the huscarles brushed aside their own barrier and closed with the enemy. The superior weapons, skill, discipline and physical prowess of Harold's front rank won. The attackers were beaten all along the line.

William and his co-commander of battles had to order their heavy cavalry to charge to the rescue. The Norman cavalry formations were slowed and disordered by their own infantry. The English re-established their shield-wall and presented a line of spear-points projecting through it. When the heavy cavalry was within range, they too received a shower of missiles. This first mounted charge seems to have been defeated before it reached Harold's line. The Norman horsemen had not been able to come forward fast, knee to knee, because of their own infantry and the steepness of the hill. Most of them did not careen into the shield-wall at all, but approached it slowly, threw their lances javelin-wise, and tried individual duels. Strong men in formation on foot armed with long axes have an advantage over single mounted swordsmen. Some huscarles killed first the horse and then the rider with successive blows. After suffering a few casualties, the Norman cavalry retired, still covering their archers and heavy infantry.

The battle had worked out so far according to Harold's plan; the English around him—he was personally to the left of the centre of his line—retrieved their missiles, cared for a few wounded, stripped the enemy dead, and awaited further attacks. On the Saxon right, opposite the Bretons, however, a different situation prevailed. William's Breton battle was more seriously defeated and was to some extent separated from the Norman centre by swampy ground. The Bretons on the left were not so directly under William's personal control as his centre and right. When they were completely repulsed by the portion of the Saxon line which they had attacked they retreated precipitously. Some of their horses decame mired. The Saxons above them, who had already broken formation to some extent, charged down killing horses and men with their great axes and other arms.

If Harold's right wing had pursued to the foot of the hill only, and returned to their position after diposing of those of their enemies that they caught, all would have been well. Instead, the English here went out of control in a wild, senseless pursuit. They might have slaughtered the section of their front, but William's own battle was practically intact and less than 400 yards away. He led his Norman cavalry against the flank of Harold's disordered right wing. Infantry caught in such a situation has always suffered severely. Harold seems to have lost about one-fifth of his entire force in two or three minutes; not many of the men caught here were able to regain the top of the hill.

The battle continued; Harold's force had suffered a severe reverse, but was far from defeated. Some scholars believe that most of the Anglo-Saxon right-flank casualties were from the great fyrd and that the huscarles did not take part in the wild rush forward. The English army regrouped and appears to have spread out to cover the original front, but with a thinner formation. William again advanced to attack with archers, heavy infantry and cavalry, and was again repulsed. Details of what occurred and the sequence of events which followed are now lost, but Harolds' army gradually gave up its never great flexibility. In the early stages of the fight they were able to retrieve their stone hammers, javelins, and perhaps some arrows. Later, William prevented this. Even without their missile arms, however, the huscarles and their supporters were able to hurl back several assaults by both cavalry and infantry.

The fight continued for several hours. William was reported killed and had to take off his helmet to restore the confidence of his own men. The Conqueror seems deliberately to have used at least once the manoeuvre that had worked well with the Bretons on his left; a part of the Norman army feigned disorderly flight, lured more sections of Harold's army into pursuit, and then crushed them. But even this did not break the spirit of the English king and those close to him.

The turning point of the battle came when William began to alternate cavalry charges of limited objectives with fire from his archers. Even when the horsemen were moving forward, the bowmen covered their attack by loosing arrows high into the air which fell at random—but in the Anglo-Saxon area. This was particularly effective against the unarmoured fyrd huddled behind the thinned ranks of huscarles and the shield-wall. The English were no longer able to occupy the whole front; the enemy archers and heavy cavalry gained more advantageous ground for their operations. The Norman cavalry charges finally began to make real headway; momentary penetrations and attacks from the flanks pushed Harold's surviving huscarles too close together. Men wielding four-foot axes needed space. Harold was hit in the face by an arrow, probably one which fell from a great height and lacked real power. He was badly wounded, but not completely incapacitated and continued to command. His army was rapidly declining in size and bodily strength; its missile capability was gone, but not its courage nor its will to fight. As dusk approached, the Anglo-Saxons occupied only the middle third of their original position; both flanks were exposed. Harold was almost blind, but stood with shield and axe in the midst of his men. His two banners waved overhead; two of his brothers were still on either side of him.

The Norman cavalry was also reduced in numbers and tired, but could now use the smooth clear top of the hill for its shock charges. Their archers were firing at ranges of below twenty-five yards. William finally mounted his fourth horse of the day—the first three had their skulls cleft by English axes—and personally led a smashing all-out careen into the area of Harold's banners. The three sons of Earl Godwin were slain together; the English

39

formation was finally broken. The Norman heavy cavalry added to its death toll with every stroke of sword and mace.

A few English were able to retreat along the tongue of land to the forest which lay to the north. They were bone-weary but the Norman cavalry which pursued them came to grief in the woods and in the two modest ravines to either side of the London road. In poor terrain and with the light failing, the great axes could still kill. One of William's advisers suggested a retreat, believing that reinforcements had arrived for the enemy, but the Conqueror was not deceived. He called off the pursuit, but knew that he had won not just a battle, but a kingdom. Harold, his brothers and most of the huscarles were dead; without them, Britain could not long resist. The conquest was virtually complete by full darkness on 14 October 1066.

Hastings was fought nearly 900 years ago, but its message of stark heroism reaches us clear and strong. Soldiers have never behaved better when all hope of victory was gone. Perhaps they left Britain an infantry legacy that was to endure through Albuera and Waterloo to the Gloucesters in Korea.

The tactical lesson of Hastings is, of course, that with the weapons of that day even the best infantry could be beaten by a combination of missile infantry and heavy armoured cavalry. The Normans and their tactics were to dominate Western Europe and extend their power even into Asia during the next three centuries.

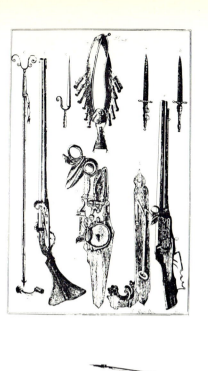

A match-lock musket and its support; two types of plug bayonets; and a long wheel-lock pistol similar to that used by the reiters

Four 16th-century infantrymen armed with, left to right, a bill, pike, caliver and a bow and arrows

This combination of leather and armour was used early in the British Civil War

A SUIT OF ARMOUR,
In the possession of Samuel Rush Esq.
A.D. 1620   A.D. 1620

British military long-arms. At the top a Queen Anne dog-catch musket. The second weapon is a military musketoon from the reign of William III; the third and fourth weapons are from the reign of James II

Two views of the lock plates and surrounding areas of the two top weapons shown full-length in the plate above

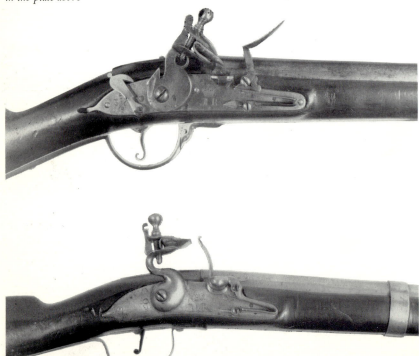

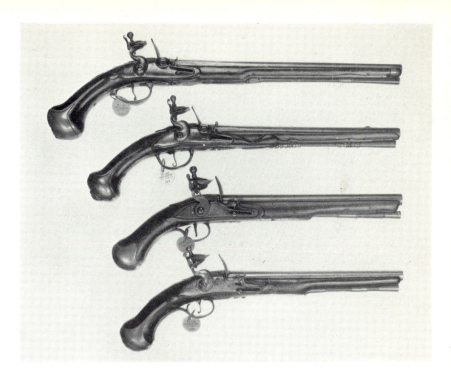

Four superb examples of British Military pistols

Puckle's gun from the Tower of London—square bullets for use against the Turks, round bullets against Christians

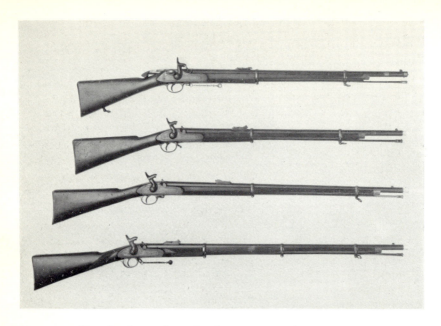

Four imported British military rifles used in the American Civil War

Four more British military shoulder arms used in the Confederate Service

III

Armoured Cavalry and its Decline

H EAVY cavalry dominated Western Europe for more than 250 years after Hastings. Infantry was less important than at any other time between Marathon (491 B.C.) and Korea (1950–3). Cavalry and infantry were present in most armies, but infantry was sometimes left to guard baggage while cavalry did the field fighting.

The battle effectiveness of these horsemen lay in their mobility and their shock potential. The last was the sum of the momentum of horses and riders charging together, actual thrusts and blows from shock weapons such as lances, swords and battle-axes, and the fear which these inspired. Armour helped in several ways not the least of which was that its weight added to momentum. It also meant security for the wearer who was reasonably free from danger of personal injury. The Companion cavalry of Alexander and the Gothic horsemen at Adrianople also used mobility, armour and shock; the principal differences between these and the chivalry of Western Europe lay in more complete and better-quality iron and steel armour of both men and horses and the greater weapons efficiency of mounted men after the introduction of the stirrup (circa A.D. 600).

Armour improved considerably after the eleventh century. Mail-makers improved their skill so that the whole body below the helmet could be covered. By the early fourteenth century visors had been added to most knightly helmets so as to protect the face. Plate armour was introduced gradually; for many decades it was a matter of personal choice, but certainly was not complete until after 1400.

At the time of the greatest relative advantage of cavalry (circa 1340), the total weight of a helmet, a few pieces of plate

41

armour, a suit of chain mail, and the necessary shock-absorbent under-garments was probably between fifty and sixty pounds, not counting shield and weapons. This was quite a load, but the whole mass was flexible and allowed the wearer to move. Even if thrown from his horse, he could rise and fight on foot, or re-mount unaided. He was nearly impervious to harm from ordinary weapons of others, but still able to do great damage with his own. His heavier specialized lance in rest could communicate tremendous force; a strong man rising in his stirrups could smite as hard with his new sharp-tempered sword as if he were on the ground. Horses at Hastings were probably too small for their loads, but breeding appears to have improved them greatly. When efficient weapons, armour and equipage were combined with strong men and horses who trained together, and with other soldiers and animals, the final result was astonishing.

The corollary to this combat effectiveness of armoured cavalry was its extreme cost. A large part of the wealth produced by the feudal systems of Western Europe was spent on armour, weapons and war horses. Only the top classes could possibly afford them, but men so equipped were the only really effective soldiers. Chivalry was based both on *matériel* and the leisure to practise with it. Men who had both, together with physical strength and agility, could fight efficiently for many years with relatively little danger to themselves. Cheaper, less protective armour and less able horses were available and used by men-at-arms—profes-sional soldiers not usually of gentle blood.

Infantry did not completely disappear from Western Europe. It was always needed in sieges; castles had become of great stra-tegic value. Flemish pikemen, Basque javelin men and archers and crossbowmen from several countries had established reputations; the armoured burghers of some North Italian cities were well thought of militarily. The enormous two-handed swords needed to cut through plate armour were best employed by strong men on foot. But in large battles infantry was generally of secondary importance between Hastings (1066) and Crécy (1346).

We should note, however, that when the armies of Christendom went to Asia Minor during the Crusades (1097–1211) a different type of war required a different weapons emphasis and new tactics. Infantry capable of discharging missiles was of paramount importance. The Turkish light cavalry relied particularly on arrows from short strong bows. These horse archers would out stand a charge, but would draw the heavy Christian horsemen further and further into hot arid terrain as their predecessors had done with the Romans. The armoured knights could resist the rain of arrows, but their horses could not. When dismounted and exhausted by hours under a boiling sun, they could be slain with shock weapons.

The answer to this tactical problem was to combine infantry with cavalry in the Christian armies. Richard I of England did this most effectively at Arsouf (1191) to beat the great Saladin. The English king actually had to maintain a battle array for nineteen days as he marched along the coast from Acre to Jaffa. He formed his first line—the men most distant from the shore—of dismounted men-at-arms and knights who had lost their horses, but placed crossbowmen immediately behind them. He used his mounted knights only for partial charges and did not let them get into isolated pockets where tired men on spent horses would be inferior to nimble, mounted archers. The armoured infantry and crossbowmen provided an unshakeable base for brief, effective cavalry charges. The Turks hovered around the tight, well-organized Christian column for days; their bows were less accurate and powerful than the Christian weapons, but superior in speed of fire. But the Christian armour, even that worn by the crossbowmen, withstood long-range arrows easily; Richard kept his force well in hand. Saladin finally had to press home an attack and was soundly beaten by a combination of heavy cavalry, armoured infantry and missiles.

Christian armies were always successful when cavalry and missile infantry collaborated, but when knights went off by themselves, even the greatest valour and personal prowess was usually insufficient. Why did Richard I and the other Christian commanders who fought in the East promptly abandon their effective combination of cavalry and infantry when they came home? Since all these men were professional soldiers, and some at least intelligent, we must conclude that they made a proper military decision based on conditions at that time. The reasons why one set of tactics applied in Asia Minor and another in Western Europe undoubtedly lay in climate, terrain and the enemy. Even in midsummer, really prostrating heat is not common in Britain, France and Germany. The open stretches of semi-desert country necessary for exhausting running fights are simply not available. Nimble, well-organized, mounted archers did not have to be encountered in mass.

BRITAIN'S GLORIOUS FOURTEENTH CENTURY

Heavy cavalry (chivalry) was in full flower in 1300. More or less gently born, well-exercised, professional soldiers encased in efficient and expensive armour, riding strong partially-armoured horses, won at Bouvines (1214), Benevento (1266) and Marchfeld (1278). In the last battle, neither commander bothered to bring his infantry on to the field at all. The successes of Flemish pikemen at Courtrai (1302) and Swiss halbardiers at Morgarten (1315) were explained away because of the impossible ground on which the knights had tried to fight. The Flemings were soundly beaten by French cavalry at Mons-en-Pevele (1304) and Cassel (1328). The Swiss had as yet no reputation outside their mountains.

The undisputed reign of heavy armoured cavalry was destined to come to an end soon. Two distinct types of weapons tactics were responsible. The more interesting and more dramatic, at least for those who read English as their native language, were those employed at Crécy and Poitiers. But to understand exactly what happened, we must review some British military history which was not understood on the Continent.

The longbow of about 6 ft 6 in. with its 3-ft arrows was not used at Hastings or anywhere else until the very end of the thirteenth century. But Edward I appreciated the potentialities of the weapon when it was used against him in his Welsh wars. His army which beat the Scots at Falkirk (1298) made good use of the longbow, still mostly in the hands of Welsh auxiliaries. Continuous fire from archers weakened the Scottish infantry squares so that English heavy armoured cavalry could smash them. Edward II lost Bannockburn (1314) when the Bruce scattered the English archers with Scottish cavalry and then beat Edward's armoured horsemen with his steady pike formations. But Edward III wiped out this bad memory at Halidon Hill (1333) by combining dismounted English armoured cavalry and archers and contriving to have his formation attacked by the Scots. The hail of arrows smothered the advancing enemy, which was able to do little damage to the formed line of armoured Englishmen flanked by still-firing archers. Once the retreat began,

Battle of Crécy – 26th August 1346

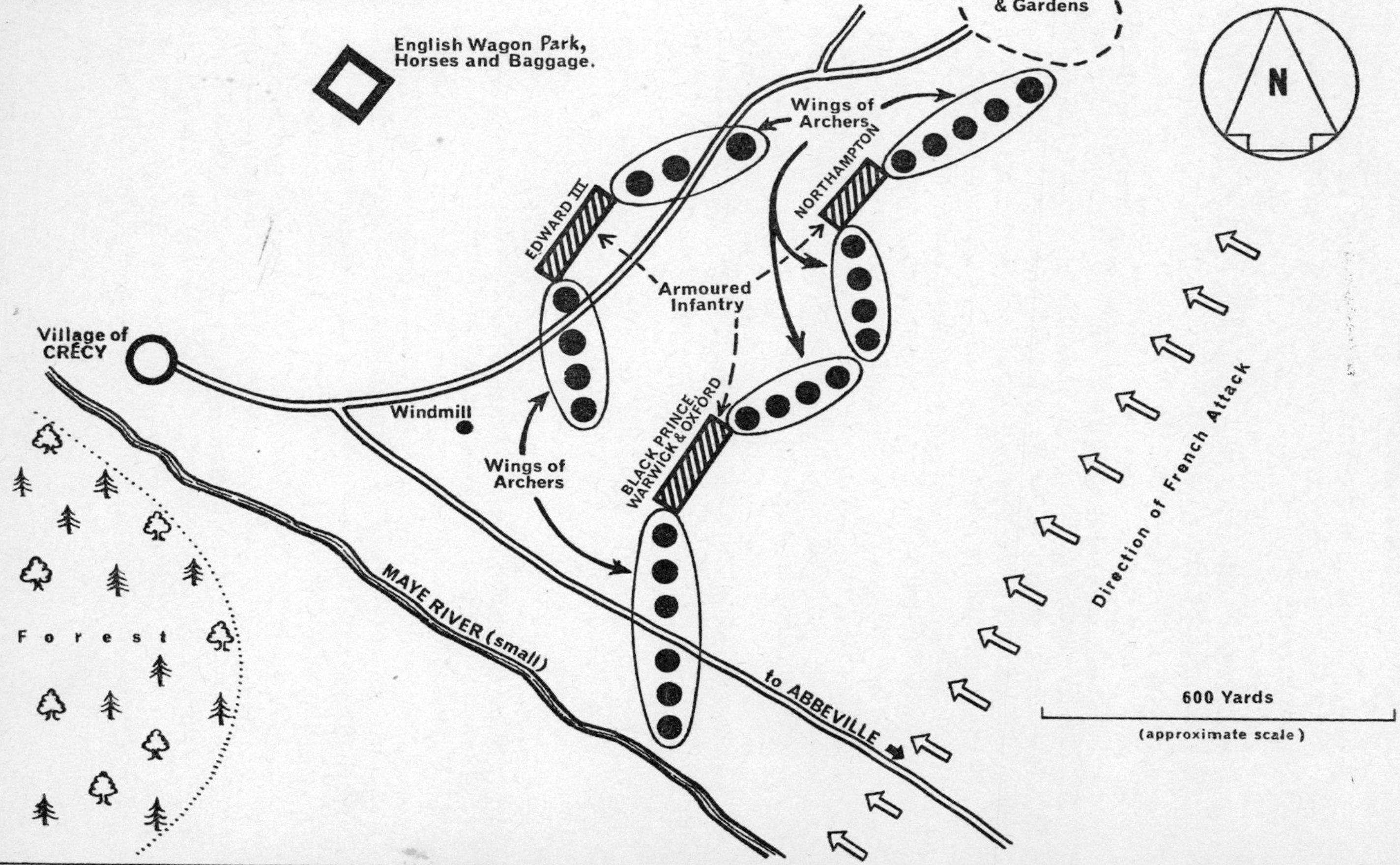

N

Wadicourt & Gardens

English Wagon Park, Horses and Baggage.

Wings of Archers

NORTHAMPTON

Armoured Infantry

BLACK PRINCE WARWICK & OXFORD

EDWARD III

Wings of Archers

Windmill

Village of CRÉCY

MAYE RIVER (small)

Forest

to ABBEVILLE

Direction of French Attack

600 Yards

(approximate scale)

Edward's knights remounted and turned the battle into a slaughter.

The new English tactics were first used on the Continent at Crécy (1346). The longbow was now thoroughly assimilated into the English army and socio-economic system. Archers were not of gentle blood, but not feudal infantry either. They were freemen who served voluntarily, in part for pay. Edward III and his young son, the Black Prince, were retreating to the coast after a raid into France pursued by a much more numerous French army. Edward probably had about 10,000 men, all of good quality. There were some 1,800 fully armoured heavy cavalry, 600 mounted infantry (hobilars) whose armour was not complete, and a small force of Welsh spearmen, probably with shields and helmets only. Edward had also between 6,000 and 7,000 English and Welsh archers with longbows. He avoided a trap in which Philip of France tried to catch his army between the Somme and the sea, forced a crossing of the river near the Channel over a secret ford at low tide, and decided to accept battle in an advantageous position between the villages of Crécy and Wadicourt.

The English position was along the crest of a low hill. The right flank rested on Crécy, a small stream and a dense forest; the left flank was secured by the buildings and orchards of Wadicourt and perhaps by an armed baggage park. Edward had plenty of time to form his command and divided it into the usual three battles. He placed two in line and the third in close support; there was some irregularity in these due to terrain, organization and other factors, but each assumed essentially the same formation. The same ratio of archers to other soldiers was maintained in the front two battles. All knights and men-at-arms were dismounted and formed with the hobilars and Welsh spearmen into a phalanx perhaps 8 ranks deep by 100 to 120 files wide. A wing of archers extended out and slightly forward from each flank of each phalanx. All three battles were concave in shape, with the support battle covering the opening between the first two. All archers were able to protect their portions of the front with slanting stakes driven into the ground and then sharpened; these projected towards the French at the height of a horse's breast. Some small deep holes were dug across the whole English front for the heavily laden French horses, whose vision was probably partially obscured by armour, to step into.

Contact was not made between the two armies until midafternoon; the French forces, which probably numbered in excess of 35,000, were strung out over a considerable distance. But the Gallic knights had such disdain for infantry that they insisted on attacking at once. Philip, the French king, ordered forward 5,000 Genoese crossbowmen to engage the English archers. The clumsy weapons of the North Italians were stronger and longer ranged than conventional bows, but inferior in range, accuracy and speed of fire to English longbows. The Genoese were so badly worsted in their brief skirmish that the French knights rode over them and, in some instances at least, cut them down.

The French armoured cavalry now charged the two forward English crescents. As they advanced, they appear to have seen the stakes in front of the archers and preferred to attack the central phalanxes armed with shock weapons. The English archers fell to with a vengeance as soon as the range was short enough. They put so many arrows into the air that the sound of them coming down not only frightened horses, but also remained indelibly in the minds of those who survived.

The result of this fire was unexpected as far as the French were concerned. An arrow discharged from a strong bow by a powerful archer could penetrate good armour only at close range; not many French knights were mortally wounded in this manner. The arrows were effective even at long range, however, when they chanced to hit weak points in the best and most complete armour and when they struck unprotected parts of both men and horses. The wounded beasts did real damage to the French; they were already loaded down with their own armour and with their armoured riders, goaded by spur and bit, and scared by the sound of the arrows in the air. Arrow-tortured animals went crazy with pain and frustration, reared into the air, and either threw their riders or came down on top of them.

But arrows alone did not decide the battle; the French came forward not once, but fifteen or sixteen times. Individual horsemen careened into the English infantry line in spite of the gleaming spear-points. There were recurring periods of hand-to-hand fighting, particularly in the right front battle—that closest to the road by which the French arrived—where the young Black Prince nominally commanded. The final British victory was gained only as darkness closed in, but was astonishingly complete. The French lost 1,542 lords and knights; casualties in other ranks were not so precisely determined, but the English and Welsh appear to have killed a total of about 10,000 men, including some fighting which occurred next morning.

Edward the Black Prince beat the French again at Poitiers (1356) using the same combination of dismounted armoured cavalry and archers fighting a defensive battle. Only a small reserve of Englishmen fought mounted. A large proportion of the French cavalry also dismounted, but were unable to deliver an effective attack on foot; their armour was too heavy and was not designed for such fighting.

After these two major defeats and some minor ones, the French would not meet the English in the open field. The Black Prince won in Spain at Navarette (1367) with a variation of his dismounted cavalry and archers technique, but the French fought out the remainder of the Hundred Years War with only one major battle. Henry V won at Agincourt (1415) with archers and dismounted armoured cavalry, even though he was forced to attack with them. During the Joan of Arc period and afterwards, the fighting took the form of sieges and irregular combats, some of it much like modern guerrilla war. The longbow continued to be important, but was used in battle mainly by the Free Companies of Englishmen who served in Italy, Spain and elsewhere for pay. The weapon was not adopted by other nations.

THE SWISS POLE-ARMED INFANTRY

Heavy armoured cavalry could also be defeated by polearms. As mentioned, the Flemings at Courtrai (1302) and the Scots at Bannockdurn (1314) won with pikes, but were badly beaten soon afterwards. Even though a well-drilled, courageous phalanx of pikemen could stop a cavalry charge, the Flemings and Scots could not manoeuvre and had little missile capability.

The infantry soldiers from the Swiss cantons, however, worked out a system of weapons tactics, organization and training which was to give them a dominance in battle against most Europeans for nearly 200 years. At Morgarten (1315) about 2,000 Swiss slew with halberds—broad light axes on ten-foot poles which also had points—some 1,500 Austrian knights in a few minutes. This fight was on a mountain road where the cavalry was severely handicapped, but the Swiss developed quickly into really competent all-round infantry which was usually willing to fight anywhere, if the price was right. They beat a Burgundian army at Laupen (1339) on a field where cavalry could and did manoeuvre and charge, but was unable to break through the array of halberd points. At Sempach (1386), the Swiss used both pikes and halberds and some light armour to beat an army of mounted Austrians who fought mostly in heavy suits of full plate. The battle was disorderly, but was fought out on open ground which gave the infantry no advantage.

In the fifteenth century, the Swiss became the foremost professional soldiers of Europe. Infantry battalions would serve on a contract basis far from home. Pikes eighteen feet long replaced halberds for at least the four front ranks; a relatively small number of crossbowmen were stationed on the flanks. The Swiss won their later battles, however, at least as much by their organization, training and physical fitness as by their weapons and tactics. A Swiss infantry unit could advance in formation for a mile at a fast pace with their pikes held horizontally in both hands above their heads with points forward. They were partially armoured, struck with almost the shock of cavalry, and inspired in their enemies the same sort of dread.

IV

The Pike and Musket

B RITISH longbows and Swiss polearms put an end to the complete supremacy of armoured cavalry in Western Europe. It continued, however, to be intermittently the most important single arm of combined armies for about two centuries following Crécy. Armour did not reach its highest development and protective efficiency until the very end of this period. The fine suits of plate of the sixteenth century could withstand not only arrows, swords and polearms, but most bullets from gunpowder weapons of calibres which could be carried by one man in the field. Horsemen in heavy plate, however, needed extensive infantry and light cavalry support.

Gunpowder weapons are said to have ended the age of armour, but if this is true it took 250 years. The first simple cannon were employed in Europe early in the fourteenth century. The English probably had small field guns at Crécy, but they were so hopelessly inefficient that they were not important in battle for almost 100 years. In finally winning the Hundred Years War, the French employed siege-bombards to take many castles; these pieces were too clumsy and heavy, however, to be used in the field. Jan Zizka of the Hussites won campaigns by mounting small cannon in wagons; his victory by means of them at Prague (1420) was hailed as something new, but his tactics were difficult to use elsewhere.

Early one-man firearms were so poorly designed, slow and inaccurate that they were more adaptable to sieges than to battles in the field. Late in the fifteenth century, however, more efficient shoulder firearms were being used in small quantities. Some of these arms looked roughly like nineteenth-century muskets. Even though they could not penetrate good plate armour at medium range, they superseded crossbows and later, during the sixteenth century, the English longbow also. Both the wheel-lock and matchlock methods of ignition were known, but the latter was preferred for military use because it was cheaper, more trouble free, and capable of giving a greater number of shots before thorough cleaning was necessary.

Another use of the new and expensive weapon was by armoured heavy cavalry which had not been able to conquer pikemen with their shock charges. German professional soldiers known as *reiters* armed themselves with two long wheel-lock pistols in addition to their regular weapons and armour. A deep, loose formation of reiters would advance against pikemen, but halt at a range of about fifty yards; the front-rank men would fire one pistol and then the other, wheel sharp to the rear, and take a new place at the back of their file. They were able to reload while other ranks fired, and fire again themselves when they were at the head of the formation. The horses had to be extremely docile and the men well-practised to reload a pair of pistols in this fashion, but apparently it did work. Even though accuracy from mounted men armed with long, clumsy pistols cannot have been astonishing, masses of pikemen were sometimes sufficiently weakened to be overthrown by shock charges. Reiters were important throughout Western Europe for several decades.

Another anti-pike tactic was developed by the great Spanish commander, Gonzolo de Cordoba (1453–1515); he mixed active, powerful sword and buckler men with his pikemen to give a greater offensive capability. When pikes met pikes, the Spanish swordsmen would slip between or under the long weapons of friend and foe alike and kill the enemy as the Romans had handled the Macedonians.

The Spanish appear to have been the first to develop a shoulder firearm that would penetrate the strongest practical armour even at a range of 100 yards. This weapon was called a musket; it weighed between 15 and 25 pounds, measured more than 6 feet in length, and was fired from a rest. As its name implies—musket from mosquito in the falcon series—it was really a small field-piece. The Marquis de Pescara won Pavia (1525) in part because of these new weapons in the hands of his Spanish infantry. The power of these new arms insured their quick acceptance in most European armies. But musketeers could not act alone;

they had particularly to be protected from armoured cavalry.

We traced briefly the Swiss polearms tactics in the last chapter. The pikes of the Scots, Flemings, and even of the Swiss through the middle of the fifteenth century were too short and heavy in the head. The true pike developed a few years later was as long as the Macedonian sarissa of 1,800 years before and probably easier to manipulate. It had a tapering eighteen-foot ash shaft and a long slender steel head which could not be hacked off with a sword. These pikes balanced fairly well and could be moved by trained men precisely in accordance with orders. In a purely defensive alignment the rear end of the weapon could be supported in the ground. The great virtue of Swiss pikemen was that they had an offensive capability, but those of most other armies were useful mainly in defence. An offensive press of pikes was possible for most pike units only under the very best circumstances.

We have traced briefly into the early sixteenth century armoured cavalry, firearms of various kinds, and pikes. Soldiers were using a greater variety of infantry weapons and tactics with reasonable effectiveness than ever before. Towards the middle of the century, however, several imaginative commanders made approximately the same organizational change towards relative uniformity. Pikemen were combined with musketeers to the advantage of both. Musketeers could not protect themselves against shock charges of cavalry, nor against anyone when their weapons were empty; pikemen were vulnerable to the fire of musketeers, reiters and even sword and buckler men. But a combination of pikes and muskets in each infantry battalion could beat not only armoured heavy cavalry whether they charged or used their pistols, but also musketeers, or swordsmen alone. Pikes and muskets were more than a match for Cordoba's pikes and swords.

The new combination was a success, but there were organizational problems. At first, pikes predominated by at least three to one. Pikemen were bigger and had more armour, which sometimes extended to the knees. They normally carried a secondary weapon, usually a stout sword. Musketeers were smaller on the average and seldom armoured; agility was more important than power. The two types did not make for homogeneity either on the field of battle or on the march, but the most pressing question was how to form so that either the pikes or firepower could be presented to an enemy as required without delay or disorder. Musketeers were sometimes taught to move in and out between the pikemen so as to fire from in front and reload in the rear. Where this type of firing was done, the formation of pikemen and musketeers together was loose so that men armed with either weapon could meet an attack or deliver one. Well-drilled combined infantry was actually able to attack other infantry; a halt was made at close range for a volley from the musketeers and then the pikes pressed forward.

Formations which allowed individuals armed with one weapon to move back and forth through those armed with the other at command were found to be too loose and too easily reduced to chaos in battle. Various arrangements of combining relatively small sections of pikemen and musketeers in the same company or battalion worked better. So long as discipline was maintained in the ranks and COs kept their heads, the required arm could usually be presented when needed.

During the last half of the sixteenth century fully armoured horsemen began to disappear from the armies of Western Europe. The finest combat armour could not normally stop a musket ball; formed, well-disciplined pikes could defeat any cavalry charge. Further, the great cost of armour was tolerable in a feudal society because it protected the men who paid for it. From 1550 on, wars were being fought and paid for mostly by kings and princes who had insufficient soldiers under them capable of providing their own armour. Some professional soldiers had it, but these suits were rarely complete. Individuals continued to wear plate armour for many decades, but fully armoured cavalry was rare. Its cost would have been out of line with its effectiveness against pikes and muskets, and it was both uncomfortable and hampering in action.

GUSTAVUS ADOLPHUS

The Swedish army as organized by their great warrior king was the most progressive in the world at the time (1600–32). Under him, field artillery finally became significant in battle. Even though French cannon had enfiladed English archers at Formighy (1450) and broken Swiss pikemen at Marignano (1515), the pieces employed were not mobile. Gustavus introduced infantry support field-pieces, made in part of leather, which could be fired more rapidly than muskets. They were not a success, but slightly heavier brass guns and howitzers were of great value because they were able to keep up with infantry and cavalry.

Gustavus also made far-reaching changes in his infantry. He shortened his pikes, decreased the amount of pikemen's armour, and increased the proportion of muskets to pikes to equality. Now that armoured cavalry was not often encountered in mass, he reduced the calibre, weight and length of his muskets. Both the old rests and musketeer's armour were abandoned. The Swedish infantry became more mobile because of these changes.

Gustavus realized that the musket was becoming the dominant weapon. For some time continuous volleys had been obtained by forming musketeers in fairly large bodies ten ranks deep. As with the reiters, the front rank would fire, fall back to the rear, reload, and again fire when it was in front. The Swedish king increased the firepower of his musketeers by using paper cartridges and a new method of loading. Musketeers could now be placed only six ranks deep and deliver two-thirds more fire. Swedish pikemen also assumed formations six ranks deep. A full-strength battalion contained 1,152 rank and file divided in three pike companies of 192 each and four musket companies of 144. Each company of either arm had a total front of 96 feet; there were several ways of positioning the companies in relation to each other and to the battalion support field-pieces. Gustavus appears to have preferred to have his musketeers on the flanks of his pikemen with the guns in the intervals between companies.

A formation of this type would have produced a maximum of firepower, particularly as the Swedish musketeers sometimes not only fired volleys two ranks at a time, but also assumed a three-rank formation and all fired at the same time. But the line of musketeers was weak against cavalry; some at least would have had trouble gaining the protection of the three pike companies usually posted in the battalion centre. Gustavus overcame this weakness by providing musketeers with another weapon, the Swedish feather. This was a short staff of wood with a pike head at either end; the whole thing was about six feet long. Musketeers who might be charged by cavalry stuck these into the ground (in the fashion of British archers centuries before) a couple of paces ahead of their front rank with the points breast-high to the horses. A Swedish pike and musket battalion could form a defensive square of great strength. The muskets were usually at the corners which were often rounded.

Gustavus also remodelled the Swedish cavalry. In 1600, most West European cavalry were still partially armoured, but were sacrificing their shock potential in an effort to use firearms. Pistols and carbines were employed on horseback in ten-rank-deep formations; horses were again of the type which would allow their riders to fire and reload.

The Swedish king cut down on firearms and reloading equipment. He eliminated the docile horses and the deep cavalry formations entirely. Horsemen were formed three ranks deep in manageable squadrons which could manoeuvre and deliver shock charges. The sabre was the most important weapon, even though firearms continued to be issued. Cavalry still had a place in war, but would function in future in three specialized roles.

Since the days of the armoured reiters, cavalry had tried to use firearms. Horsemen armed with pistols, carbines and musketoons were invariably less effective with them, when mounted, than foot soldiers with muskets. But if cavalrymen dismounted, they were in theory at least the equal of infantry. Dragoons in the seventeenth century were mounted infantry. Their strategic mobility was greater than ordinary infantry, but they were handicapped when fighting on foot by lack of infantry practice and a desire among dragoon officers to function as true cavalry.

A more important role for horse soldiers was in reconnaissance and screening which could be done best by unarmoured light horsemen. Formal organization and training were not so necessary as intelligence, dash, experience and horsemanship. Cavalry has always been important for such work, but the religious wars of the period, where fighting was often confused, emphasized it.

The final role which cavalry played throughout the ascendancy of pike and musket infantry was similar to the tactics of horsemen at Adrianople and Crécy. A mounted formation in motion had momentum. If this was maintained right through contact with the enemy and supplemented by shock weapons, its combat effectiveness was still great. Even though cavalry could not normally break steady pike and musket infantry, it could destroy foot soldiers caught in disorder, or badly shaken by artillery. It could also operate against other cavalry. Maximum shock in battle required heavy horses, large men and, above all, the use of momentum. Firearms could be a disadvantage, but some armour could add to the effectiveness of heavy cavalry. Gustavus, before his untimely death in battle at Lutzen (1632), had already established the Swedish School of cavalry thought which emphasized charging home at speed with sabres.

THE BRITISH CIVIL WAR

Britain was to some extent out of the main stream of military developments on the Continent. Although some of the British Civil War leaders had served under Gustavus, Maurice of Nassau and other Continental commanders, the war started with a minimum of experience in the ranks. In addition, there was at first too much armour and too many pikes in the infantry and a too great reliance on firearms in the cavalry. The Royalist horsemen under Prince Rupert had a considerable advantage because they had greater mobility and more dash.

Cromwell had no military experience before the Civil War, but learned rapidly—perhaps in part because of previous study. His Ironside Cavalry was remarkable not only for its composition, but also for its organization and equipment. After a period of trial and error, it became really effective. Even though at first it relied too greatly on firearms and sometimes tried to receive Prince Rupert's horsemen at a stand, it soon learned its job. The troopers had some defensive armour, but abandoned entirely their early and faulty practice of relying on firearms. They stopped trying to check their own momentum and beat Rupert's best at Marston Moor (1644) and Naseby (1645) by their greater solidarity and discipline.

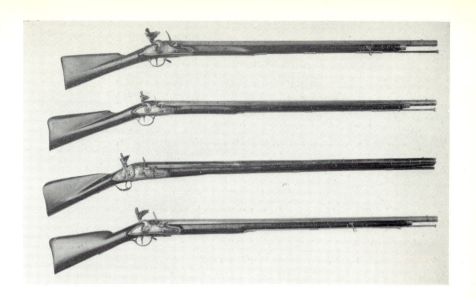

17th and early 18th-century weapons. The third from the top was issued by Monk to his 'Coldstreamers' in 1660 before they surrounded the Houses of Parliament

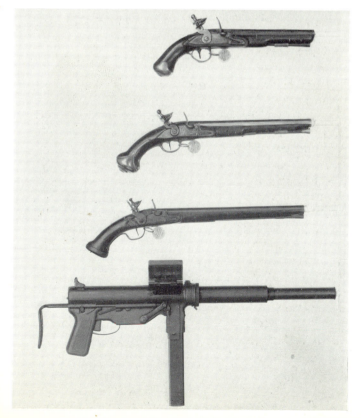

Three early British military pistols and the United States M3 SMG with a silenced barrel. The longest of the pistols is early 17th century and may have seen service in the British Civil War

An early German tank destroyer (World War I): a field gun mounted on a truck

A German crew with their Model 1908 Maxim MMG—usually an efficient combination

German Maxim Model 1908 MMG with crew in gas masks. The mount could be adjusted for elevation over a wide range and also used as a sled

British soldiers with a tank, field guns, SMLE rifles and Lewis ARs

An Italian soldier in the trenches (World War I) with a rifle which could be fired from below the level of a parapet so that the firer did not expose himself. Note the periscope sighting arrangement

The three main allied MMGs of World War I. The French 8-mm. Lebel heavy air-cooled Hotchkiss, the Model 1917 ·30-'06 water-cooled Browning and the British ·303 water-cooled Vickers

V

Marlborough and Frederick

THE last years of the seventeenth century produced a series of related changes in infantry weapons and tactics. The matchlock was finally replaced by the flintlock; all-weather leather pouches holding forty to sixty paper cartridges were issued to all infantrymen. The new muskets and ammunition meant quicker shooting even when surprised, without sacrificing reliability throughout a battle. Infantry now had a more useful and dependable firepower.

The invention of the bayonet was of even greater importance. Musketeers were given a short sword which could be mounted in or at the muzzles of their weapons, thus converting them into tolerable pikes. Even though a musket and bayonet was not as good as a pike for shock action, a homogeneous unit armed with muskets and bayonets throughout proved superior to any combination of muskets and pikes. Fire was beginning to dominate shock in both weapons and tactics, but the new bayonets were still important.

The name *bayonet* comes from Bayonne in the Basque section of France. In mid-seventeenth century, this area produced a short, round-handled sword. A French infantry commander from Bayonne, Seigneur de Puysegur, said in his memoirs that he ordered a quantity of these and issued them to his French musketeers on the Flemish border in 1647. They could be fitted into the muzzles of muskets for use as bayonets, but prevented further firing until they were removed. The idea made slow progress in France and may have originated independently elsewhere, but plug bayonets, as well as a few sleeve and ring types which did not prevent the muskets from being loaded and fired, were in almost universal use with military muskets by 1700.

Sleeve bayonets had obvious advantages over the plug type, but were not widely used in the British army until after 1714.

The demise of the pike brought about the end of infantry armour. Foot soldiers were to fight with flintlock muskets and bayonets only, for the next 150 years. Further improvements in their weapons and ammunition came about gradually; lighter, shorter, handier weapons made infantry tactics easier, simpler and more controllable. The standard infantry unit throughout Western Europe was the battalion, which generally formed six ranks deep. Gustavus's three-rank infantry line was more efficient for delivering fire, but lacked solidarity.

These new battalions which did not have either long clumsy pikes, or smouldering lengths of match attached to every man, as well as tubs of it in wagons, gave greater strategic mobility to the commanders capable of taking advantage of it. Firepower had increased not only because the new muskets were better, but also because there were more of them, now that pikes were gone. These firearms may not have been accurate beyond 80 yards, but they could kill at 300. The set-piece battles of the pike era, in which both armies remained for days in battle array even when moving, were no longer necessary.

The new reliance on missile weapons which could be discharged many times produced a greater possibility for winning against odds. In the pike days, an inferior infantry force could be destroyed quickly by a larger one, and at small cost to the larger. Efficient firepower changed this; a battalion could hold off a brigade and inflict severe casualties upon it. A weaker force, if properly handled, could pin down a stronger one for a considerable period. Opportunities for strategic and tactical manoeuvre and generalship were enlarged.

Cavalry was still important for the three purposes mentioned in the last chapter, but on the field of battle it was required to deliver shock charges which took full advantage of speed and momentum. The sabre became the dominant weapon; firearms were of little use to men who actually fought mounted.

By slow and limited improvements artillery had increased its importance in battle. As noted, Zizka and Gustavus pioneered the employment of small pieces which could accompany infantry and cavalry, but the importance of artillery mobility tended to be forgotten. All cannon in the eighteenth century were more efficient than before, but most field pieces were large, slow and hard to move. All had, however, specialized ammunition and could be handled efficiently by well-trained gunners.

A number of wars of various sizes were fought with these new weapons and by these tactics, including the first of world-wide scope, the Seven Years War (1756–63). Terrain and supply conditions rendered many battles non-typical; some reputations were built more on logistics than battlefield command. These were particularly true in the New World and in the East, although Wolfe, Washington and Clive might have been outstanding anywhere. Reviewing the period as a whole, however, the military reputations of Marlborough and Frederick appear to stand out above the rest. Rather than consider many battles and sieges generally, we will follow in some detail the weapons tactics of both men, each in his finest battles. Marlborough's Blenheim (1704) and Frederick's Leuthen (1757) illustrate the genius of each at his best.

BLENHEIM

The War of the Spanish Succession began in 1703; it was predominantly fought by Austria, the Netherlands and Britain against France. Marlborough was senior Allied commander in the Low Countries, but was subject to control by a Dutch military commission. During the first year of hostilities, the main area of manoeuvre was Belgium. In 1704, however, French grand strategy appears to have called for holding actions there, while a combined French-Bavarian offensive knocked Austria out of the war. If this happened, the Allied forces west of the Rhine would have been unable to stand against the great French numerical superiority.

Marlborough decided to forestall his enemies by moving far to the east, combining with an Austrian army there, and beating the French and Bavarians in battle. This was not easy to achieve because of the possible veto by the Dutch commission and the distances involved. The commission wanted 'big manoeuvre, little fight' campaigns in flat country where fortress towns limited results; it certainly did not want its allies moving hundreds of miles away to the banks of the Danube. But the great British general prevailed, in part by concealing his ultimate intentions, and sent his army across the Rhine at Bonn on 23 May 1704.

This march to the Danube has been called the greatest military manoeuvre of the century. Marlborough managed it without loss of morale and preserved the physical condition of his army. It was a co-ordinative and logistic achievement of unique proportions for that period; troops marched by regular stages along different but parallel routes and lacked nothing, not even new boots.

Marlborough took Donauwörth on 2 July and established himself firmly on the Danube. He made contact with the Austrians under Eugene, Prince of Orange, but still had to win his battle; manoeuvre alone was not enough. He knew that a French and Bavarian army which was somewhat superior in numbers lay at Hochstadt.

Instead of advancing in the approved, methodical, permanently-aligned manner of the seventeenth century, Marlborough and Eugene moved quickly west along the northern bank of the Danube and surprised their enemies, in a strategic sense. On 2 August 1704, the opposing forces met on a rolling plain two miles wide with the Danube to the south and foot-hills to the north. The small village of Blenheim on the bank of the river was held by the French as the southern anchor of their position; the Bavarians were to the north and west.

Marlborough's strategy was to attack Blenheim in heavy force and direct Eugene to attack the Bavarian centre and left. Eugene was to work round the Bavarian flank, if possible. Marlborough probably intended the French and Bavarian commanders—they collaborated as equals rather than having one senior to the other as in the Allied army—to believe he was trying to execute the famous Cannae manoeuvre by attacking on both flanks. At worst, the two thrusts were to hold the enemy while the Allies prepared their main attack, which was to be in the centre where the French and Bavarian armies joined.

For three hours the two preliminary attacks were carried on with great vigour. The fighting in and about Blenheim was particularly severe. The first attack was delivered by a predominantly British force about the size of a modern brigade. This was repulsed after bloody fighting, during which the French reinforced their Blenheim garrison considerably. Marlborough then delivered another attack which was even stronger. The

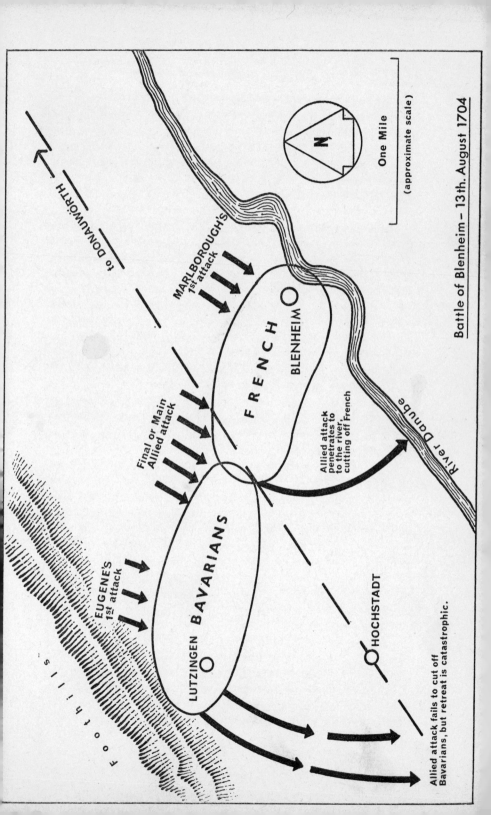

Battle of Blenheim – 13th. August 1704

enemy had initially an advantage in regard to position; the garden walls and houses gave them a fortress, but it was far too small to accommodate the French forces which were soon engaged in this area. The later fighting was done mostly in the open.

For the first time, one major army met another with the infantry of each depending almost entirely on firepower, on missile weapons rather than those of shock. Heavy lines of musketeers advanced against one another with French formations sometime partially sheltered. Six-, four-, and three-rank alignments were used; there was a lot of firing, usually of the volley type by ranks and at close range. Some units fired a final volley and charged with bayonets, but this sort of thing was rarer than long musketry duels between battalions. When Marlborough's infantry was retiring for the second time, some French cavalry endeavoured to sweep round Blenheim and get in amongst the disorganized foot soldiers. They were prevented from doing so by a covering force of Austrian cavalry. The village was not taken, but a large proportion of the French army was pinned down in the area.

Eugene was following more or less the same plan on the Allied right and making more headway. In the centre there was as yet only artillery fire, although some of these weapons were as large as twenty-four-pounders. Marlborough had not only drawn a good deal of the enemy strength to the flanks, but also prepared his own decisive blow. Suddenly, the Allied commander broke through the middle of the enemy line using both cavalry and infantry. The French army was separated from the Bavarians. The two enemy cavalries reacted quickly, however, and moved almost together to throw back the Allies and restore their own line. The crisis of the battle occurred when Marlborough led his cavalry to meet that of France and Bavaria. The Allies charged home at speed in a long, relatively thin line—probably a series of lines—relying on their sabres. The French and Bavarian horsemen endeavoured to use firearms while at a stand. Momentum and shock weapons won completely.

The French army was isolated and pinned against the river. After hours of stubborn fighting, the original garrison in Blenheim and all the reinforcements fed into the place were captured. Only a few well-mounted French horsemen, who made off west, and a few more cavalry and infantry, who were able to swim the river, escaped. All French artillery and baggage was taken. Similar plans for capturing the Bavarian army miscarried because of dust and smoke. But that force was useless for months because of actual casualties, loss of equipment and demoralization during a frantic retreat. Blenheim was one of the most decisive victories in history.

Tactically, the battle is important because infantry fought almost entirely with firepower. The pikes were not missed. The winning cavalry tactics, on the other hand, involved shock from both momentum and weapons. A line of troopers two or three ranks deep was able to exert more shock power than the older deeper masses. Firearms in the hands of mounted soldiers at a stand were nearly useless.

LEUTHEN

Frederick the Great came to the throne of Prussia in 1742. He inherited a fine showy professional army of no great patriotism, and improved it over a few years by drill, strict discipline, field training and actual war into one of the most outstanding forces that the world has ever known. The Prussian army had an unusual strategic mobility for that time, based on its greater ability to march, react to orders and to care for itself logistically.

The Prussian king improved his individual arms by a few minor changes in weapons; he replaced wooden ramrods with steel so as to give speed and sureness of loading. But his greatest military virtues were dependent upon drill. Not since Roman times have soldiers spent so much time practising in peace what they were to do in battle. Frederick's artillery and infantry could handle their weapons efficiently under all conditions. His infantry, particularly, drilled not only in battalions but in both smaller and larger units. In the words of a later time, it could move, fight and communicate.

Frederick knew from his study and early experience that great masses of horsemen many ranks deep were inefficient, because their momentum ceased when the front ranks suffered severe casualties. Besides, they were difficult to control. He had his units train and fight in squadrons of about 120 troopers, two ranks deep. The Prussian organization and system of command was such, however, that many squadrons could act together in a perfectly articulated whole. The lateral interval between squadrons could be reduced to as little as five yards, but packing them one behind the other was avoided.

Frederick went further in the realism of his cavalry training than any other commander. His units deployed from column into line, charged, wheeled and went through other convolutions at speed over rough terrain as well as on smooth ground. Casualties among horses and men were frequent, but the ability to exert maximum shock boot-to-boot on any practical battlefield was achieved.

The Prussian king anticipated by fifty years the rest of Europe by making the horses which drew his field artillery organic to his lighter piece units. This was not horse artillery by a British Victorian definition, but was a great step forward compared to Frederick's contemporaries. He was usually opposed by more and heavier guns, but put his guns to better use and kept them up with the rest of the army more constantly. He followed Gustavus in assigning light pieces, usually three-pounders, to individual infantry battalions.

The Prussian king changed his mind in regard to infantry firepower after his early battles. Initially, he had followed Marshal Saxe, who thought that muskets did little damage save at assault range. Frederick soon realized, however, that his drill was such that his infantry, at least, could fire volleys at moderate ranges to disorganize their opponents and still charge with loaded muskets as well as bayonets later on. Prussian battalions were divided into eight companies and were normally arrayed three ranks deep. They fired volleys in various ways, but preferred to use a system by which an entire company of all three ranks fired together and then loaded in unison. The other companies would be doing the same thing but on a different time schedule, so that there were company discharges at an average rate of one every two seconds, or faster.

In order to understand fully Frederick's victory at Leuthen, we should review his triumph at Rossbach earlier in 1757. He won there with a force of about 24,000 over a French and Austrian army of nearly 64,000 by catching the enemy in the act of attacking the Prussian left flank. Frederick took full advantage of his greater manoeuvrability to deploy in line of battle against the head of the enemy column. Cavalry smashed the enemy cavalry screen using shock only; the Prussian artillery and infantry used their concentrated firepower on the opposing infantry columns, which came apart. The Prussian cavalry entered the fight once

FRENCH & ALLIES
1st Position

FREDERICK'S
1st Position

Village of ROSSBACH

Allied Cavalry (not properly formed at time of Prussian attack)

2 Miles
(approximate scale)

N

Key

Allied Infantry
    ,,   Cavalry

Prussian Infantry
    ,,   Cavalry
    ,,   Artillery

Battle of Rossbach – 5th November 1757

more, against the infantry this time. The battle was over in some forty minutes, but was a complete victory for Frederick who suffered considerably less than 1,000 casualties while inflicting about 8,000 on his enemies; all the rest fled in disorder.

Leuthen was a different story. Frederick was again outnumbered, about 40,000 to 75,000, but the battle was the reverse of Rossbach. The Austrian commander took up a strong defensive position and was not going to try complicated manoeuvres which had a way of ending badly against Frederick. The Prussian army attacked, using Frederick's now famous oblique order. Actually, this amounted to marching across the Austrian front—what his enemies had done at Rossbach—and making a heavy attack by his own right flank on the enemy's left. He protected his inner flank with a cavalry screen and threatened the Austrian right. This sort of thing was possible because Frederick's cavalry, infantry and artillery was under such tight control, and because of advantageous terrain. He formed his line of battle from his marching columns without a halt; the manoeuvre was covered by a low hill. Most commanders of this period required hours to organize their army for battle (Marlborough and Eugene used up three hours at Blenheim). Without hesitation Frederick attacked the Austrian flank with almost his entire force. Even the cavalry screen in front of the Austrian centre and right smashed an enemy mounte forced which endeavoured to attack Frederick's inner flank.

The Prussian king took the Austrian line at a serious disadvantage. The better controlled Prussian cavalry, which had defeated the Austrian cavalry screen, was able to get into the rear of the enemy left flank. Prussian artillery and infantry attacked the other end of this part of the Austrian infantry and forced it back upon itself. Frederick's mobile and efficient artillery and his well-drilled infantry firepower slaughtered the clumsy Austrians packed together in a mass of battalions. The enemy left was defeated before the right came up to be beaten in turn. Frederick's superb shock cavalry completed the job. The Austrians lost as many in dead and prisoners as the Prussian army had at the beginning of the action, about 40,000 men. But the Prussians suffered 6,200 casualties themselves, in severe fighting. The Austrians were outmanoeuvred, but fought stubbornly.

Tactically, Frederick and his army are probably the finest

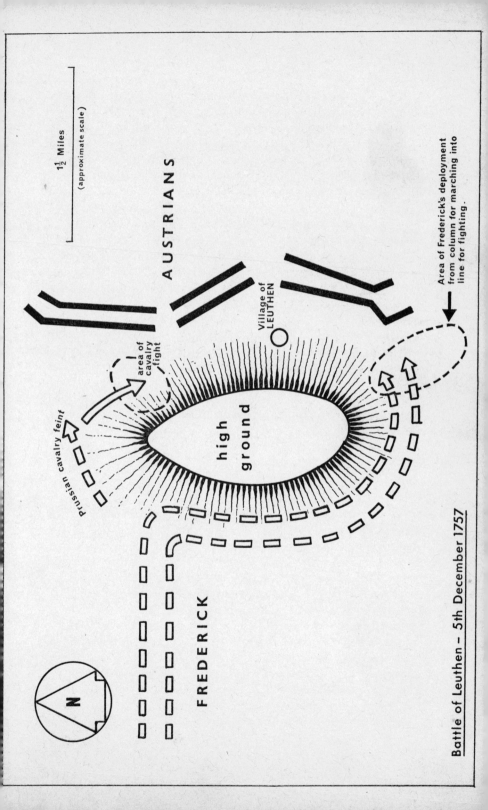

N

1½ Miles
(approximate scale)

AUSTRIANS

Village of
LEUTHEN

area of
cavalry fight

Prussian cavalry feint

high
ground

FREDERICK

Area of Frederick's deployment
from column for marching into
line for fighting.

Battle of Leuthen – 5th December 1757

examples since Roman times of what professional, thoughtful organization and incessant drill can achieve. Every man of every infantry platoon, cavalry squadron and artillery brigade not only knew exactly what he was supposed to do, but did it precisely and without hesitation at command. The entire army had extreme strategic and good tactical mobility. Even in defeats—these were inevitable because of numerical odds against them—the Prussians could draw off without fatal injury and continue the campaign.

On the other hand, Frederick appears to have lacked an appreciation of the value of light forces of both cavalry and infantry. Even though in other ways his intelligence system was excellent, his cavalry reconnaissance was often poor. But these things were of small importance. At speed and boot-to-boot, his troopers and their horses were the best in the world. He also realized more clearly than any other commander of his era that a musket, even when equipped with bayonet, was still best used as a missile weapon. His infantry was beautifully organized and under perfect control, but it won with firepower. His artillery was equally efficient. A Prussian army under its great warrior king appears to have had no serious weaknesses. His infantry–artillery team had great missile facility and his cavalry an astonishing shock potential.

VI

Napoleon, Wellington and the American Civil War

THE French Revolution changed many things throughout the world, including the techniques of making war. Through 1792, the nations of Europe financed their wars more or less as private ventures. Republican France resorted to national war in a modern sense. Universal conscription was introduced; the resources of the entire French nation were harnessed in a united national effort.

The army created was of unprecedented size, but at first lacked weapons, training and most of the advantages of professional military organization. It soon remedied these defects, however, because of the inherent industrial strength of France, the professional military knowledge of some soldiers from the old regime, and the fine raw personnel brought into the service by a conscription which applied equally to all classes. There was no shortage of gifted officer candidates from the ranks who had natural ability, intelligence, ambition and even education. Each French soldier realized that he could rise to the rank of marshal, if he did his jobs well enough. Even more important, the patriotic spirit captured in the stirring Marseillaise brought out personal and group valour.

In the early days of the Republic, infantry was the predominant arm; artillery had not yet been fully developed, and cavalry was weak in numbers and in training. The only significant weapons of the infantry were muskets and bayonets. The French took full advantage of both and evolved a way of fighting suitable to their numbers, weapons and enthusiasm. One company of each infantry battalion was composed of soldiers selected for their physical activity, ability to load and fire their muskets, and function as skirmishers (tirailleurs) when necessary. In battle, many similar units went forward in an irregular line against their more formally deployed enemies. The French tirailleurs aimed and fired individually, taking advantage of any available cover. They were supported by French artillery and could withstand even major efforts to clear them away because of their numbers, their élite status, and their individual bravery.

These tirailleurs and their artillery support would engage the whole of the opposing front for some time. They inflicted casualties and threw formations into disorder. Even more important, they concealed the location of the main French attack. When the time was right, other less skilful, but no less patriotic, French infantry came forward in deep columns. These struck relatively narrow sections of the enemy line already weakened and disorganized by the tirailleurs and artillery. A French column would smash through the opposition, often without firing a shot. The enemy usually broke before contact. The more numerous French infantry then won the mêlée that followed.

An analysis of these column victories reveals that the French were winning mainly through psychological shock. They were threatening to use the bayonet, but rarely actually using it. They were victorious by virtue of their apparent mass and fearsome appearance. One of these French columns could not exert hydrostatic pressure as the Theban phalanx had done at Leuctra. Unlike cavalry at a gallop, men in fairly loose ranks can stop in an instant, if their courage fails or casualties pile up ahead.

After 1796, Napoleon and other French commanders greatly improved their military techniques. The French under Napoleon dominated Continental Europe as never before, because of a military competence at all levels and a new system of weapons and tactics. First, there were changes in artillery *matériel* and use; Napoleon provided the highest proportion of artillery to infantry ever used successfully by a mobile army. Powerful, long-ranged pieces supported the tirailleurs; light guns came forward with the French infantry columns and sometimes delivered grape and canister at ranges of under 200 yards. Napoleon was also a master of artillery concentration on a narrow space for maximum effect.

The second general improvement in the French army was in connection with their cavalry. Well-trained and disciplined men

Enemy Line
Continental Type

French Tirailleurs —
50 to 100 yards from enemy.

'X'

←Light Artillery

←Infantry

←Light Artillery

←Infantry

Procedure:

● First, tirailleurs engage all along the enemy front supported by medium artillery.

● Second, infantry columns accompanied by light artillery come forward to attack one or more points 'X' in the enemy line. These points may or may not have received concentrated fire from medium artillery.

● Third, light artillery go into action at ranges of 150 – 300 yards against enemy line where columns will strike. Tirailleur aimed fire, medium artillery, light artillery close range fire and finally the threat of infantry bayonet shock usually caused the enemy to break before contact.

Medium artillery –
700 to 1000 yards from enemy

Schematic representation of French
Battle Tactics: Napoleonic period.

were provided with good horses; the same three types already discussed were used. Light cavalry was for reconnaissance and screening; the cuirassiers and other heavy horsemen for shock charges in battle; the dragoons started out as mounted infantry, but soon became true cavalry intermediate between the other two types and were to some extent suitable for both missions.

The third general improvement in French armies under Napoleon was in relation to the infantry. His tirailleurs became more effective with discipline and training; their missile accuracy improved and their ability to manoeuvre in the open became more easily controlled. The columns also improved with professional training and active service.

Napoleon displayed personally an appreciation of overall military situations never exceeded in history. He was able throughout his military career to manoeuvre superbly on a large scale and strike in unexpected, but critical, places. About 1809, however, his battle tactics began to be more massive and less mobile. He employed even heavier concentrations of artillery and used more cavalry and infantry on narrower fronts. His later victories were frequently gained by wearing down the opposition with repeated bloody attacks in the same area concluded by a final blow of the Imperial Guard which was an élite organization of infantry, cavalry and artillery usually held in reserve.

While Napoleon was winning, and less often losing, grand dramatic costly battles in the heart of Europe, a British commander by the name of Wellesley, later the Duke of Wellington, compiled an all-victorious string of more modest combats. Wellington beat the French continuously in the Peninsula and finally drove deep into Southern France in 1814. His forces aided enormously in forcing the Emperor's first abdication. Wellington defeated Napoleon utterly at Waterloo in 1815 to put a quick end to the rekindled Imperial ambitions.

Wellington probably knew more of tactics than any other man in history who was also of first rank in strategy. He was also a master of transportation and supply. Under the Duke, the British army beat each tactical manoeuvre of the French in detail. First the tirailleurs: Wellington sent against them skirmishers of his own who were nearly as numerous and better armed for their job. Many British and Allied skirmishers were provided with rifles. This was the first time in military history that these

A British ·303 water-cooled Vickers MMG on an extemporized AA mount

A 37-mm. Model 1916 gun as used against the Germans in the Meuse-Argonne offensive (World War I)

US infantry with the Springfield Model 1903 calibre ·30-'06 rifle and bayonet in the foreground (World War I)

Outpost sentries on duty. This place was destroyed by enemy shellfire a few minutes after the picture was taken. Forest of Paroy

An unusual picture showing French rifle-armed infantry mingling with British MMG crews

US artillerymen about to fire one of the primitive mortars widely used in 1918

A US soldier firing his BAR in combat in the Philippines in 1945

US Marines at Iwo Jima (World War II). Note particularly the Model 1919A4 MMGs, the model M1 SMG, the grenade and part of a combat shotgun which appears just above the action of the MG

weapons were used effectively on the battlefield in large numbers. The French tirailleurs never reached Wellington's main line and certainly did not mask any points at which the French columns would endeavour to strike.

The Baker British military rifle of this period was, of course, a flintlock muzzle-loader, but was accurate in slow independent fire because it used leather-patched spherical bullets which loaded easily and were spun properly on the way out. This rifle had only the same inaccurate maximum range as the musket—about 450 yards—but a good shot could hit a man at 200 yards more frequently with a Baker rifle than he could with a musket at half that distance. In an emergency requiring rapid fire, after the bore of a rifle was dirty, unpatched bullets from paper cartridges could be forced down the bore with strong, relatively short steel rammers almost as easily as with loose musket-balls and the Brown Bess.

When the French infantry columns did come forward, Wellington's own infantry met them in two-deep lines, which usually advanced a short distance before halting in a good firing position. The missile advantage of musket-armed infantry stationary in line over similar troops in a moving column is obvious. Every man in both ranks of the lines could load and fire easily as if at practice. The French columns were constructed in various ways, but no more than one-fifth of them could fire at all.

We must avoid the usual error of thinking of this line versus column tactics as a mysterious invention. The theoretical superiority of the line was well known, but only Wellington's infantry had the organization, discipline and sheer bottom to remain calm and deliver regular, full volleys. Blucher and his brilliant young Prussian Chief-of-Staff, Gneisenau, freely admitted the great advantage that the British lines had over French columns, but pointed out that their own troops, even in three-deep lines, did not have the discipline, training and individual stability to hold such formations and didn't try to use them.

Why was British infantry able to function in this manner?

Part of this unique ability came from natural talent and six years of victorious battle experience under Wellington. But there was a technical reason also. Only Wellington's infantry during the Napoleonic period actually practised sufficiently with live ammunition in their rifles and muskets to know how to deliver effective

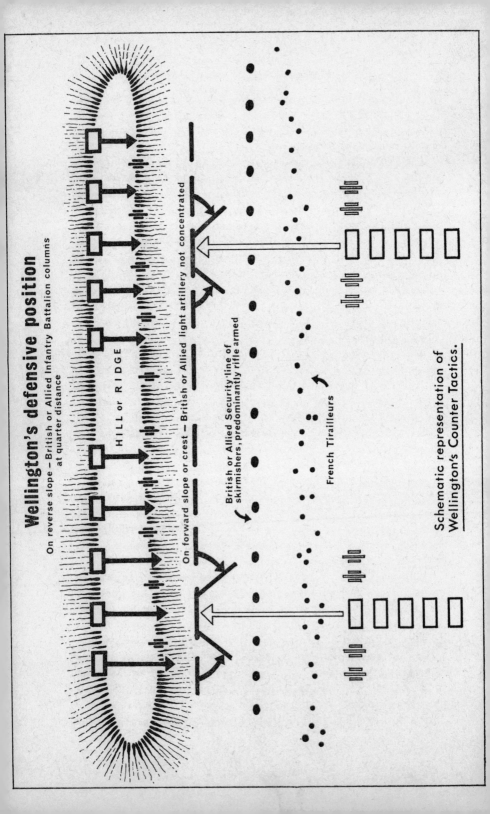

Wellington's defensive position

On reverse slope – British or Allied Infantry Battalion columns at quarter distance

HILL or RIDGE

On forward slope or crest – British or Allied light artillery not concentrated

British or Allied Security line of skirmishers, predominantly rifle armed

French Tirailleurs

Schematic representation of Wellington's Counter Tactics.

fire for as long as necessary. A single round cost at that time almost as much as food for a full day; only Britain could afford enough target practice to gain efficiency. Some well-trained British battalions are said to have been able to fire full battalion volleys as rapidly as once in nine seconds. In battle, however, Wellington's infantry fired in volleys by half companies and more slowly.

British missile tactics against French columns revealed the essential weakness of the latter. They could not really exert much shock, although all former enemies had assumed that they could. When the head of a column was continually being shot down by the rolling platoon fire of British, Hanoverians and Portuguese infantry in line, the column just stopped. Once this happened, a segment of the Allied line would wrap around the close-packed Frenchmen and slaughter them with firepower. Frequently, the French would try to deploy into line under fire, but were never able to accomplish this; they always broke and ran first.

Now for Wellington's counter-measures against Napoleon's artillery. As we have seen, the Emperor had not only more pieces, but also some of the most powerful field pieces—the new French twelve-pounders—ever used successfully in battle. Wellington made no effort to copy the French in the composition of his armies. He was content with fewer and smaller guns and did not often use concentrated fire. He generally dispersed his artillery throughout the area occupied by his infantry. No matter where the French columns might attack, they would come under some Allied artillery fire. Wellington did not allow his artillerymen to fire at the opposing guns, because the accuracy of the weapons of that day and the destructiveness of their projectiles at long range did not normally give sufficient return for effort, ammunition and deterioration of the pieces fired.

Wellington protected his main line infantry against preliminary artillery fire by deploying it on the reverse slopes of hills and ridges; this was almost completely effective in the days before indirect laying and control of artillery fire by observers. In the few places where his infantry had to be in the open, he ordered his men to lie down in line. When light artillery came forward with French columns, it was the special target of Allied riflemen; more than half of all pieces that did this were captured before they were able to get into action at all.

Wellington did not encounter Napoleon's heavy cavalry until

Waterloo. Dragoons and lighter types were employed by the French in the Peninsula. The Duke had heard, however, all about the shock attacks of French cuirassiers and was ready. He formed his infantry into squares when cavalry approached and withstood many charges with firepower and the threat of bayonets. A kind of defensive psychological shock was produced by the line of bayonets on muskets which won for the infantry. If the enemy cavalry had actually carried through their charge, offensive and defensive shock would have met. But almost no horsemen did carry through; they swerved *around* the sixty-foot squares.

Wellington adopted a novel expedient at Waterloo for preserving his guns (he never lost one in his entire career). The Duke had his field artillery where it could fire on both cavalry and infantry attacks. He positioned it on the low crests behind which his infantry was sheltered. When infantry came forward, Allied infantry in line moved in front of the guns at the last moment and defeated it in the usual way. When French cavalry charged, British artillerymen kept their guns firing until the horsemen were almost to them and then temporarily abandoned their pieces. They ran back and threw themselves under the bayonets of the infantry squares.

The French cavalry appeared to take scores of Allied guns, but could neither bring them away nor destroy them. The short-range fire of the infantry squares was immediately directed upon any Frenchman who tried. As soon as the French cavalry retired, the artillerymen returned to their guns and opened fire. Ammunition was available just behind the infantry; the gunners took their implements with them and, of course, brought them back.

Waterloo was followed by forty years of comparative peace. Throughout this period, the flintlock musket remained supreme. Around 1855, however, mechanical and industrial advances began to play a large part in war. The most important military development of this period was the introduction into major armies of an infantry rifle which made possible fairly accurate fire on large targets such as a battery of artillery at 1,000 yards without hurting the speed of loading. These rifles still loaded from the muzzle, but fired an elongated, hollow-base bullet that slid more or less easily down the bore. The inflammation of the powder, caused by the detonation of the percussion cap under the hammer, expanded the base of the lead bullet into the grooves of the rifling, so that the bullet received the proper spiral motion on the way out.

The Crimean War and the American–Mexican War were fought primarily with the old smooth-bore muskets, but the new weapons—usually called Minie rifles after one of the several men who figured in their development—were of extreme importance in the American Civil War. These accurate, easily handled muzzle-loaders made battlefield cavalry charges all but suicidal; horsemen just could not get to infantry capable of delivering as many as ten full accurate volleys after their assailants were within range.

A similar change had to be made in the battle tactics of artillery. Even though some field guns were now rifled, and fired elongated projectiles more accurately and to greater ranges, their increase in combat efficiency was negligible. Their great disadvantage was that the bursting charge in the new shell was only black powder. The projectile broke into a small number of pieces, usually from three to six. The infantry of both sides learned that the artillery was ineffective when firing at beyond canister range. Infantry could beat artillery, if the latter was in the open within range of the new Minie rifles. By the end of the war, artillery was reduced to a subordinate role. The most effective pieces were light muzzle-loading smooth-bores, used like large shotguns right with infantry.

The Minie rifles also doomed close-order columns as attacking formations; even two-deep lines suffered greatly, if exposed over considerable distances. The skirmish lines of the Napoleonic period —actually the old Ranger tactics of American Colonial days— were found to be best even for heavy attacks. The terrible losses at Fredericksburg and Gettysburg tended not only to spread out formations on later battlefields, but also caused both sides to dig field works at the slightest provocation.

We must examine a half-truth in regard to weapons in this war which says that it began with smooth-bore muzzle-loaders and ended with breech-loading, metallic-cartridge repeating rifles. Although some smooth-bore muskets were used early in the war, particularly by the South, they were never standard. Breech-loading infantry rifles were tried on a small scale and found to lack power, range and reliability. All were withdrawn; the infantry finished the war with the new-type Minie muzzle-loaders.

Cavalry carbines are a different story. The Union horsemen

tried out more than twenty breech-loading systems and finally adopted the Spencer, which was not only a breech-loader, but a magazine repeater as well. It fired a metallic cartridge with priming contained in the rim around the base. An infantry version of this same weapon had been abandoned because the breech mechanism could not stand the pressure of a powerful cartridge, but low power was satisfactory for cavalry. Some Union cavalry commanders did complain, however, because their new weapons put them at a disadvantage against Confederate cavalry which had short muzzle-loading Minie rifles of British and Austrian manufacture.

Throughout the Civil War, the defence was stronger than the attack. Even a defeated army could use the new Minie rifles to prevent an effective pursuit. Field fortifications added to the defensive advantage. The soldiers of both sides were largely farmers and well acquainted with spade and axe. A half-dozen hours would provide trenches with pine log reinforcements. The troops of both sides were patriotic and sometimes capable of astonishing offensive bravery in the open, but they were always tough on the defence in sheltered positions. Many had been experienced marksmen before they entered the army. Attacks on prepared positions were costly and seldom succeeded.

Victories in the field were so nearly evenly divided that the war was ultimately won through attrition and the breakdown of Confederate civilian transportation. The industrial revolution had come into war with a vengeance. Supplies and munitions multiplied in weight and variety; railways, steamships, and even electrical communications, were now of great importance. Wellington had made use of the power of Britain's industry and commerce, but Grant won with these plus Northern manufacturing horsepower, foreign recruit-purchasing and dollars. In the future, wars would still be decided by men with weapons, but the importance of home-front efforts in many different fields was to increase in geometric proportion.

VII

Chemical and Industrial War

THE Franco–Prussian War (1870–1), and the Russo–Turkish War (1878–9), were fought with weapons both old and new; on the whole, the old predominated. Black powder was used for propelling missiles and for the bursting charges inside most artillery shells. Field pieces ran back on discharge, making accuracy difficult and rapid fire impossible. Breech-loading infantry rifles were known, but only partially successful; all were large-bore, low-velocity weapons. No satisfactory infantry repeating rifle was available. Horse cavalry was still running around waving sabres and lances.

On the other hand, war was now dependent on railways, telegraph lines and munitions supply systems based on the vast new manufacturing potentials of integrated economies. Missile power due to numbers of accurately made weapons and millions of rounds of efficient ammunition had reduced shock weapon utility on the battlefield nearly to zero. As we have seen, the new bullets and rifling in small arms forced artillery to retreat temporarily beyond its effective range and ended the glorious career of mounted cavalry in battle. Explosive artillery projectiles suddenly drastically decreased the combat potential of wooden fighting ships.

From the very beginning twentieth-century war was different from all other major conflicts in dozens of ways. The material progress of the human race in the last quarter of the nineteenth century was truly astonishing and was based on new inventions. But chemical, mechanical and industrial engineering and production techniques were also responsible. Scores of civilian areas of progress were adapted to military ends, but the purely military inventions and improvements were also important. Space prevents a discussion of all these, even in the field of weapons, but we will describe in some detail the three most important: the modern military rifle, the MG, and the modern high-explosive-firing field gun. All were in service before 1900.

Modern military rifles combine a number of improvements that are in themselves old. Rifling, magazines to contain additional ammunition and elongated bullets of reduced diameter have been known for centuries. But these devices were not practical before the development of technological skills in manufacture and stronger chemical propellants with better burning characteristics. Within a few years, however, several armies were provided with essentially similar, but different rifles and ammunition. Almost all were bolt-action, box-magazine weapons firing a bullet of approximately ·30-inch bore diameter and 175 grains weight at a muzzle velocity slightly in excess of 2,000 f.p.s.; this meant a lethal range of at least 2,500 yards. Ballistics in this class could be achieved only by smokeless propellants, and bullets with an outer jacket of metal harder and more heat resistant than lead.

A rifle of this type allowed a soldier of average skill to fire at targets as far away as he could see with a fair possibility of hitting them. He could get off at least ten aimed shots in a minute. The ammunition was sufficiently light so that the soldier himself could carry a good deal of it. The rifle could fire several hundred rounds before cleaning was absolutely necessary. These new rifles increased infantry firepower and also the capability of one protected man on defence to defeat several attackers. The new rifles further reduced the effectiveness of all mass infantry and cavalry formations in the open during daylight.

On the heels of these new infantry rifles, or actually preceding them, were the first MGs. The idea of multiple missiles delivered by a machine, but as if several archers or musketeers were firing together or in quick succession, is old; volley guns were among the first military firearms. Museums contain rapid-fire weapons from the early flintlock era. The mechanical problems involved in the production of an efficient repeating weapon, however, were insoluble until after the American Civil War. The French mitrailleuse, which was used to a considerable extent in the Franco–Prussian War, is usually considered the first successful MG, although it failed more often than it succeeded. The American Gatling gun was produced earlier, but was not used significantly in war for some time. Both could send streams of bullets at a target in the manner of modern automatic weapons, but they were artillery pieces in size, weight and mobility. The French weapon was normally assigned to the artillery and used like a field gun, not for infantry support. Since it fired essentially rifle-type ammunition, it was deficient in range and power when opposed to Krupp field pieces.

The Gatling and the mitrailluese were mechanical MGs in which the operating power was supplied by the crew; there were many similar weapons of this same type. Then Hiram Maxim, an American working in Europe, finally designed and perfected an automatic gun in which the ammunition provided the power for working the mechanism. Various model Maxim MGs were adopted in Britain—the name was later changed to Vickers—Germany, Russia and other countries. Automatic MGs were much lighter and more mobile than mechanical types. The new MGs all fired the same ammunition as used in the infantry rifle of that country and could deliver several hundred bullets per minute for a considerable period. No one yet appreciated the ultimate potential of MGs in battles, nor even how best to use them in combat, but the weapon itself was available and reasonably free from operational troubles.

The third truly significant new weapon developed in this era was the modern field gun. Artillery was handled in the American Civil War with imagination, gallantry and dash, but the pieces and ammunition were efficient in combat only at canister range. Two major changes were necessary to keep artillery abreast of the times. The first was really effective explosive shell; as mentioned, black powder bursting charges did little damage. Detonating bursting charges—high explosives—not only gave more blast, but split shell casings into many more fragments which moved at velocities higher than rifle bullets. Smokeless propellants also gave greater range, precision and penetration; a complete round was loaded into a single cartridge case small arms fashion, up to sizes which taxed the strength of one man to lift.

The second major field piece improvement was the incorporation of a recoil absorbing device, usually a cylinder under the barrel. The old guns ran back on their wheels over the ground after each discharge; these pieces had to be rolled up, loaded and aimed after each shot. The new devices allowed the gun to remain in place with only the barrel moving to the rear and returning by means of strong springs. The fired cartridge case could be ejected automatically during recoil and the breech left open for the insertion of a new round. The aiming process was also speeded up, since the gun did not move and the layers could remain in position during discharge. The crew required for actual operation of each gun was reduced, so that the extra men could be used in bringing forward ammunition.

Two corollaries of the new recoil cylinders were better sighting equipment and small arms proof shields to protect the immediate gun crew. The new pieces could fire several times as many rounds in a given time to longer ranges with much more precision and effect. The way was clear for effective indirect fire—firing on targets out of sight of the gun crew—with adjustments in aiming controlled by observers located at a distance from the piece, but communicating with the crew by telephone.

The new tactics for employing these major new weapons lagged behind the weapons themselves principally because there were no big wars. The new military rifles were used effectively in late nineteenth-century colonial wars. Four early Maxim MGs used against the Matabeles (1893–4) helped fifty Britons to win against 5,000 natives who suffered 3,000 casualties in an hour and a half. Eight Cal ·303 Model 1895 Maxim MGs are said by Colonel Chinn to have killed 15,000 dervishes at Omdurman (1898). But in the era of Kipling and Lord Roberts, victories because of better weapons, discipline and leadership were taken for granted; a few British soldiers were continually accomplishing prodigies against numerically superior natives. No one bothered to pick apart these early MG victories to discover tactical principles for the future. Similar modern weapons, training and organization were not pitted against one another for decades following 1871.

The Spanish–American War (1898) and the Boer War (1899–1902) cannot be considered typically colonial because white men with modern weapons fought on both sides. But they were not modern either. In the earlier conflict, American fleets quickly isolated Cuba, Puerto Rico and the Philippines from logistic support; the war was small by modern standards. South African terrain and the skill of the Boers in irregular combat made up to some extent for their lack of heavy equipment and industrial support. Distances, climate and the absence of modern transportation may even have led to a false conclusion in regard to the continued strategic efficiency of horse cavalry. The Boers were astonishingly mobile on their horses, but did their main fighting on foot, usually from concealed and partially fortified positions. The conflict was bloody, but proved little of military value, save the efficiency of the new rifle bullets when directed by skilled marksmen, and the final complete degeneration of tactics involving formed soldiers in the open during daylight.

The first big war of the twentieth century and the first war where the new weapons predominated was the Russo–Japanese War (1904–5). Both sides had reasonably efficient modern armies supplied with the new weapons and ammunition; each was backed by transportation and industrial systems more powerful than any in existence fifty years before. Smokeless propellants, high-explosive bursting charges and all the new weapons which used them were suddenly available in unprecedented quantities. The results foreshadowed what was to happen ten years later in Europe.

The siege of Port Arthur and the battles around Mukden were different from anything that had ever happened in war before. The new weapons soon taught everyone how costly it was to remain visible for any length of time within range of the enemy. Soldiers seldom had formed enemies at which to shoot; the infantry of both sides took whatever cover was available and improved it with the spade. They shot at fleeting movement and at likely points for concealment. The Russians, particularly, relied on their heavy water-cooled Maxim MGs. Streams of bullets sought out targets on the apparently deserted, entrenched battlefields. Rifles and MGs in the hands of the defence converted daylight attacks by unsupported infantry, regardless of how delivered, into mass suicides. Mounted cavalry on a battlefield had become an anachronism.

The impending stalemate due to small arms improvements did not actually occur. Artillery, practically a forgotten arm forty years before, blasted defensive positions so that friendly infantry could move forward. Even though foot soldiers could dig in to a depth that made them safe from MGs, they were vulnerable to high-explosive shell. A few guns located far back and behind a hill could now deliver 100 shells a minute in a small area. Heavy howitzers—the Japanese had eighteen eleven-inch pieces which fired 550-pound shells—could smash into any concrete fortifications that the Russians had at that time.

203 METRE HILL

Let us examine in some detail a part of the siege of Port Arthur, the main Russian naval base in the East. After an indecisive naval action, the Czar's Pacific Fleet was bottled up here. Temporarily, the Japanese navy dominated the local seas, but the Russian Baltic Fleet was on its way around Africa. If the Japanese could not take Port Arthur, or at least take a point from which they could direct artillery fire on the Russian warships in the harbour, the two Russian naval forces could conceivably unite and place the Japanese at a disadvantage.

On the other hand, if the Russian Pacific Fleet in Port Arthur could be destroyed before the arrival of their Baltic Fleet, the Japanese would be able to concentrate against the ships from Europe in heavier strength. To take Port Arthur from the land side in the time available would have been extremely difficult, but 203 Metre Hill offered exactly what was required to direct accurate fire on the Russian Fleet. This position was heavily fortified with concrete-reinforced earthworks and subterranean dormitories and storehouses. The Russians realized the importance of this hill and had a garrison there of 2,200 of their best troops under Colonel Tretyakov, a courageous and resourceful officer.

The fight lasted eighty-three days in all. The Japanese had a preponderance of artillery and plenty of men and ammunition, but the Russians had both more MGs and more skill with them. The attackers literally blasted the top of the hill into chaos; the 550-pound shells from their big howitzers were particularly effective. One killed the gallant Russian commander; another exploded 1,000 badly needed hand-grenades stored below a key strong-point. The fighting was often hand-to-hand in trenches and in mines. Grenades were used freely by both sides. The attackers finally won, but at a cost of more than 10,000 killed and wounded. An eye-witness wrote, 'There have probably never been so many dead crowded into so small a space since the French stormed the great redoubt at Borodino. . . . There were practically no bodies intact; the hillside was carpeted with odd limbs, skulls, pieces of flesh, and the shapeless trunks of what had once been human beings, intermingled with pieces of shells, broken rifles, twisted bayonets, grenades, and masses of rock loosed from the surface of the earth by the explosions.'

Once the hill was taken, the Japanese sank the Russian Pacific Fleet, while still in the harbour, with indirect fire. Later, they sank or captured the Czar's ships from the Baltic, and won the war in the field. The new weapons had changed combat tactics, particularly infantry tactics, although many West Europeans did not yet realize the fact. Further, a non-white nation had beaten an important European military power for the first time in centuries. We should note, however, that the Japanese were using Western weapons and field manuals which were word-for-word translations of those employed in Europe. Her officers were thoroughly educated in British, French and German tactics and strategy, but had applied their knowledge and weapons with an imagination and efficiency of their own.

VIII

World War I

THE conflicts which occurred throughout the world between 1914 and about 1920 were economically, politically, and in the realm of human experience the most tragic ever fought. Total casualties, direct and indirect, ran into many millions. Britain lost at least ten times as many men as in all the Napoleonic wars and more than three times her WW II total. WW I put an end to a way of life throughout the world. Even in a purely military sense, the dislocation of old systems was greater than in any other war until that time.

In spite of the world-wide nature of even the WW I land conflict—the Palestine, Macedonian and Mesopotamian Campaigns cost 174,000 British casualties with 214,000 more at Gallipoli—the major fighting was in north Central Europe, principally near the borders of Germany. Let us sketch briefly the major strategy and the actual fighting on both the German Western and Eastern fronts.

In the West, the German General Staff had a master plan for overcoming France and Belgium quickly; it was named after their Chief-of-Staff who put it together about 1902, Field Marshal Alfred von Schlieffen. It called for an oblique-order attack not unlike that of Frederick at Leuthen, but on a much wider scale. The under-strength German left was to hold from the Ardennes to the Swiss border while the powerful right flank swept through Belgium and reached the Channel; this force was then to wheel round and isolate Paris.

The Schlieffen Plan was changed gradually by increasing the proportionate strength of the German left, the holding flank, and changing its role from semi-passive to active. The offensive which was finally delivered too closely resembled an attack at maximum power all along the line. The headlong German rush of 1914 was defeated by its own lack of proper central direction, the changes in the original plan, and the greatly increased power of the defence. Even though the Allies were to some extent outgeneralled and outfought, they inflicted severe casualties because of the range, power and speed of fire of their new weapons.

The German plan for the envelopment of Paris from the west could not be carried out because their strength in this area was both insufficient initially and suffered too heavily. A Franco–British counter-attack on the Marne saved Paris. The Western front soon extended from Switzerland to the Channel. Four years of the most costly war ever waged ensued; men and munitions were sacrificed in gigantic siege operations. Attrition, rather than strategy and tactics, determined the winner.

The German General Staff originally planned to hold off Russia with as small a force as possible while they won in the West. The early fighting led, however, to local German reverses. Someone dug a name out of the retired list of German generals; Hindenburg was appointed to command in the East. Reinforcements were found for him and a Chief-of-Staff by the name of Ludendorff. These two achieved the colossal victory of Tannenburg in which the Germans outmanoeuvred, outsupplied and outfought the Russians. Total Russian casualties were never determined, but may have been above 200,000—prisoners alone were between 92,000 and 125,000. The victory was complete and the German Eastern front temporarily stabilized, but the Austrians ran into reverses in Serbia and Galicia.

Germany took a calculated risk in the West in 1915, transferred large forces to the East, and won there. The final Russian or Eastern front extended almost north and south from the Gulf of Riga to the Rumanian border. Russia's Brusilov offensive in the summer of 1916 won some ground and caused about 600,000 enemy casualties—400,000 of these were Austrian prisoners—but ended in disaster for Russia and collapse for Rumania, a country which entered the war on the side of the Allies at the wrong time. Russia degenerated into revolutions; fighting of sorts continued in the East, but the war was to be decided in the West.

The mass slaughter between the Swiss border and the Channel leaves us only hallowed but horrible names; Ypres, the Somme and Verdun mean little today save as places of sacrifice. Mountains of munitions produced casualties by the 100,000 but the territory gained was measured in yards. In the early fighting, all armies more or less ignored the lessons of the Boer War and the Russo–Japanese War. Even though the Germans had more MGs than all other countries combined, they still did not appreciate their extreme power and had none organic to infantry companies. They placed too great a reliance on artillery-supported infantry in the open and tried to deliver formal attacks by full regiments with companies moving forward more or less in column. Against heavy fire which could not be silenced by their own artillery, German soldiers became skirmishers and were intended to crawl forward and then charge. Where this would prove too costly, a night or dawn attack was recommended in their field manuals.

British infantry in 1914 had great skill with rifles and fine fire discipline, but only a few MGs, not well integrated into their tactical plans. Their effective employment of aimed rifle fire stopped the German mass attacks, but heavy casualties destroyed the small, well-trained professional army. The wartime infantry which took its place lacked rifle skill and needed MG support. After a period of trial and error, this was provided by the Machine Gun Corps, a separate organization created to use the water-cooled Vickers-Maxim MGs. LMGs, principally Lewis guns, were left in infantry units. British HMGs were particularly effective in indirect fire.

The French infantry began the war with an almost superstitious faith in the bayonet and in the emotional qualities of the French soldier. There was a theory that below 400 yards enemy-aimed fire would 'become impossible' and French casualties would decrease. This was sheer fantasy. French casualties were extremely severe against an enemy who relied heavily on defensive firepower from MGs and magazine rifles.

The contending armies all realized the importance of the new artillery, but they differed in the types they favoured. The French, and to some extent the British, had great faith in direct fire from relatively light, fairly high velocity field guns of about 3-inch bores (18-pounders and 75 mm.). Practically all the French mobile artillery was initially of this type. The Germans had some pieces of approximately this size, but relied more on heavy metal. They used large howitzers of great power to smash through the Belgian fortified line along the lower Meuse. Masses of concrete were

A German soldier in Russia camouflaged so as to blend in with the snow with an MG 34 also camouflaged (World War II)

German MG 34 and crew in Russia. This weapon is mounted on a tripod and is being fired from a box of ammo not attached to the gun (World War II)

A German MG 34 with bipod mount on a sled firing from a drum magazine (World War II)

Old water-cooled Maxim Model 1908-15 MMG reactivated for AA defence in the Pas de Calais area in France, 1943

A German 8-cm. mortar crew in a defensive position (World War II)

German infantry with their auxiliary transport, a one-mule cart

German troops practising for the invasion of England during the summer of 1940. They gave the code name of Sea Lion to this operation but never carried it out

A German mobile AT gun crew with the reducing bore 28-20-mm. high-velocity weapon (disassembled) that was of considerable value early in World War II. These are mountain infantry photographed early in the attack on Russia, probably in Galicia

German soldiers handling a captured model 1910 Russian Maxim MMG on an estuary next to the Black Sea

destroyed surprisingly easily by shells 16·5 inches in diameter. Even for field use the Germans sacrificed mobility for greater explosive force. Artillery and ammunition for it assumed a greater and greater importance as the war progressed.

Horse cavalry played a more important part early in WW I than some of us realize. Of the 407 divisions in the European armies in 1914, 72 were composed of cavalry. They were of no consequence whatsoever for fighting mounted, in Europe, but had a mobility in Russia and the Balkans which gave some justification for their retention. Some mounted fighting occurred in the Near East.

In the West, after the continuous lines were formed, both sides began to analyse their new weapons and the tactics which the trenches imposed. Manoeuvre in the old sense was now impossible; there were no flanks. But these could be created, at least in theory, by breaking through the line of the enemy. This was essentially the offensive strategy of the rest of the war, if we grant that there was any. The lines were soon so strong and deep, however, that they were proof against any attack; MGs well dug in could inflict appalling casualties. The only way for the offence to get forward was literally to blow up with artillery the entire enemy defence system. New systems of trenches could be dug more quickly, however, than they could be obliterated by artillery and taken by infantry.

Western Front warfare was really one vast siege operation. Surprises were difficult to achieve; even limited advances could be accomplished only with an enormous expenditure of munitions and thousands upon thousands of lives. Artillery now dominated the fighting and produced on the average about 90 per cent of all casualties, but the stationary and creeping barrages needed to allow infantry to get forward created a belt of ground much easier to defend than normal terrain and extremely difficult to cross by any available means of transportation.

The foremost tactical lesson of WW I was the great importance of defensive MGs, particularly the heavy, water-cooled Maxim types. The extra-heavy-barrelled French Hotchkiss MGs were air-cooled, but not more mobile. These weapons, in small fortifications known as nests, were indispensable because they could provide almost continuous fire and cover an arc of as much as 180 degrees. As the war progressed, ways of preserving weapons of this type and their crews throughout the long, terrible artillery barrages were carefully worked out, particularly by the Germans. British indirect fire skills have already been referred to. The maximum combat effectiveness could only be obtained from MGs through careful training and imaginative planning. On defence and to support attacks with barrage fire, HMGs were almost perfect.

These weapons were, however, too heavy to move easily and too bulky for offensive use. The ammunition that they normally expended even over a short period would be difficult to supply. Lighter, air-cooled LMGs that could be carried by one man were introduced in the major armies for offence. The French Chouchat, the Anglo–American Lewis, the German Bergmann, and the U.S. BAR were all lighter than the water-cooled types and capable of fairly accurate burst fire from a prone position with bipod mounts.

Trench warfare required other new arms too, particularly mortars for high-angle fire. Several sizes and types were designed and often had their first real trials in combat. The British Stokes trench mortars were made in sizes as large as 12 inches but lighter weapons of simple design were generally more useful. Mechanical explosive throwers not using propellant powder were used with varying success. Field pieces that were so light that they could be carried in an emergency by one man were also employed. A French 37-mm. infantry gun, weighing 40 pounds, was extensively used by U.S. troops.

The possibility of personal surprise in the trenches caused all armies to reintroduce a number of individual weapons, mostly to give men confidence. Trench knives of several types became common. Pistols were widely issued as secondary arms, particularly in the German and U.S. armies. The American army developed and used in combat a slide action (pump) shotgun which took a bayonet and could be deadly with buckshot at ranges below 75 yards.

All the weapon innovations discussed so far were relatively simple and depended on principles in use for some time. There were four others of a more sophisticated type which were based upon new advances in chemistry and engineering. All four had considerable lethal power, plus a psychological shock potential because they inspired terror.

The first of the new weapons in point of time was the fighting aircraft. We think now entirely in terms of aeroplanes, but the German dirigibles of WW I could carry more bombs further than any heavier-than-air machine of that era. Even then, however, tactical bombing and strafing was done from planes which could also direct artillery fire, observe the enemy, and photograph for intelligence purposes. Air power could not create break-throughs nor win battles, but was important, particularly late in the war.

The Germans resorted to poison gas on 31 January 1915 against the Russians, but used it more effectively near Ypres on 22 April 1915. Thousands of Canadians and French Senegalese died horribly, but Ypres did not fall, in part because men urinated on their handkerchiefs and used them for makeshift masks. The means of fighting with poison gases improved not only in the gases themselves, but also in their delivery, but so did the defences against them. They were never as effective again.

The Germans first used high-pressure flame-throwers in the Verdun offensive on 21 February 1916. Even though deadly, these weapons had a limited range and produced extreme counter-fire from all enemy personnel and support weapons in the area. Neither flame nor gas could effect a break-through and create flanks, as their proponents had prophesied.

The last of the big new weapons was the British tank, which was first used in action on the Somme on 15 September 1916. In theory, tanks were the answer to trench warfare; they could master MG nests. A quarter of a century later, they were to revolutionize battles and restore manoeuvre. Their WW I accomplishments, however, were more modest. We will deal with tanks at some length after discussing the infantry tactics which preceded their effective introduction.

At Waterloo each surviving line infantry battalion remained together throughout the battle. The battalion CO controlled the entire unit; a British square was about sixty feet on a side. Every man stood or marched shoulder to shoulder according to precise commands in a single cohesive unit. Even in the looser American Civil War and Franco–Prussian War formations, battalions were still together mostly under the eye of the battalion CO. Subordinate officers were necessary to see that orders were properly executed, but did not have much independent responsibility. They took minor parts in a normal battle unless they succeeded to battalion command.

WW I changed all this; the range and accuracy of modern weapons led to concealment and dispersement. Even though thousands of men were sometimes crowded into relatively small areas, battalion COs could rarely see any significant part of their commands at one time. The kind of direction possible at Waterloo and Gettysburg was out of the question here.

WW I armies had to change their way of obtaining obedience, with subordinate commanders granted more initiative and taught more self-reliance than ever before. On defence, direct command could seldom be exercised above company level. On offence, depending on circumstances, platoon commanders frequently had to think for themselves. The nations which had strong battalion loyalty kept it, but also emphasized the solidarity and unity of companies, platoons and sections. In the loneliness of trench warfare, where the isolation of relatively small units, and even individuals, is the rule rather than the exception, regimental pride and *esprit de corps* were not enough. Efficiency in this sort of combat depended on the family loyalty within small units that were commanded by NCOs. An infantryman at Waterloo could not do less than his duty without those around him knowing. In WW I, a man could often just occupy space, expose himself as little as possible, and do no fighting at all. Even in attacks, dragging the heels was possible.

The Anglo–German battle on the Somme and the Franco–German fight for Verdun, both in 1916, led to combined casualties of about 1,200,000 and 900,000 respectively. Obviously, all three armies had solved the problem of how to get men to fight without close supervision. Morale remained astonishingly high in the British and German armies. In these ghastly battles, tactics within infantry units were much the same in all three armies. Defences were based on the soldiers who survived the preliminary artillery barrage selling their lives as dearly as possible. Even a few heroes could create a living hell for the offence.

When infantry attacked behind a barrage, they climbed out of their trenches and tumbled forward, taking advantage of any cover there was. Support weapons heavier than LMGs had trouble crossing blown-up terrain. Severe casualties were almost always inflicted by the opposing artillery, but forward progress was stopped by enemy MGs, usually in isolated, but often mutually supporting positions. As the war progressed, HMGs were sometimes protected by concrete or timber-and-earth which reduced their fields of fire but generally increased their power of resistance to infantry attack, particularly when fields of fire interlocked.

THE TANK

By 1916, scientific systems of trenches could be quickly constructed—but could also be obliterated by artillery. Strong points containing MGs were more difficult to locate beforehand, either from the air or the ground, and to destroy. Individual MG nests, fortified or not, were costly to take once an advance had begun. The problem was to neutralize efficiently and quickly these small centres of defensive power.

One solution was the tank, which combined shock and firepower with protective armour and mobility over difficult terrain; these depended upon caterpillar tracks and internal combustion engines. Tanks were invented, in a practical sense, by several Britishers working together, but Lt Col Ernest D. Swinton was the most important of them. As mentioned, the British army used tanks first on the Somme on 15 September 1916. They were not a real success; only forty-two rather imperfect small machines protected by boiler plate were employed in a twelve-division attack. They did spread terror, however, among the German infantry which actually saw them.

Tanks were used frequently thereafter, but were usually disappointing; French machines often incinerated their crews. Then at Cambrai on 20 November 1917, 324 British tanks were properly employed in a successful mass attack without preliminary bombardment and won a lot of territory cheaply (compared to other WW I offensives). Two German divisions were smashed on a front of 13,000 yards; an irregular penetration to a maximum depth of about 10,000 yards was achieved at a cost of only 4,000 British casualties and 65 tanks by enemy action. A total of 135 additional machines failed in one way or another.

Tactically, tanks which supported infantry or led it were important because they could defeat emplaced MGs either by firing their own MGs and light field guns (usually six-pounders), or by physically crushing the MG and its crew. A tank could master any emplaced MG not enclosed in so much concrete that its own effectiveness was greatly decreased. The heavier type were death-traps after infantry was able to get up to them.

In theory, tanks in mass, supported by infantry and perhaps even horse cavalry, could have led to deep penetrations and break-throughs; they could have created the long-sought flanks and conditions under which manoeuvre was again possible. As always in war, however, counter weapons were soon found. The early British machines were slow-moving and had armour only sufficiently thick to withstand usual 7·92 mm. Mauser rifle bullets. German infantry already had some 'K' rifle ammunition with hard-core bullets for shooting at steel sniper shields; these would penetrate tank armour at close range. Newer tanks had heavier armour, but the Germans introduced a Mauser 13·2 mm. bolt-action rifle which would get through the armour of any WW I tank. Flame-throwers could also destroy tanks, but only at close range.

The most effective AT weapons of WW I were artillery, either in normal counter-barrages to hit tanks as well as advancing infantry, or left in protected and/or concealed positions to fire directly on individual machines at nearly point-blank ranges. All AT tactics combined, however, fell far short of producing the tank casualties these monsters inflicted on themselves; they were prone to become mired inextricably or to break down after the fashion of early automobiles. Tanks combined the shock, mobility and armour of the old heavy armoured cavalry with HMG firepower, but still had many weaknesses.

The infantry which fought in Western Europe and elsewhere during WW I began to use in a new way an old tactic of combat which developed into several different theories of fire and movement. In sieges of old, archers would cover with their fire men who attacked. A major part of an assaulting infantry unit, including ARs, would concentrate fire on the opposition while a smaller part dashed forward in the open. The idea was that defenders would not expose themselves, if they were pinned down by enemy bullets hitting in their general area. Properly applied after supporting artillery fire had done its job, this infantry fire and movement could succeed where a full-scale advance would have been utterly defeated. It was particularly successful if MG positions could be neutralized beforehand by artillery, grenades, or tanks.

Another new infantry manoeuvre with roots in the past was infiltration. Late in the war the Germans were successful with an offensive in which loose probing columns took the place of assault waves. Like a number of German tactical developments, the theory probably came from others, but they perfected it in practice. Ludendorff's great spring offensive in 1918, which was delivered against numerical and munitions odds, was based on infiltration by small units relying particularly on LMGs. They penetrated wherever there was a weak spot and opened fire from flank and rear. Isolated Allied elements were destroyed later, mostly by artillery once their exact locations were evident.

INFANTRY ORGANIZATION

Space has not permitted any detailed discussion of organization until this time, even when it has been known. We can now treat these matters more carefully. All armies have had to be organized. Even a number of Boy Scouts require some internal unit structure to be controllable. The Roman legion was not unlike a modern division; army corps came into being in Napoleonic times. All WW I armies were divided into divisions of roughly 10,000 to 20,000 men. Usually there were three infantry regiments or brigades in each infantry division plus artillery and other support units.

The U.S. army was late in the field and was trained, armed and to some extent organized, on the basis of British and French experience. Even though the U.S. infantry division was really double strength and square—two brigades of two rifle regiments each—the regiments were similar to those of other armies. Each contained about 3,400 men divided into a regimental MG company, three rifle battalions, and logistic support forces. Each rifle battalion contained four identical rifle companies.

Each U.S. rifle company had at full strength six officers and 250 EMs divided into an HQ group and four rifle platoons of an officer and 58 EMs each. Each platoon as of July 1918 had four dissimilar sections theoretically intended for hand grenading (12), rifle grenading (9), rifle fire (17), and using ARs (16 men with 4 ARs), but every man save the AR gunners had a rifle and bayonet. There were 235 U.S. Model 1903 or 1917 rifles, 73 pistols (U.S. Model 1911), and 16 ARs in each company. The

ARs were the British Lewis, the French Chouchat, and the newly arrived BAR, but all fired the U.S. ·30–06 cartridge. The MG company organic to each infantry regiment contained six officers and 172 EMs divided into an HQ and three platoons; each consisted of 47 men and 4 HMGs, usually the British Vickers or the water-cooled Browning Model 1917. Both used, of course, the ·30–06 cartridge.

Infantry regiments provided a maximum of low-angle covering fire for themselves; MGs were particularly valuable for this. Advances were no longer to be made all in one wave 'over the top'. Each platoon under severe fire was to advance one part at a time while the others covered it with fire. The ARs could do this well, for each had the firepower of several rifles. Men would spring up, sprint a few yards, and go down again to resume firing to cover their companions when they came forward in turn.

WW I infantry units at all levels were much the same as today in MGs, ARs, rifles and grenades. They were quite different, however, with regard to other organic support weapons even at brigade level. Mortars and even the little 37-mm. infantry guns were handled by artillerymen directly responsible to the division CG. Larger artillery pieces and tanks, when available at all, were similarly organized. As mentioned, British HMGs were not infantry, but a separate corps.

In spite of many new features, WW I had many aspects that we now consider old-fashioned. Horses were more important than motor vehicles in transportation. Bombings from the air killed a total of about 2,133 in Britain and Germany combined. Tactical aircraft were almost as limited in their relative destructiveness. Tanks gave promise of military efficiency, but accomplished nothing strategically decisive. More ideas in new weapons failed than succeeded, including some that have been improved since. For us today, the importance of what happened in WW I has been decreased by WW II.

IX

World War II

THE years following WW I were chaotic throughout the world, but the power and ability of human civilizations soon began to assert themselves. Science and industry, particularly in the Western Democracies, led the way with giant strides; production soon exceeded anything known before. The twentieth-century march to superlatives was again in new-record territory and accelerating. Most people thought only of peace and personal gain; everyone had had too much of war.

History seems to prove, however, that war is inevitable. Those who wrote and thought of past war naturally projected their conclusions into the future. If war did come, it would surely be waged by the major nations with their total national strengths. How would the new systems of transportation and production and the continuing parade of inventions and new processes change total war? In the 1920s, thinking along these lines was not popular. But the giant economic boom came suddenly to a halt in 1929 and was followed by serious dislocations which gave rise to several aggressive nationalistic patriotisms. The world was headed inexorably for more fighting.

Military theorists between WW I and WW II were not always logical. The area in which conjecture was most likely to border on fantasy was in relation to military aircraft. Air power was going to be important in all future wars, but the imaginative proponents of the air arm claimed that it had already made conventional armies and navies obsolete. Douhet, Mitchell and Seversky expounded in varying degrees this new philosophy. Men in authority did not take the theorists too seriously, but many people in the West did think it wasteful to spend money on conventional means of making war, if airplanes only were needed.

Single bombs were supposed to sink battleships or destroy cities. Gases and germs were considered non-realistically, always with delivery by air.

Tanks were also overemphasized; visionaries had entire armies riding in tanks which were individually self-sufficient for days of combat. These vehicles and their crews would do all the moving and fighting; they were supposed to need no supporting infantry or artillery. This extreme idea was far beyond performance of any vehicles, even on drawing-boards.

On the other hand, tanks had come to stay. War in the future had to include them. The three best-known disciples of practical tank warfare were all professional soldiers of ability. The foremost, Major General J. F. C. Fuller, had been in responsible positions in the British Tank Corps from 1916 to the end of WW I. He converted to some extent his fellow-countryman, Captain B. H. Liddell Hart, to his views on the tank. These two, plus Colonel Charles de Gaulle of more recent fame, wrote of the war of the future more accurately and reasonably than the air-power enthusiasts. Fuller and Hart were translated into German and played significant parts in the organization and training of the new German army which was started about 1934.

Had WW II come without any preliminary conflicts, the major belligerents might have entered combat with a poor idea of what to expect. The Spanish Civil War (1936–9), the Sino-Japanese War which began in 1932, and the bloody battles between the Russians and the Japanese in the East in 1938 and 1939 served, however, as testing grounds not only for new weapons, but also new ways of employing them. In this fighting, planes were not the whole answer, but tactical air-power was an important auxiliary to ground forces. Even a few aeroplanes, if properly handled, could temporarily isolate a combat area and influence fighting with bombs and MG fire, but air superiority did not always assure victory.

In these small wars, a few tanks, even though reliable and powerful for their time, did not necessarily make the offence stronger than the defence. Tanks were not available in really large numbers, but their shock power in mass was amply demonstrated. Twelve could accomplish more than twice as much as six. Terrain was always important; where tanks could not move freely, they could be destroyed by field guns. Even when they had free movement, if brave men could remain concealed until the machines were close, they could be knocked out with hand-thrown AT grenades, usually incendiary affairs of simple manufacture.

The small wars between WW I and WW II also emphasized the ever increasing importance of automatic arms. The old water-cooled HMGs were still valuable in spite of their weight and lack of mobility because they could deliver sustained, accurate fire. Air-cooled LMGs firing full rifle-power ammunition were also needed; they appeared in each squad and began to form the basis for all infantry tactics at that level. In Spain, the SMG firing pistol ammunition began to rival the standard rifle for useful issue to individual soldiers. These weapons were superior to bolt-action rifles for fighting at close range and inspired confidence. One air-cooled AR, five rifles and five SMGs appeared to be about the perfect proportion of weapons in a rifle squad in the Spanish War.

Propaganda and military psychology were also gaining in importance. The soldiers of Frederick the Great fought well without much national feeling, because their tactics left them always under the control of professional officers and NCOs; besides, most of them could not read and had no radios. By the time of the French Revolution, most men were thinking. Patriotism made the French armies of the Republic and the Empire formidable, but continual exposure of their descendants in WW I to modern battle, casualties and lack of success broke the morale of many French units. Outside influences could then undermine their sense of duty. Serious consequences were avoided, but the same strains in Russia led to Bolshevik Communism.

In the post-WW I turmoil and the economic depression of the early 1930s, other movements of both the Right and the Left came to power. Propaganda could be as useful as arms and was far cheaper. In future conflicts, efforts were sure to be made at least to sow discord in a potential enemy. The value to the dictators of democratic indecision within an enemy country, due to differences in public opinion, was fully appreciated by the dictators. If disaffection could be fanned into guerrilla activity, the gain was tremendous and the cost negligible. Unfortunately for democratic theory, people could often be influenced towards other forms of government. Proper indoctrination with various types of propaganda cleverly cut to fit individual situations could inspire extreme devotion to the most diametrically opposed ideas.

In the later 1930s, Germany, Italy and Japan were obviously bent on military expansion. Each had taken over territory by force, or by the threat of force; they made little effort to conceal their military ambitions and were obviously preparing for war. The German army reoccupied the Rhineland in 1936; Austria was annexed in 1938; and Czechoslovakia seized in 1938 and 1939, all without serious fighting.

Britain and France finally realized that there would probably be no end to Hitler's ambition short of world domination. The Democracies began to rearm in earnest, but the German army and air force were already the strongest in the world. WW II began when Hitler invaded Poland on 1 September 1939. An astonishing series of victories was achieved by the Germans who were using new offensive tactics. Poland was conquered in seventeen days, while Denmark and Norway fell in a single day and in twenty-three days respectively.

On 30 May 1940, the German army launched an attack against Holland, Belgium and France. France and Britain reacted as if they were trying to save territory in the old WW I manner and moved their strength north and west to support the Belgian and Dutch armies defending their borders. A heavy German armoured column then crossed the Ardennes hills and struck in behind these advancing Allied elements, cut their communications and lines of supply, and finally reached the Channel. In eleven days this force had covered 220 miles; on 20 May the German 2nd Panzer (Armoured) Division advanced over fifty miles.

The enormous pocket containing British, French and Belgian soldiers collapsed. The evacuation of Dunkirk saved most of the British personnel, but their heavy equipment was lost. The rest of France surrendered forty-three days after the German attack commenced. In all this fighting, the Germans were outnumbered in men and tanks; but were much better organized and led. Their *matériel* was, on the average, no better than that of their enemies in quality, but they were taking more advantage of its potentialities.

The German victories continued; Yugoslavia was conquered in twelve days, Greece in twenty-one, and Crete by air in eleven.

Hitler, by diplomacy and the threat of force, took over Rumania, Bulgaria and Hungary. Nazi Germany extended from the Arctic in Norway to the Black Sea. Hitler's domination over Western Europe was even greater than that of Napoleon or Charlemagne. Britain held on doggedly, alone, but the only major land fighting was in North Africa.

Hitler attacked Russia on 22 June 1941. For weeks the Germans were victorious; they penetrated for hundreds of miles and took prisoners, tanks and guns in enormous numbers. Japan attacked the U.S. on 7 December 1941 and began its own remarkable series of victories which extended almost to Australia. The Axis countries had won many victories on land, but slowly the tide began to turn. In Russia, neither Moscow nor Leningrad fell; the Russians counter-attacked late in the winter and won back some territory. The seesaw fighting in North Africa and the slowing of the Japanese advance in the Pacific coincided with the stabilizing of the Russian front so as to absorb a large part of German military power. North Africa was invaded from the west (8 November 1942) and won; Italy was invaded and knocked out of the war. Russia recovered territory permanently and in large blocks.

The Normandy invasion was made on 6 June 1944; the St Lo break-out began on 25 July. Save for the Battle of the Bulge (16 December 1944 to about 15 January 1945), the Germans lost steadily not only because they were fighting on two fronts, but also because of British and U.S. strategic bombing. The end came in May 1945.

Japan reached its highest degree of territorial success in the late spring of 1942, but lost naval and air power in the Coral Sea (7–8 May 1942), and at Midway (3–6 June 1942). The land tide turned in the bloody fighting which followed the invasion of Guadalcanal by U.S. Marines (7 August 1942). U.S. and Commonwealth forces slowly rolled the Japanese back towards their homeland and would probably have been ready to invade it late in 1945, if two atomic bombs on Hiroshima (6 August) and Nagasaki (9 August) had not brought the war to a close.

SCOPE OF THE REMAINING CHAPTERS

Through WW I, we considered weapons and tactics from a general point of view. In the brief discussion of the years between the great wars and the outline of WW II, I have given only a few details about them. We will now consider by nations, or small groups of nations, both what they did in WW II and have done since, with particular emphasis on present arms, organization and proposed tactics.

For millenia, weapons were almost entirely personal arms. At Cannae, at Hastings, and at Crécy, nothing was used that a man could not lift. Even at Waterloo, the heaviest field pieces were man-handled into battery. Weapons today include rockets weighing many tons and capable of travelling thousands of miles; conventional artillery pieces of great range and size, planes of many varieties, and armoured vehicles of astonishing dissimilarity. A detailed discussion of these new weapons and the ways they may be used is not only impossible, but out of continuity with the earlier sections of this book. We will confine our examination of WW II and modern weapons and tactics principally to the smaller weapons similar to the arms of the past. In the chapters remaining, we will focus our attention mainly on infantry arms at battalion level and below. Tactical air-power, armour and artillery will be referred to only in connection with its support of, or opposition to, the men who actually face the enemy with weapons they carry and use in battle.

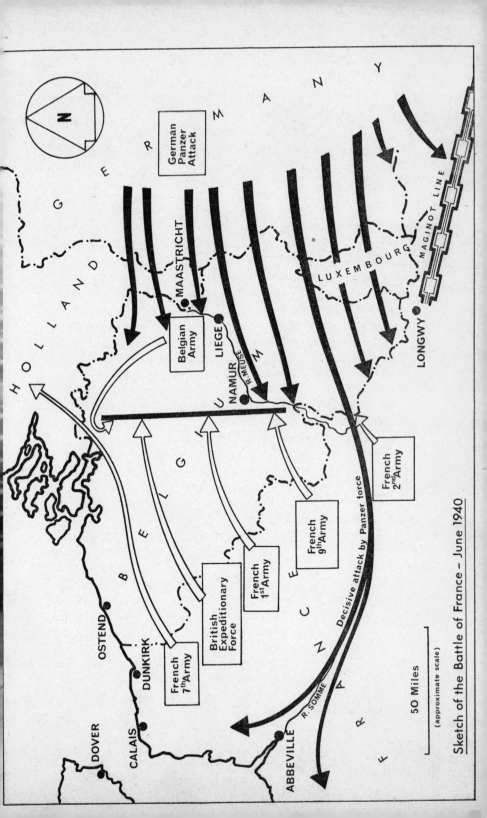

Sketch of the Battle of France – June 1940

X

Great Britain

THE British army retained stability and common sense during the military theorizing between WW I and WW II. British commanders did not believe that every soldier had to have either a tank or a plane to be effective. Small Colonial actions were to some extent responsible; rifle and MG fighting still took place from time to time. Another factor on the side of sanity was the existence of strong regimental traditions in the British army. Bigness and newness were held in check by the family affection, loyalty and spiritual continuity felt by British soldiers towards their units.

On the other hand, British 'top brass' was certainly guilty of some backwardness. In spite of the writings of General Fuller and Captain Hart, the trend in armour was towards thin-skinned vehicles, open at the top. These were the famous BREN carriers which were full-tracked and had fair mobility and speed. They were organic to rifle battalions, however, and had little power. Most British tanks in the Battle of France were in the hands of mechanized cavalry brigades which lacked the supporting infantry and artillery found in the German Panzer divisions.

Even though British forces in France in May 1940 were out-generalled and out-manoeuvred, together with the armies of France, Belgium and the Netherlands, British infantry held its own in combat. The successful evacuation from Dunkirk did not crush the morale of the army and had heroic aspects. But the war which stretched ahead was grim; a lot of military rebuilding was necessary. The *materiel* immediately available was extremely limited. In spite of her recent losses, Britain set out to create a mass army second in size in her history only to that of WW I.

The fighting in 1940 proved that infantry was still required in

Light AT rifles of Germany (top, high velocity 7·92 mm.) and Britain (calibre ·55 Boys). These were effective against most tanks early in World War II, but were not much use later on

The famous German MG42 with bipod mount

The equally famous US BAR as used in World War II and Korea

A US Army 75-mm. RR team in action in Korea

All these weapons were used to a considerable extent by the US Army and USMC in the Korean conflict. The rifleman has an MI with GL attachment installed on the muzzle

A Marine Corps flame-thrower in action against an enemy pill-box in Korea

A USMC 75-mm. RR team in a road-block position in Korea. Note the two M2 carbines, the M3 SMG, the grenades and the telephone

From top to bottom, the British BREN AR, the British Sten SMG, the German Model 1898–37 rifle and the German MP44 assault rifle

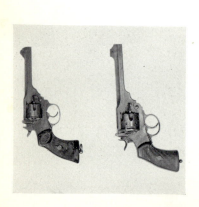

*From top: British 380 Webley revolver;
Webley 455; FN Browning Model 1935;
Swiss Sig or Neuhousen*

war, but armour was also necessary—large units required both to be efficient in combat. The armour to infantry proportion, and the organization of the two arms into a single command, was to vary considerably during the rest of the war, but neither fought alone. The fine British armoured divisions which emerged from this period of reorganization contained infantry, usually three rifle battalions and a motor battalion. All infantry divisions ultimately had supporting tank units. But before we discuss large organizations, we should review infantry weapons and the way they were combined, for maximum efficiency, in small units.

The British infantry rifle in 1942 was the No. 4, basically the SMLE (Short Magazine Lee-Enfield) slightly redesigned, but many weapons from WW I were reissued. All these rifles fired the ·303 British rimmed cartridge, first introduced about 1889. The situation was complicated by the arrival of U.S. Model 1917 Enfields of British design, but chambered for the U.S. ·30-'06 rimless cartridge. The U.S. weapon was practically indistinguishable from the Pattern 14 British Enfield which fires the ·303 British. In the North African Desert, at least, the ·30-'06 Enfields were given a band of red paint halfway to the muzzle.

Early WW II fighting established the extreme importance of an LMG or AR in each rifle section. The British BREN was available; it had been developed by the Royal Small Arms Manufacture at Enfield from a Czech prototype produced at Brno. The name is compounded of 'BR' for Brno and 'EN' for Enfield. This AR was first-rate and a real improvement on both the Lewis and Hotchkiss LMGs; it was already in the hands of troops in considerable quantities and fired, of course, ·303 British ammo.

SMGs were useful in the Spanish Civil War but were not widely issued in British armies until after the Battle of France. There were a few Lancaster weapons on hand in 1940, but these were used mostly by the navy. U.S. Thompson SMGs, however, were lighter, handier, and available almost immediately in large quantities. They were popular, particularly with Commando raiding parties.

Britain began producing in 1941 SMGs of her own design known as STENs. There were several models, one of which was 'silenced'. All were simple, cheap to make, and light; the later models were remarkably effective and reliable, but never appealed to the eye because of their welded construction. They were chambered for the 9-mm. Parabellum; the Thompsons took Cal·45 U.S. ammo.

Infantry support weapons in production in 1940 included two- and three-inch mortars and Boys Cal·55 AT rifles. Tank armour increased in thickness so that the AT rifle gradually became useless, but the two mortars were employed throughout the war most effectively. The unique British PIAT (Projectile Infantry Anti-tank) was introduced in 1942 and was a cross between a low trajectory mortar and a standard RL. It had a 29-mm. bore, but threw low-velocity bombs of larger diameter, which projected from the muzzle before being fired and weighed 14 or 20 lb. These could stop any tank if they hit the track or engine compartment because of their powerful shaped charges. BREN guns could be mounted on tripods for use as MMGs and also for firing at aircraft. Larger AA and AT weapons were available, but not organic within infantry battalions.

The ·303 Vickers water-cooled MGs are worthy of special mention. The British army followed their WW I custom and kept these in MG battalions under divisional control; they were not organic even to infantry brigades. These weapons were heavy, but extremely effective for both direct and indirect fire. Their low cyclic rate and water-cooling allowed continuous fire for extended periods where required. When assigned in pairs to rifle companies, experienced crews could give fine support fire. They were particularly good for defensive use, even under unfavourable conditions. Towards the end of the war, a MG battalion of 697 of all ranks had one heavy mortar company with 16 4·2-inch mortars and three MG companies with 16 ·303 Vickers guns each.

An infantry division also contained a specially armed reconnaissance regiment—really a battalion (793 TO&E strength). There were normally three artillery regiments for general fire plus one for AA and another for AT. A brigade of tanks was either organic or assigned; there were supposed to be three brigades of infantry, but sometimes there were only two. Each brigade had an HQ defence platoon (32), and three rifle battalions of 786 of all ranks each.

The rifle battalions were essentially 36 ten-man rifle sections, each armed with a BREN, eight rifles, and an SMG (carbine) for the section leader. These small-fire teams built around an AR made up the great fighting potential that British infantry demonstrated throughout the last four years of the war. There were three sections in each platoon plus an HQ of seven with a Cal·55 AT rifle and a two-inch mortar; the AT rifle was discontinued about 1943. There were three platoons in each rifle company plus an HQ of eleven which had three PIATs, when they became available. A rifle battalion had four rifle companies plus a three-inch mortar platoon with 6 weapons and a carrier platoon with 10 to 14 BREN gun carriers. This battalion HQ also had AA, AT and assault pioneer elements which charged considerably during the conflict.

The BREN carriers had a limited fighting capacity, but were good for protecting personnel from incidental small arms fire and for general off-road transportation. They, or a similar lightly armoured tracked vehicle made by Lloyd, could carry not only BREN guns, but AT rifles, two-inch mortars, ·303 Vickers MGs and three-inch mortars.

A British rifle company with a full TO&E strength of only 125 was one of the smallest in WW II, but its direct firepower, dependent mainly on 9 BRENs, was high on a *per caput* basis. The relative absence of support arms meant that company and platoon COs could concentrate on what they knew best. The British method of employing infantry was to have it specialize in direct aimed fire at company level and below.

Even a British rifle battalion with its organic weapons and carriers was still lighter than most. Lightness plus the carriers gave good combat mobility, but required a closer association between infantry and other arms than was normal. To an outsider studying the Normandy invasion organization, it is not always clear exactly who commanded what at some intermediate levels, but the arrangements worked with no apparent inefficiency.

The well-known determination of British infantry in WW II on offence and defence, and its ability to use aimed fire both from rifles and ARs, was backed up by fine support from armour, artillery and engineers. British attacks like that at El Alamein and defences such as the intermediate fighting around Caen were well-coordinated efforts by all arms. The British army also demonstrated unusual flexibility in improvising special combine forces. The Jock columns in the Desert—named after Brigadier

Jock Campbell, V.C.—are perhaps the first modern battle groups; they combined infantry, artillery and armour under one relatively low-level commander.

THE ONE WEAPON AND ONE AMMO IDEA

At the end of WW II, Britain found herself with different makes and models of small arms, most of them obsolescent. There were rifles, LMGs, and MMGs which required ·303 British, ·30-'06 U.S., and the 7·92-mm. German rifle ammo. The ·303 British rimmed cartridge was not really efficient for modern weapons. Six varieties of ammo for SMGs and pistols were standard issue 1945.

During WW II, Britain and her allies suffered from too many different, but similar, small arms and types of ammunition. A single weapon and cartridge which could be used as a substitute for many different SMGs, ARs, and LMGs would have many advantages. Even before the birth of NATO, Britain instituted programmes to develop both a new cartridge and an all-purpose weapon to fire it. The results were the EM-2 and the ·280 short British rimless cartridge (actually a 7 mm.). The loaded round was shorter, lighter and less powerful than the cartridges of standard military rifles; the original 120-grain bullets were driven at about 2,200 f.p.s.

With the coming of NATO, both were proposed as the new standard for the alliance. This combination of weapon and ammo caused a controversy that was heated, protracted and not always logical. The real point at issue was whether there was to be one weapon and ammo or not, but the U.S. never admitted this. The SMG proved its value conclusively under some conditions during WW II, but an SMG cannot be designed within practical weight limits which can fire full rifle power ammo accurately in bursts.

The EM-2 firing the original ·280 ammo was light, short, handy, and capable of accurate burst fire at close range—the essential qualities of an SMG. It could also deliver from a prone position with a bipod mount a heavy volume of fire accurately at ranges out to 600 yards. If one weapon was to replace both SMGs firing pistol power ammo and rifles and ARs using full power rifle cartridges, this was it. More power would mean too much recoil and inaccuracy in SMG-type burst fire; less power would not allow sufficient range for use as an AR or LMG. Britain solved the one-weapon problem as well as it could be solved.

The EM-2 and its original ammo received support from Canada, France and some other NATO armies, but was contrary to U.S. ideas of long-range power and was opposed by most Americans. Conferences achieved nothing; even though the ·280 was beefed up in bullet weight and velocity—finally 138 grains and near 2,600 f.p.s.—until it was no longer suitable for SMG use, the U.S. was still against it.

Britain needed new small arms badly; the Labour government then in power decided to go ahead on its own. The EM-2 and the Cal ·280 was placed in limited production and issued experimentally. A few months later, however, Sir Winston Churchill returned to power. The army was ordered to reconsider and adopt some cartridge acceptable to the U.S.

The U.S.-sponsored 7·62-mm. NATO ammo was officially adopted in December 1953. This cartridge has full rifle power, but is a little shorter and lighter than most of the old standard rifle ammos. No agreement was ever reached in regard to weapons; no nation ever adopted a single arm which replaced SMGs, rifles and ARs within its own armed forces. All kept separate SMGs and LMGs, even when adopting a new NATO round rifle which could often perform some squad AR functions. The 9-mm. Parabellum became standard throughout NATO (save for the U.S.) for pistols and SMGs.

Britain accepted the 7·62 NATO with good sportsmanship and adopted the then new Belgian FN rifle chambered for it. Both were immediate successes; most British small arms and tactics specialists now seem genuinely pleased with what they have.

The actual model FN rifle now called the SLR (Self-loading Rifle) is indicative of England's whole weapons philosophy. The FNs issued in the West German army had a switch allowing burst fire: all British FNs can fire single shots only. Burst fire from a 9-pound rifle is impractical and inefficient according to British standards because of its lack of accuracy. On the other hand, the capability of the SLR to deliver fast single shots SMG fashion led to a temporary replacement of most SMGs in rifle companies. The average soldier can score more hits in a given time at short range on several life-sized targets with the SLR than he can with bursts from an SMG. So long as accuracy can be retained, Britain was delighted to have the extra power of the 7·62 NATO cartridge.

Some Britishers were fearful that the SLR would not shoot as accurately as their Rifle No. 4s. The service rifle championship matches were fired for the first time in the summer of 1960 with the new rifles. Both the average and winning scores were the highest on record, although the only rules changed were reductions in times allowed. The British in one of their rapid fire matches go from standing to prone and fire 10 shots in 30 seconds rather than in the 40 seconds previously allowed with bolt rifles.

Some time after adapting themselves to the NATO round and the FN rifle, the British standardized on the L2A3 SMG, also known as the Patchett (the name of its designer), and the Sterling (the name of its first producer). It fires, of course, 9-mm. Parabellum ammo. This weapon is compact, light, and fires both single shots and bursts accurately; it takes a bayonet, but was not at first widely issued in infantry units. African and Asian experience has modified this somewhat. There are now (1964) 24 regular issue SMGs in each 132-man rifle company. At present these are issued to soldiers not primarily fighting with their personal arms, but provision has been made for alternative issue of SMGs instead of SLRs in rifle sections.

Some of the pistols and revolvers formerly issued to British infantry have been superseded either by SLRs or L2A3s. The present British service pistol is the Model 1935 FN Browning which also fires the 9-mm. Parabellum, but there are each only six in rifle company.

British infantry in WW II relied heavily on BREN guns. Since the magazine was on top, they could be fired more easily from low cover and held more rounds than any AR with a magazine at the bottom. These fine LMGs weighed about 25 lb. and had a lower cyclic rate than any other similar arm, save the U.S. BAR using its slower lever position (340 r.p.m.).

When the SLR replaced the SMLEs, careful consideration was given to a similar AR using a heavier barrel and bipod mount. Several different models were issued experimentally, but the heaviest appears to have weighed no more than 14·5 lb. They were light, handy and graceful to look at, but when hits were counted on targets at 500 yards none did so well as the BRENs. The British converted some BRENs to fire 7·62 NATO ammo and produced new ones chambering this cartridge. Current plans call for the gradual replacement of the BRENs with belt-fed GPMGs designed by FN, although a new model of the BREN, weighing 19 lb. and firing the NATO round, has been used with considerable success in the jungle.

The support weapon situation in each rifle company has changed considerably since WW II. A rifle company (132) now has an HQ (12), a support platoon (24), and three rifle platoons (32 each). The support platoon has an AT section with two Gustav 84-mm. RRs and a mortar section with two 81-mm. mortars. Both these weapons are relatively new and have not yet completely replaced the older 3·5-inch RLs and 3-inch British mortars.

A rifle platoon now has an HQ (8) and three rifle sections (8 each). There continues to be one 2-inch mortar as well as a 3·5-inch RL in each rifle platoon headquarters. Each section has a GPMG with bipod mount and seven SLRs. There is a tentative plan to place one 84-mm. RR in each section also, but this would have several disadvantages, if platoons are to be kept light and rifle-armed. So far, only BAOR (British Army of the Rhine) infantry units are so equipped. All BAOR sections have an organic vehicle of some sort to alleviate the weight problem; their primary prospective mission is meeting and defeating Communist forces composed, in large part, of armour.

This British 2-inch mortar deserves special praise; it is a simple little weapon but has outlived all its WW II companions. It resembles the Japanese knee mortar, but is smooth-bore and cannot have range varied by powder differences or by changing the depth to which the shell sinks in the barrel; there are no adjustable sights. A veteran British NCO can shoot one of these surprisingly well; it is as accurate as anti-personnel rifle grenades used in other West European armies and much more powerful. It weighs 15 lb. and discharges a 2·5-lb. bomb either directly or at a high angle. Future use calls, however, for smoke bombs and parachute night-illuminating flares. The 84-mm. RRs are better for HE projectiles.

Each rifle company HQ now has three conversion kits which can be used to change any GPMG—there are ten of these in each company—into the equivalent of the old ·303 Vickers. The new GPMG mounted on a solid tripod is a much better MMG than the BREN so mounted, because it is belt-fed and has a quick change barrel. For the first time in the seventy-odd-year history of MGs in the British army, MMGs can be organic within rifle companies.

Throughout the last century and a half, Britain has consistently stressed small arms accuracy. Wimbledon and Bisley are familiar to all riflemen. In dozens of wars, small and large, marksmanship has contributed to British tactical efficiency. In WW II, British snipers frequently gained an important ascendancy over their opponents. In heavy action, rifle companies and platoons delivered fewer bullets, but directed them more accurately. BREN gunners realized their responsibility to their sections and knew how to deliver aimed fire. They would expose themselves as necessary to see their targets. Their short bursts may not have sounded like the ripping of an MG-42, but they usually scored more hits.

But automatic weapons can never be more than a part of the answer to the aimed fire problem. Men who will dare to deliver well-aimed shots with their personal arms (rifles or carbines), and have the ability to hit what they aim at, are still important. The SLR, with its 20-round magazines, make this sort of fire extremely costly to the enemy at below 300 yards. There are other ways of fighting; squirting bullets fast in the general direction of supposed targets has been effective in the past, but Britain relies heavily on accuracy.

Colonel I. W. Gore-Langton, Commandant of the Tactical Wing at the British School of Infantry, explained the British point of view. 'We realize that frequently in modern war the enemy isn't visible. But the real value of one's own infantry is still to shoot men, or at least to concentrate fire in small areas containing motion. During the days, or even weeks, when infantry isn't firing at visible targets, it's really just standing by. Area fire can be delivered more efficiently by other means. When one needs infantry badly, that is when the enemy is visible, nothing else will take its place. This condition may last for a few minutes only, but it's what you call the pay-off. If our chaps do well aiming at the enemy, we will win. All the rest of the time is really secondary. The infantry has to be there continuously, but its major contribution is its aimed fire delivered at the climax of battle.'

The Colonel, whose right sleeve is empty as a result of WW II infantry combat, then went on to explain that area fire may be psychologically important, particularly with inexperienced troops. He found that three BRENs were required to make as much noise as one MG-42. He believed, however, that one BREN was as good as two MG-42s for shooting at men under combat conditions

A nation desiring to take full advantage of aimed fire must first teach its soldiers to shoot. There is no short cut; both time and money have to be spent liberally. The British continue to do this willingly, for they have found an additional advantage to this procedure. Young men learn faster and reach a higher level of skill not only as marksmen but also as modern soldiers when they train in part under the informal conditions found on ranges. Senior NCOs and even officers give 'big brother' type personal attention. They don't coddle the boys; British NCOs are unusually good 'chewers-out' when this is required. But each recruit knows his superiors are interested in his individual progress and want to help him. In Britain, an infantryman's pay is dependent on his shooting ability.

The actual course of rifle instruction given varies somewhat from one recruit training centre to another and according to facilities and personnel. All soldiers receive, however, the same basic fundamentals and plenty of practice. The emphasis is on making recruits into competent shots with the SLR, the GPMG and the L2A3 at known ranges on bull's-eye targets. Once a man has the ability to shoot accurately, this proficiency can be converted to combat-type firing problems. The British infantry has recently remodelled its field exercises along U.S. TRAINFIRE lines. If a soldier begins to shoot poorly, however, he is put back to relearn holding and squeezing. Towards the end of this field training, entire squads compete with each other under conditions which are reasonably uniform from one to another, but are arranged on different time schedules so that a squad is not able to anticipate what is coming next. Every soldier practises and requalifies each year.

For many generations, the basic British infantry unit was the battalion. Smaller formations could operate independently, but there were supply and administrative handicaps and a lack of organic support weapons. For a few years, platoons were considered to be fully capable of independent action and proved it in Malaya, but present thinking appears to emphasize the company which now has adequate organic support weapons. Long separation from the parent battalion would require considerable ingenuity and improvisation in regard to logistic support, but British soldiers have been doing this for a long time.

Offensively, a British rifle company now needs only sufficient support from battalion and higher level echelons in the form of artillery, armour and tactical aircraft to neutralize similar enemy arms. The current support platoon and the three rifle platoons from Britain's tradition-inspired infantry regiments firmly believe they can outshoot, out-grenade, and even out-bayonet if necessary any comparable units in the world. A company would normally attack with two rifle platoons in line and the third in close support. Depending on terrain, the attack would probably be made under cover of fire from the support platoon which would be kept together. The new company weapons give additional capacity to a company CO to solve emergency problems which he would lose if he assigned his support weapons. At close range, the SLRs, perhaps assisted by SMGs, give deadly aimed fire where nothing else can be completely effective. The delivery of this fire is, as Colonel Gore-Langton says, the real purpose of infantry. Britain's all-professional army, with its training and traditions, is better prepared to meet these moments of truth than any other in the world.

Defensively, a British company must still receive some assistance from battalion and higher echelons, but they now have their own medium mortars and fine new RRs. They can produce quickly their own MMGs which are so important for both direct and indirect fire in all modern defensive systems. Both real and fake strong-points would be established with fortifications in accordance with terrain, *matériel*, and time. But the final potential of infantry can only be developed when soldiers see their enemies across the sights of their personal weapons. British tacticians have met firmly the Maginot Line type of defensive thought and rejected it. But they also appreciate the human tendency not to fight. This can be conquered by training and team morale. For any defence to hold against modern attacks, every man must fight either as a part of a weapon crew, or with his personal arm. The new GPMG is as accurate as the BRENs were and capable of delivering more fire. An 84-mm. RR in each section would certainly be valuable in defence; they are as accurate as rifles and as powerful as the WW I 18-pounder field guns.

These brief sketches of companies on offence and defence depend on reasonable numerical equality with the enemy. British military theory of a relatively small, highly efficient professional army which is mobile not only tactically, but also strategically, is in accordance with modern world conditions and British traditions in the time of her greatest relative strength. A force amply powerful for most missions can be moved to any spot on the globe in a few hours. Recent uses of this striking power indicate the value of the concept. British military capacity is sufficient for normal combat in which great powers do not fight each other. If total war should come, Britain would fulfil her NATO commitments, but will not have mass armies of the WW I and WW II type. Forces of this size could not be supported by any industry and economy which might survive even limited nuclear attacks.

XI

United States Army

THE American tradition of citizen soldiers, in part inherited from Britain, lasted into WW II. WW I was fought mainly by hurriedly trained amateurs. Public interest in and appropriations for the Army were extremely low in the early 1930s, but a small dedicated group of officers struggled effectively to keep organization, weapons and tactics up to European standards.

As the war clouds began to form in 1937, the Army was still weak in numbers, but capable of rapid expansion. There were enough officers and NCOs to train and direct a far larger force. Weapons of WW I, many never actually used, were available in large quantity. Some new arms had been developed and were soon in production, notably the U.S. M1 semi-automatic infantry rifle. Organization was revised after field tests of large size in 1937 and 1939. The fall of France in June 1940 gave impetus to a real build-up which soon included conscription. Eighteen months later, after the Japanese attack on Pearl Harbour on 7 December 1941, war was declared on Germany, Italy and Japan.

The American economy had been producing for Britain as well as the U.S. before the end of 1940. Pre-Pearl Harbour aid to Britain was in the form of weapons, ammo, other munitions, and civilian commodities frequently delivered on the other side of the Atlantic. The Japanese attack on Hawaii was not entirely unexpected, for the U.S. was really already in the war, but was far more successful than anyone thought possible.

Once war came, the U.S. had to wage it on two fronts, but a promise was made to Britain and Russia for the U.S. Army and its semi-independent Air Force to participate in the European war first and to fight in the Pacific with what was left. The American navy operated, of course, in both oceans, but was principally concerned with the Pacific where they suffered such a staggering initial defeat.

Britain and the U.S. planned and carried through a gigantic air campaign against Germany and her allies. This strategic decision made by Winston Churchill, Franklin Roosevelt and their top advisors give air action priority over ground operations. The wisdom of this emphasis is open to question, but the U.S. ground forces were less strong than they might otherwise have been. On 6 December 1941, General Lesley J. McNair, later Commander of U.S. Ground Forces, estimated that an army of 200 divisions would be necessary and could be produced; only 91 were activated with 89 actually maintained through the war. Russia probably had 400 divisions in combat in 1945, but did not have a strategic air force, a two-ocean navy, or the man-power-consuming task of supplying active theatres and allies halfway round the world.

U.S. participation in WW II has already been outlined briefly. For the Army, the North African invasion (8 November 1942) was followed by that of Sicily (10 July 1943), Salerno (9 September 1943), and Anzio (22 January 1944). Once the long fight for Italy was well begun, U.S. and British forces began to prepare for the Normandy (6 June 1944) and Southern France (15 August 1944) landings. All were successful and led eventually to total victory in Europe in May 1945. Similar landings were made in the Pacific; not one was ever defeated. Perhaps no test of military organization, weapons and tactics can be so severe as an opposed landing on a defended shore. Why did these invariably succeed?

Part of the answer lay in naval craft, aeroplanes, munitions, vehicles, and communications; organization, planning and continuing logistic support were also important. But the spearhead which actually did the fighting was the combat infantry. If this had not been first-rate, the rest could have accomplished nothing useful.

In WW I, U.S. infantry divisions were large and had a square structure as described. The triangular concept—three regiments plus support arms to a division with three battalions plus support arms to each regiment—was finally adopted in the middle of 1940. At about the same time, armour became semi-independent. For a time, all tanks were separated from infantry, although the

German Panzer Divisions were known to have heavy infantry components. Even though the Air Force went its separate way, armour did not and became less independent as the war progressed. For a while, an armoured division had a TO&E strength of 232 medium tanks and 126 light tanks in six battalions with three battalions of infantry carried in half-tracked APCs and three battalions of self-propelled artillery (54 105-mm. howitzers). After 15 September 1943, however, tank strength was reduced to three tank battalions (177 medium and 51 light tanks) and the extra tank battalions made available for assignment to infantry divisions. Although tanks were valuable almost everywhere the Army fought, even in the Italian mountains and on Pacific islands, only Patton's magnificent thrust from St Lo to the Rhine rivalled the German Panzer penetrations earlier in the war.

An infantry division contained three infantry regiments each; it had three rifle battalions plus supply and other components, with one or two organic artillery companies—always an AT company and sometimes a cannon company—with infantry type artillery. The AT company had at first twelve 37-mm. AT guns, but when enemy armour became heavier, these were changed to 57-mm. AT guns, and then 75-mm. self-propelled guns. Finally, according to TO&Es at least, the AT company had nine 90-mm. gun tanks. The regimental cannon company had a chequered career with both towed and self-propelled weapons and ended with nine 105-mm. howitzer tanks. These artillery companies were not always readily employable by regimental commanders and sometimes just joined the divisional artillery or armour.

U.S. rifle battalions throughout WW II had three rifle companies and one heavy weapons company. The support weapons in the heavy weapons company, or sometimes in battalion HQ, changed as the war progressed. In 1942, there were four 81-mm. mortars, four Cal ·50 HMGs, and eight Cal ·30 water-cooled MMGs (Model 1917). Each rifle company also had a weapons platoon which usually had two Cal ·30 MMGs (Model 1919A4) and three 60-mm. mortars. RLs were added in 1943 and RRs in 1944, usually to the company weapon platoon. Flame-throwers were available throughout WW II, but were not suitable for a lot of it.

The rifle strength of each rifle company was in its nine rifle squads, three each in the three rifle platoons. Each rifle squad was composed of twelve men armed (after 14 May 1942) with one BAR and eleven rifles. A rifle company at full strength varied between 193 and 242 of all ranks. Personal arms outside the rifle squads consisted of rifles, carbines and pistols. To save space, these will be discussed in the next chapter, predominantly devoted to the U.S. Marine Corps.

The European Theatre fighting consisted mostly of large offensives followed by a period of defence. The invasions were preceded and supported by enormous bombardments by air and naval units. Once ashore, even small attacks were backed by air superiority and the unique power and articulation of U.S. artillery. Tanks usually participated in both initial offensives and counter-attacks and were co-ordinated into infantry plans.

In such circumstances, infantry rifle companies tended to sweep along, take objectives, or in some cases not take them, in accordance with factors beyond their control. Rifle company tactics were dwarfed and twisted by the presence of more powerful weapons. Even if it were not followed perfectly, the theory of offensive fighting was that each twelve-man rifle squad had a two-man scout (Able) section, a four-man fire (Baker) section with the BAR, and a five-man manoeuvre and assault (Charlie) section. The squad leader would normally be with Able until the enemy was located and fixed; he was then supposed to signal his assistant squad leader in Baker for fire according to his quickly conceived plan, and lead Charlie in an attack by short rushes. This was an adaptation of the fire and manoeuvre theory evolved in WW I and used by all trained infantry since. When properly and intelligently conducted, it allows an offence to win against fire. Too often, the squad leader was pinned down with Able; two or three medical or psychological casualties made the whole thing impractical. Even if it did work, Baker and perhaps Able did not join in the final assault by Charlie.

Many alternatives were proposed and tried—with and without sanction of higher authority. One of the simplest and most effective was the marching fire offensive impressed so forcibly on his command by General George S. Patton, Jr. Supported by fire from every larger weapon available, infantry went forward in a thick skirmish line firing at anything that appeared to be capable of containing enemies. Even BARs and LMG teams joined in this marching fire; no one was supposed to go to the ground unless the whole attack had to be interrupted because of superior enemy strength.

Marching fire infantry is more exposed to counter-action, and is less able to take advantage of terrain and organic teamwork, than fire and manoeuvre tactics, but has the priceless advantage of concentrating force. A marching fire attack had several times as many men in the first wave and a much greater capacity for shock. It tended to keep men together. In modern war there is a stringing out phenomena both physically towards the enemy and in fighting effectiveness. Some soldiers were only partially trained civilians who had grown up in a democratic, non-regulated society. Rigid adherence to discipline and regulations was never achieved, although U.S. infantry did become surprisingly battle effective.

Another type of infantry attack was that delivered with tank support. Three to seven or more tanks would join each rifle company in an attack and greatly increase its chances for success. The tanks could go first, or closely support the infantry skirmish line; it was also possible for infantry to ride on the tanks. Regardless of the procedure, tanks could quickly overcome, by direct fire, centres of defensive strength while infantry protected them from close-range AT weapons. In some cases, the tanks actually had aboard artillery observers able to bring down heavy indirect fire on stubborn resistance.

Rifle company defensive tactics were not emphasized before combat actually began. U.S. units were primarily organized for offence; in defensive situations, they tended to grow. This happened even in companies; personnel sometimes tried to substitute extra *matériel* for dangerous personal exposure. There was sometimes a tendency to over arm and over protect by earthworks not always carefully concealed. But supporting artillery planned defensive fire missions of great power that could be brought down immediately where required. Barrages could be shifted from one place to another quickly and efficiently.

In theory, a rifle company took up its assigned area, made a thorough survey, planned a unified position with a security line, a MLR, CPs, and the like, and went to work. As in all defensive situations, well-arranged MGs can give a belt of resistance which the enemy can breech only after delay and casualties. U.S.

The new US 90-mm. RR

A modification of the US M14 fully-automatic rifle

A simple Viet Cong single-shot smoothbore weapon of village manufacture

US M60 GPMG

The Stoner 63 rifle

French infantry rifle Model 1949-56 and the AT rifle grenade

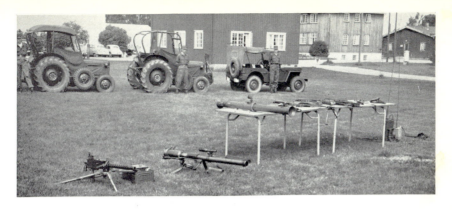

Norwegian rifle company weapons; in the foreground, the US Model 1919A4 MMG, the 57-mm. RR, and the 3·5-in. RL. In the background, two Norwegian tractors and a jeep

Spanish CETME assault rifle being fired from the shoulder

The Netherlands' AR-10 assault rifle being fired from a prone position with bipod mounts

A British infantryman firing an ENERGA AT rifle grenade from the SLR

A British soldier firing the new GPMG from a bipod mount AR fashion

The unique British 2-in. mortar being fired in the open. Note the lanyard trigger arrangement in the soldier's right hand

water-cooled MGs were lighter than most other similar weapons and extremely effective, but, as the war continued, the air-cooled type, which was even lighter, less bulky and easier to conceal, gained in favour. There were often more of both than TO&Es called for; mortars were arranged as required. Direct fire from BARs and rifles completed the picture; both weapons were capable of accurate fire in their classes. The U.S. M1 rifle was the only widely issued semi-automatic of WW II that was entirely satisfactory.

Defensively, tanks were sometimes not well handled; they are not ideal for such operations When an enemy attack came, infantry commanders committed their tanks too early. The desire to reduce casualties led to the sacrifice of armour, and sometimes impaired the development of proper small infantry unit defensive tactics based upon their own organic direct and indirect fire weapons. U.S. infantry could and did fight stubbornly on many occasions, but usually depended more on co-operating artillery than other armies.

The Pacific infantry fighting differed in several respects from that in Europe. Manpower in the Philippines was limited and of unequal quality. Infantry *matériel* was mostly adequate in quantity, but to some extent obsolete; terrain and climate were difficult. The heroic defence of Bataan emphasized human courage, the value of area fire from automatic weapons, and artillery and air support. General MacArthur's Philippine command was soon without aeroplanes and never had the logistic support and preponderance of artillery that U.S. forces came to expect later.

The long Guadalcanal fight was at first somewhat the same. The Japanese naval victory at Savo Island and hostile planes interrupted the flow of munitions, men and supplies to the beach-head; success hung by a thread for weeks. Units were of skeleton size; rifle companies and their supporting elements were all within yards of each other in steaming, disease-ridden jungle. Battle ranges of less than twenty-five yards were not unusual; field fortifications were often limited to groups of foxholes in among tree roots. Small arms were important and grenades a necessity, particularly at night. U.S. soldiers and Marines beat their Pacific enemy by equalling him in tenacity, in spite of terrible conditions, and slowly restoring a superiority in weapons and tactics.

As the island war wore on, U.S. forces began to hold with infantry and win with artillery. They had more and better weapons, better fire control, and more ammo, although the Japs were astonishingly effective with their mortars and had one fine small-calibre gun, a 47-mm. high-velocity dual-purpose weapon. The pattern of fighting which finally emerged in these island invasions was an intial bombardment from the air and sea, involving expenditures of ammo in WW I amounts plus thousands of HE rockets. Once ashore, U.S. Army units took full advantage of better organic weapons, support, artillery of all types and superior logistics. They literally blasted the Japanese from the surface of the earth. Army commanders were, on the whole, careful of infantry and would have liked to use them just to move up behind a totally destructive barrage. It did not work out that way; the enemy went underground, fought viciously and had to be burned out or destroyed with explosives. For a time, the Japanese engaged in suicidal counter-attacks (banzai charges) of little efficiency, but these were replaced by defences to the death in which the enemy sold their lives as dearly as possible. Well disciplined infantry, armed principally with small arms—their Jap 6·5-mm. Nambu LMG was remarkably good—could not win without support, but could do a lot of damage before it was destroyed.

KOREA

The Korean conflict, which began in July 1950, was a fierce war of movement for almost a year, and then dragged on into 1953 in static defences. United Nations forces could have beaten those of the Communists in a few days if the full U.S. strategic air potential had been employed. Self-imposed restrictions kept the fighting local, but the handicap of not being allowed to interfere with Red Chinese communications beyond the Yalu was fatal for a clear victory.

In the first phase of the war, well-organized and well-armed North Korean divisions attacked with Russian logistic support. They had modern artillery and armour. In the defensive motions which culminated in the Pusan perimeter defence, lightly supported, understrength, and under-trained U.S. infantry was driven back by powerful thrusts of all arms, including fine Russian T-34 tanks. Tactics became confused in actions which emphasized expedients of all types; one U.S. general handled a bazooka in the forefront of battle to set an example to men not mentally ready for combat.

The Pusan 'bridgehead' was saved, largely by the arrival of the 1st Brigade, USMC, and order somewhat restored. All units had to adopt 360-degree defensive positions, even several miles behind the front line. Rifle companies learned flexibility and to take advantage of organic and assigned supporting weapons without entirely forgetting their own direct fire. U.S. forces concentrated on plastering areas with both flat and high trajectory fire and then taking them with fire and movement, but usually by units larger than rifle squads.

General MacArthur's brilliant offensive (26 September 1950), which included sea-borne landings far behind North Korean lines, freed all South Korea. U.N. forces reached the Yalu and demonstrated to the full the potentialities of their new weapons. Mobility on land and water was the key. Terrain was not really suitable for armour, but tanks and self-propelled guns spear-headed columns of vehicles. Men did not fight mounted, but they rolled forward fast between combats and achieved an apparent victory. Tactical air power and superb artillery were almost always present; U.S. logistics were now near WW II efficiency.

The intervention of the Chinese Communists (25–26 November) changed all this. They were better soldiers than the North Koreans and far better organized and led, even though their weapons were primitive by U.S. standards and their logistics based mainly on animal and human muscle. These new enemies did a remarkable job considering their handicaps, but failed to achieve a victory of staggering proportions. They did push back all U.N. units long distances, but broke only ROK divisions. After several more fluctuations, a line was finally stabilized not far from the original 38th parallel.

The long period of static war which followed was hard on U.S. forces. The Chinese demonstrated the old military virtues of discipline, courage, alertness and experience, even though they had inferior weapons, poor air and artillery support, and primitive communications. As the Korean conflict wore on, and total U.S. casualties surpassed those suffered in WW I, the Army had more and more trouble convincing young draftees that the issues involved were worth the sacrifice of their lives. Men were unwilling to remain for long in combat. There is no substitute for good soldiers; veteran enemy units with combat experience had advantages over new recruits who were continually being rotated into U.S. organizations already in action.

The enemy, because of their air and artillery inferiority, dug a line of defence across the Korean peninsula more than twenty miles wide and well camouflaged. The defenders lived in mines far beneath the surface safe from any form of non-nuclear explosives. These chambers were large enough to accommodate whole companies, apparently without serious deterioration in health and morale. The Chinese mounted artillery and mortars in their subterranean defences which were almost impossible to spot—and extremely difficult to hit, if spotted.

Even though the fighting during the peace talks at Pangamandung was on a geographically small scale, both sides made vicious attacks and counter-attacks. Patrolling was carried on almost every night. This phase of the war was particularly favourable to the Chinese, because they were now almost all veterans who knew every foot of the terrain. The U.S. defensive tendencies of WW II reappeared. Support arms grew far beyond TO&E strengths. Even on patrol, many COs preferred to rely on artillery and mortar fire support systems rather than their own weapons. A sedentary attitude similar to the Maginot Line state of mind is said sometimes to have occurred, even in fairly open fighting: 'Let the artillery do it!' U.S. field works were too obvious, often too deep for proper use of individual weapons, and so protective that they obstructed both observation and fire.

On the other hand, no defence in any war has been supported by artillery so well organized, registered, controlled and supplied with ammo. Fire could be placed on any specific sector quickly and in large volume. Bunkers and covered sections of friendly trenches permitted infantry COs to call down proximity fuse artillery barrages on themselves in which the shells would burst at a predetermined height above their positions and send down only shell fragments which were capable of killing anyone in the open, but not penetrating the roofs. U.S. infantry and artillery at all levels had a natural aptitude for handling weapons, communications gear and support vehicles.

Chinese infantry, in spite of their combat experience, never gained the commonsense fighting ability of Western soldiers.

They often reacted poorly in a crisis and allowed themselves to be killed needlessly. Combat fatigue due to long-continued life underground or exposed to overwhelming artillery fire may have played a part in this. The U.S. rotation policy in Korea may not have produced maximum efficiency, but it did give American officers and NCOs a broader base of combat experience than is now possessed by any other army, including that of the Chinese.

U.S. INFANTRY TODAY

The relatively light Pentomic divisions of the early 1960s have been replaced by heavier ROAD (Reorganized Objective, Army Divisions) divisions. Armour, artillery and infantry, as well as reconnaissance, engineer and other units, are now combined in these semi-flexible units; a task force for various purposes can be formed within any division as circumstances require. An infantry division usually has two tank and eight rifle battalions as well as artillery and other elements, but these are not permanently combined into regiments or brigades. All ROAD divisions have more organic aircraft of several types than ever before; to a limited extent they can provide their own tactical air support.

Each rifle battalion now contains 830 of all ranks divided into an HQ (290) and three rifle companies (180 each). A reconnaissance platoon (33), a 4·2-inch mortar platoon (43), and an AT guided missile platoon (18) are organic in the battalion HQ. Each rifle company has a weapons platoon (36), three rifle platoons (44 each) and an HQ (12). The weapons platoon has two 106-mm. jeep-mounted RRs which can be manhandled and fired from the ground, and three 81-mm. mortars. The four 4·2-in. heavy mortars at battalion level, plus the nine 81-mm. mortars, three from each weapons platoon, give this force a good organic indirect fire potential. All thirteen mortars can be used together for efficient concentrations of fire. One of the reasons for the abandoning of the 60-mm. mortar was that its short range did not often allow it to be used in co-ordinated battalion firing. Rifle company COs don't lose their 81-mm. mortars beyond recall when they need them, but they are relieved of complicated technical training and specialized direction in combat. Provisions are being made at company level for mortar and artillery FOs; they will have an APC in each infantry company soon.

Each rifle platoon is divided into three rifle squads of ten each, a weapon squad of eleven men, and a platoon HQ of three. Each rifle squad has two ARs, which are the bases of the two five-man fire teams. The other eight men are armed with six rifles and two M79 GLs. The weapons squad has two LMGs and two 90-mm. RRs. All weapons squad and HQ personnel carry rifles, save the four men primarily assigned to LMGs and RLs; these have pistols.

U.S. infantrymen are carefully trained so that rifle companies and platoons are continuously under the control of their COs. Oral commands are supplemented by signals, whistles, telephones and radios. Offensively, a rifle unit can advance with its three sub units in line and the weapons unit in close support, or all in column. The wedge and the V can also be used. In the vicinity of the enemy, squads would move forward by fire teams, each covering with fire the movement of the other. The weapons squad of each platoon would aid in building up this covering fire. The two MG are good against personnel and the two light, powerful RRs extremely effective against bunkers as well as armour.

Movement has undergone some adjustments. The old leapfrog individual rush tactics are still in favour for open ground, but Patton's marching fire is also taught. When infantry attacks, along with artillery and armour, platoons might be carried in APCs throughout a part, or even most, of such an assault. But within 300 yards of contact, infantry should be in the open where it can protect tanks.

Defensively, mortars, missiles, RRs and MGs with interlocking fields of fire would handle most of the load until ranges were below 400 yards when AR, rifles, and the new GLs begin to be really effective. Defensive fortifications and arrangements for artillery barrages would mushroom in a few hours. American commanders should take full advantage of their fine support weapons at all higher levels and almost limitless supplies of ammo. But infantry leaders know that munitions won't do the whole job; each battalion must be ready to meet the enemy right down to grenade and bayonet range. The last seven inches, the length of the new M14 bayonet, is the most important of all. Only by being willing to fight to the finish for this strip of land can an army win against a major opponent.

XII

United States Marines

WHY discuss separately the two types of American infantry? First, because Marines are not the same as the Army in organization, weapons and techniques. Second, because of the unique size of the USMC—at present larger than the entire British military establishment. Third, because American Marines are extremely important in the general defence of the Free World. They will be the first to fight, if a big war does come. Meanwhile, they hold down smaller aggressions. A powerful, Marine landing team of remarkable self-sufficiency can be delivered anywhere on the surface of the earth in hours.

U.S. Marines, like the British Royal Marines, were originally soldiers assigned to fighting ships. The USMC was small and organized mainly for shipboard duty until the end of the nineteenth century. When the U.S. decided to prevent European colonial expansion into South and Central America, however, the nation also had to preserve the stability of some of the governments in that area and prevent injury to foreign nationals and their property. U.S. Marines were landed to maintain order, so that the great military and commercial nations of Europe would have no valid excuse for sending their own armed forces.

Small disorders of limited duration were handled in this way, but sometimes Marines had to operate for longer periods and beyond artillery and normal logistical support range of their ships. USMC detachments grew in size; the Corps developed more individuality. By slow stages the Marines ceased being just an auxiliary of the fleet and became a mobile force organized, trained, equipped and provided with traditions which enable it to carry on small land wars with naval support only, and to take important parts in larger ones alongside British, U.S. and other allied armies as they did in WW I, WW II and Korea. Marine fighting power is based on an astonishing assortment of support weapons including aircraft and artillery with an atomic capability and a strategic mobility never known in the world before.

But at the end of the line, the all important eye-to-eye fighting force which would be in contact with the enemy, is rifle-armed Marine infantry. Their weapons and techniques are different from the U.S. Army because the two organizations have different missions. At the beginning of WW II, a Marine rifle platoon had six BARs rather than two, because their Caribbean experience had shown the worth of this type of weapon tactically. A Marine rifle squad was never without its BAR; after April 1943 it had two in each of them. Combat experience in the Pacific led to three fire teams and three BARs for each thirteen-man squad; this became official in March 1944. Because of these additional BARs, Marines have had greater direct firepower than any other similar units.

Another obvious organic dissimilarity between the Army and the Marines in WW II and Korea was in the proportion of direct to indirect (high angle) fire. Marine rifle companies in WW II and Korea had three 60-mm. mortars, exactly the same number as in the Army. But the Marines had more MGs, three to two— and then six to two from March 1944. Even after the Army introduced a weapons squad in each platoon between WW II and Korea, the Marine rifle company still had a six-to-three MG advantage. The two LMG weapons squad in the Army is a post-Korean development.

On the other hand, support weapons firing ammo above rifle calibre are generally either present in smaller numbers or at a higher level in the Marine organization. The Marine Corps believes that heavier weapons provide greater flexibility, but prefers to have them at battalion level. USMC rifle companies have no mortars at all now. Although RLs have been common in both Army and USMC organizations for twenty years, RRs have never been organic within Marine rifle companies. The Army had them at company level in Korea and now has two 90-mm. RRs in each rifle platoon.

There are, of course, many similarities in weapons, organization and tactics between the Army and the USMC. Perhaps the greatest is in the basic small arms. As mentioned in the previous chapter, we will now discuss briefly weapons common to both Army and Marines. The U.S. M14 NATO round rifle has finally replaced the M1. All Marine recruit training since the spring of 1962 has been done with the new rifle; all active-duty Marine Corps combat units now have the M14.

The Marine Corps did not have to adopt the same rifle as the Army. They chose the M14 because in the opinion of their experts, who have fought personally from the equator to the arctic, it was the best in the world for their purposes. They considered not only its fighting capabilities, but also maintenance and resupply of ammunition. In extended manoeuvres and field exercises, the M14 appears to be in every way the equal of the M1 and superior in lightness, ammo capacity and handiness. The 20-shot magazine can be changed without unloading the chamber. Comparative recruit training indicates that the new rifle can be mastered as easily as the M1; qualification scores with it are slightly higher.

The M14, as now issued in both the Army and Marine Corps, has two features which the Army is said to have opposed initially. Rather than order two separate models of the same thing, a conference was held. An Army intention to eliminate the bayonet was abandoned. The Marines also insisted that the new rifle should be able to project rifle grenades. This is of particular importance to the Marines because of their greater need to designate precisely targets for supporting artillery, tanks, and even aircraft. Coloured smoke grenades are easy for squad leaders to carry, allowing them to call for fire on targets not easily pointed out in any other way.

The principal difference of opinion in regard to the M14 is in connection with the type that can fire bursts usually referred to as the M14 Modified. The Marine Corps initiated the development of this weapon after the M15 was abandoned. The M14 Modified is presently the squad ARs of both the Army and the USMC. Can these replace tactically the old 20-pound BAR? The new weapons are not so accurate in bursts, but this may not be significant in battle. Off-the-record opinions from both soldiers and Marines with combat experience conflict: some of both services still favour the BAR.

Those who think the M14 Modified superior appreciate most its lightness. The Modified rifle, with folding bipod, weighs under 11 lb. unloaded, approximately half the weight of the BAR. This is a real advantage in transporting the weapon and in using it under some circumstances. The M14 Modified can deliver close-assault fire more handily than the BAR. The interchangeability of magazines between the standard rifles and those capable of full automatic fire is of value, particularly if a squad is pinned down and needs heavy bursts to gain fire supremacy. Riflemen can toss loaded magazines to their AR gunner. The new weapon has a cyclic rate far higher than the BAR; at desperate shock ranges, this might be an advantage. Most important of all, the M14 Modified is a better weapon for firing accurate single shots.

Soldiers and Marines who feel that the M14 Modified is not so effective as the BAR under combat conditions, stress the difficulty of directing accurately the second and subsequent shots in any one burst. The weapon is too light and its cyclic rate too high (750 r.p.m.). Recoil is above the point of support, so that the rifle is unstable. No man can hold the M14 Modified on a silhouette target from the shoulder at even fifty yards. From a prone position, it is difficult to get a second hit from a single burst on 6 ft × 6 ft targets at 200 yards no matter how the firer tries to control the weapon. This rifle just cannot deliver the accurate, sustained burst fire of the BREN, BAR and other good squad ARs.

This whole burst fire problem may not have a meaningful solution until the new weapons are tested in combat. If a man armed with an M14 Modified wants to put his shots precisely, one after another, into silhouette targets at any range up to 500 yards, all he need do is to turn his fire selector to semi-automatic and fire fast single shots. It is possible to deliver fifty of these per minute under combat conditions. Since the enemy is seldom exposed, bursts may be preferable psychologically. Burst inaccuracy might have the advantage of distributing the fire over a greater area.

The new U.S. M79 GL is also common to both the Army and the Marines. This short stubby single-shot weapon has a maximum range of approximately 400 metres and is more accurate than rifles firing grenades, but the power of the projected HE grenade is below that of the standard hand-thrown missile. The M79 probably has other more effective types of ammo which are still classified.

Personal defence weapons in the U.S. forces consist of pistols, SMGs and, in the Army and Air Force, two types of carbines (Cal ·30 M1 and M2 and the Cal ·223 AR15 or XM16–A2). The Marine Corps does not like SMGs for combat and has discontinued using carbines. Most Marines who would be handicapped in their regular jobs if they had to carry a rifle now receive only the U.S. 1911A1 semi-automatic pistol. The U.S. M3A1 SMG, which also fires Cal ·45 ammo, is issued only for special missions. New, lighter and more compact SMGs and pistols chambered for the 9-mm. Parabellum would be preferable, but the total cost for weapons, holsters, magazines, ammo and training manuals is simply not justified by the small amount that these would be used.

Now for the support weapons. Both the Army and Marines have the new U.S. M60 MGs which fire, of course, the 7·62 NATO round. They are lighter and less bulky than the old Brownings; barrel changing is now easy. An M60 MG, with integral butt stock and bipod mount, weighs approximately 23 lb. It could replace the M14 Modified as the squad AR, but mobility would suffer. Ammo resupply might also be a problem.

These new MGs, when mounted on substantial tripods, fit nicely into the Marine Corps' MG theory which is different from that of the Army. Marines maintain that MGs are not just heavier, more reliable squad ARs. The M60 can deliver efficiently bursts at visible targets AR style, but it can do a lot more also. The Army has given up indirect MG fire, but the Marines can use two, four or six M60s operating together from tripods according to complicated, but efficient, 'traverse and search' plans with special sights to cover areas suspected of being occupied by the enemy in spite of visibility.

The 81-mm. and 4·2-in. mortars and 106-mm. RRs are widely used in both the Army and USMC, although at different levels. These have changed little over several years; the mortars are essentially what they were in WW II, while the 106-mm. RR is a development of the WW II 57-mm. RR. There are also 3·5-in. RL in both; their great disadvantage is that their maximum effective range is limited to about 300 yards, with accuracy dependent upon the gunner's proficiency. A shaped charge projectile from one of these can penetrate tank armour, but a single hit may not be fatal. These are the RLs used in Korea; they are bulky and clumsy but hinge in the middle for easier carrying. A new lighter type will soon be issued in each rifle squad when tanks are likely to be encountered. This 66-mm. M72 Light Assault AT weapon (LAAW) weighs, complete with one round, only 4·25 lb., but is effective for AT and bunker missions. The LAAW has greater range and accuracy than the 3·5-in. RL, but does not have an anti-personnel nor a smoke round.

There are some other organic infantry support weapons which deserve mention, even though recently abandoned by regular units. The most controversial is the fine, accurate 60-mm. mortar still common in NATO. It was less powerful than the roughly comparable 81-mm. type, but our Allies and some of our own veterans complain of the weight of the larger weapon and a reasonable number of rounds for it. The 57-mm. and 75-mm. RR and the 2·36-in. RL were all effective in their day, but are now superseded by more powerful weapons without comdlaint. The water-cooled Browning Cal ·30 MGs have been gone since Korea, but still have their advocates. They could fire longer bursts more accurately than the M60s, which were particularly useful for indirect fire.

In WW I, the Army and Marines used almost the same organization and techniques. In that conflict, the infantries of the world learned about modern war. Men could not advance against modern weapons, or even put their heads up above cover, unless they achieved fire superiority. This meant firing sufficiently fast and accurately as to pin down the enemy and prevent him delivering accurate counter-fire. Given fire superiority, an attack could be delivered without unacceptable casualties.

Every army sought a system of achieving fire superiority and then advancing without losing it. This fire and movement theory has evolved differently in various armies. We have already discussed that used over the past twenty-five years in Britain and also in the U.S. Army. We will now discuss the Marines.

Early in WW II, the greater number of BARs in each rifle platoon led to more use of this weapon. When casualties mounted, survivors tended to cluster around their most effective arm. The three-BAR, thirteen-man rifle squad was better for practical fire and movement and also allowed closer supervision of firers. Each leader from fire team to company controlled only the three men subordinate to him. Marines had a minimum of men who failed to fire their weapons and advance in accordance with orders on offence, and succumbed to bunkeritis on defence.

Three of these thirteen-man squads, along with a small HQ, continued to make up a rifle platoon for twenty years. In 1964, a fourteenth man armed with a GL (M79) was added. There has never been a weapons squad in a USMC rifle platoon. A rifle platoon now contains 47 Marines, three fourteen-man squads and a five-man HQ. It has in addition to the nine ARs and three M79 GLs a total of 33 rifles and five pistols. The five pistols include those carried as individual weapons by the grenadiers who also carry the M79 GLs.

A rifle company has consisted of three rifle platoons, a company HQ, and weapons platoon since before WW II. The HQ unit now has nine men and the support weapons platoon 53 men as well as six 3·5-in. RLs and six MMGs. There are a total of 203 Marines with 142 M14 rifles, 27 M14 Modified ARs, 34 pistols, and nine GLs.

Marine rifle battalions have been organized in several ways over the past twenty-five years. To March 1944, there were three rifle companies, a weapons company and an HQ. The weapons company was eliminated for the last year of WW II, but the essential support arms and personnel from it were assigned to battalion HQ. The weapons company was restored before Korea, but the Marine rifle battalions which first fought there had only two rifle companies. In 1957 the weapons company was again incorporated into the HQ company, but a fourth rifle company added. Full strength now is 1,197 officers and other ranks, with 385 in the HQ company which also has eight 81-mm. mortars, eight 106-mm. RRs, eight 3·5-in. RLs, and eight flame-throwers.

In WW II, Marine rifle companies had more BARs and MGs, but were lighter in other support arms. This was certainly an advantage in the war fought against the Japanese for individual islands, particularly in the early stages. The Army followed at least in part and unofficially the Marine Corps lead in this. In Korea, the Marines continued their more powerful direct-fire rifle platoons and emphasis on individual weapons, especially during the mobile war phase. Today the three fire team squad and the direct-fire rifle company are still the basis of all Marine planning. The emphasis in rifle companies is on rifles, ARs and rifle ammo MGs; company COs are not normally accomplished instructors for mortar and recoilless artillery crews, but are able to direct assigned specialists in the use of these arms for maximum overall combat power. Company commanders frequently have other weapons attached to their units on a temporary basis, including even tanks, but rifle companies will fight mainly with their organic arms.

The teaching of techniques at any level is particularly complicated in the USMC because of wide variations in possible combat terrain, climate and enemy. Further, the Marine Corps may have to go ashore against opposition of varying strengths and complexities which require different counter-measures. Finally, even though the Marine Corps has an all-volunteer personnel available for more months of training than in most Western armies, time is still limited.

First emphasis is given to fire; all Marines are small-arms specialists able to deliver fire accurately and in volume under all circumstances. The second emphasis is on movement both before and during an attack. This is more complicated because Marines want to take full advantage of the speed and mobility of their water and air transportation facilities and their astonishing array of ground vehicles. They train, however, 90 per cent on foot; leg muscles are still extremely important.

Each Marine rifle unit, from a fire team to a company, can move in line of next subordinate units, or a column of them. They can also proceed at platoon and company level in a wedge (one subordinate unit forward and two back), a V (two forward and one back), or in echelon with either flank leading. Variations of all sorts are taught, particularly in regard to columns. Both assigned supporting weapons and vehicles are fitted into manoeuvres and combat concepts.

Communications are the essence of modern tactical effectiveness. If you cannot communicate, superior plans, training and weapons may mean little. In Marine manoeuvres today, each fire team leader is continuously in touch with his squad leader. The three squad leaders will be in direct communication with the platoon commander and the platoon commanders with the company CO. This triangular concept allows extreme flexibility and articulation. Voice, hand signals, telephones and radios of various types are all used.

U.S. Marines have an aggressive approach to war. Their

primary mission could be to strike quickly and hard beyond normal support. They must be offensive specialists in order to get ashore at all. Landing and follow-up operations put a premium on audacity. The first wave of Marines brought in by landing craft, or dumped from helicopters, must dominate by fire, manoeuvre and shock action all local opposition. Ground must be taken, but the small units must also be ready to go over to a temporary stubborn defence, if the enemy is found to be strong. They must protect resupply operations. Neither helicopters nor most landing craft capable of bringing in the large quantities of *matériel* needed in modern war have much armour protection or firepower of their own.

A Marine company offensive would depend upon terrain, support, the enemy and other factors; it would generally be composed of several phases. First, the company commander would plan his attack, brief his subordinates as required, and order a concentration of attacking and supporting elements at a given time in the area chosen. Second, the company would probably move forward to the line of departure either before or during preliminary support fire on all spots suspected of containing the enemy. The attack proper would begin when the leading elements moved across this line. The most common formation would be a V, two rifle platoons in line and the third in close support. The two leading platoon commanders might place all three squads in line, or have two in line and one in support according to circumstances. The MG section of the weapons platoon might be split into three teams of two MGs each and attached to each of the three rifle platoons. The RLs would be placed in accordance with AT and bunker requirements.

The advancing rifle platoons would not fire until fired on; they would then reply with everything they had. Once a fire fight starts, the paramount requirement for continuing an offensive is to gain fire superiority quickly. The enemy must be killed or driven deep into his foxholes. Burst fires from automatic weapons always sound dangerous and are of great value here. Targets for aimed fire will probably be scarce.

Once fire superiority is gained, the attack would continue by fire and movement. Enough units would sustain the necessary level of fire while others worked forward. Initiative by leaders at all levels is important in order to adapt the method of advance to terrain and take advantage of all favourable features. Short rushes by single men, fire teams and squads can be used until an adequate force arrives within assaulting distance of the objective.

The final assault through the objective should now begin without delay. There has been a shift away from the old technique of advancing by short rushes over the last 150 yards. When men went to the ground so close to the enemy, the attack lost cohesion and was difficult to control. The new idea—it is the same as Patton's in WW II—is for the entire assault force to move forward firing. If possible, fire supremacy is retained, even though supporting weapons will probably have to shift their fires to the enemy rear. This walking fire is not accurate; even though many riflemen fire from the shoulder while stationary for the moment, they rarely have clearly defined targets. But if they can retain fire supremacy for a few more seconds, they can go in viciously with grenades and bayonets. Men who have confidence in their ability with these shock weapons of final decision have a tremendous advantage when they overrun an enemy position. Bayonets do not create many casualties, but the shock action inherent in a charge to the shortest possible range is extremely important.

Once an objective is won, the attack will not penetrate further. Pursuit would be by fire only, unless new orders arrive to continue the advance. Our Communist enemies use various tricks to draw attacking troops beyond their support and into ambushes. If careful air and surface reconnaissance revealed nothing of this nature, and there was no counter-attack, Marines would probably receive orders to continue. Meanwhile, the attacking elements would have reorganized, brought up their support weapons, and prepared a defensive position.

Marine defensive formations are, of course, dependent upon terrain and other conditions. In modern war, security must always be thought of on a 360-degree basis. In helicopter and beach landings which penetrate a fair distance, a rifle company or even a platoon must be prepared to hold out alone and surrounded. The same thing can happen on an atomic battlefield. A Marine company CO is always ready to deploy his force around a small area and hold it. Positions for the six MGs would be chosen so as to give interlocking fires, particularly between the two guns of each MG section. RLs would be placed where terrain suggested

The Danish Madsen AR and crew with a tripod mount to convert it to an MMG

A Danish 81-mm. mortar crew firing on manoeuvres

Two Danish jeep-mounted 106 RRs and crews in a typical setting

The jeep-mounted 106-mm. RR and Spanish soldiers

Turkish soldiers and their bolt-action Mauser rifles

A Belgian soldier with a heavy-barrelled FN rifle called the FALO with bipod attached

A French soldier firing an AT grenade from the Model 1949-56 French service rifle

A FALO team firing from the prone position

The compact Turkish service pistol which fires a 9-mm. short cartridge

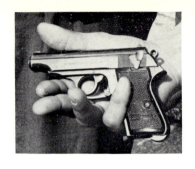

A Turkish soldier and his Hotchkiss Squad AR

This Turkish soldier has a US Model 1919A6 MMG

Turkish soldiers with a Cal ·50 HMG

the possibility of an attack by enemy armour. Riflemen and AR gunner in their fire teams would complete the perimeter in an irregular manner dependent upon terrain. CPs and communications would be established; all personnel would be protected by foxholes, with more ambitious entrenchments a possibility later. But earthworks of the WW I and final Korean type are not contemplated. A company would retain enough territory within its initial defences to give up something, if hard pressed, and still hold out. A CO would not hold so much ground, however, that he had to deploy his entire command in his perimeter defences and could retain no reserve.

The Korean fighting revealed weaknesses in isolated company positions because of ammo and fire support shortages. The USMC was more successful during the dreadful first winter of Chinese counter-attacks by forming battalion perimeters which could hold out longer not only because of greater personnel, weapons and ammo strength, but because a battalion was more capable of retaining morale and offensive spirit.

A Marine rifle company in a battalion perimeter or larger defensive formation would protect an area between two points which would have to be held primarily against a frontal attack. A company would still occupy this line in a flexible manner, but would have more support. Fortifications would vary with time available and other factors—foxholes and slightly larger MG positions can usually be dug in a few minutes. Communications could also be established and some camouflaging done particularly around the CPs. If there was time, a more ambitious set of defences could be laid out and constructed, including even a second or alternate set of positions slightly to the rear of the first.

This flank-to-flank defence would also rely on the six company MGs, but individual fire teams would be important. It is dangerous in modern war to expose yourself to the extent necessary to fire efficiently from a foxhole, because of the storm of lead and steel which usually accompanies an enemy offensive. It is suicide, however, to remain passively at the bottom. Human experience includes no more searching test of courage, but discipline, *esprit de corps*, and the fire team system will keep Marines fighting.

The Marines were 100 per cent ready in the Cuban crisis of October–November 1962. Their continuous training consists in part of giant manoeuvres far from home. Units of all sizes practise what they would do in war; they gain both know-how and confidence. There are permanent Marine bases in the U.S. and its possessions and well-equipped temporary stations far from American shores. The 2nd Division/Wing team—total organic, assigned, and support strength in excess of 43,000 men—has its home at Cherry Point and Camp Lejeune in North Carolina, but one heavily reinforced battalion, in the form of a complete landing team from this division, is continuously with the U.S. 6th Fleet in the Mediterranean. Another is always in Porto Rico. Units of various sizes are on the move over wide areas; landings are carried out under all-weather conditions from Greenland to Brazil and from Panama to Turkey.

The Marines are ready to fight, move and communicate anywhere at any time. Their fire teams and larger units will continue efficient and vicious in spite of heavy casualties. These men have no illusions. They are all volunteers and know that they are not good insurance risks. They have chosen their way of life because of patriotism, courage and a desire to be U.S. Marines. When you see them at various stages in their training from recruits to combat-ready landing teams, you cannot help but be thankful that the Free World can produce men like them. Their traditions go back a long way, but their present key personnel learned their jobs at Guadalcanal and Iwo Jima, in delivering the Naktong counter-attacks, and in the magnificent fighting around the Chosen Reservoir.

XIII

Germany and West Germany

GERMANY was defeated in 1918, and lost her ability to make war. Her armies were demobilized and her battle fleet given up along with a lot of military *matériel*. The treaty of Versailles drastically limited the size of the German army and the weapons which it could use. These conditions were adhered to until Hitler came to power in 1933. Germany began to rearm, at first covertly, but openly after 1934. The Wehrmacht and the Luftwaffe were born and grew prodigiously. The German General Staff flourished again.

The military achievements of the German nation in the next few years are astonishing both in quality and quantity. There were basic strengths in science, in idnustry, and in the German people; there was a magnificent group of veteran officers and a national spirit that did not consider itself defeated in 1918. But the transformation of the small, predominantly infantry force of 100,000 of 1934 into the articulated fighting machine of all arms which conquered more than half of Europe by the end of 1941 is hard to believe even in retrospect. The new armed forces were both absolutely, and relatively to other nations, more powerful than the Imperial German forces of WW I.

Even more important, the Germans used early in WW II new concepts of war which allowed victories to be won quickly and with a minimum of bloodshed. These involved both grand strategy which is beyond our scope and new weapons and tactics. Most important of the latter were the Panzer tactics involving vehicles not even thought of until 1935. The first German tanks were tried out in Franco's Spanish War and found to be too light. Their armour was too thin and their guns too small compared to the heavier Russian models.

New heavier German tanks were designed and put into production. Similarly, German field, AT and AA artillery was tried out in Spain and modified where desirable. The great 88-mm. dual purpose (AA and AT) gun was conceived in the Spanish War. New aircraft were also developed.

Matériel developments were overshadowed, however, by new ways of using the weapons. The German army invented and perfected what later became known as Blitzkreig (lightning war). If war was to come—and German ambitions made it inevitable—the new General Staff and all veterans of WW I wanted to avoid another bloody fixed-position stalemate of the 1914–18 type. The Germans followed the disciples of armour, principally Fuller and Hart, further than any other army was willing to go. But with typical Prussian thoroughness, they kept their feet on the ground and still relied on infantry. They produced integrated teams of all arms, not just tanks alone.

The quick German triumphs already discussed perfected and standardized the new way of fighting. Spearheads of tanks smashed deep into and through enemy positions: tactical aircraft, particularly the Stuka dive-bombers, operated against known enemy strong-points and were immediately available for use against any defences that developed unexpectedly. Motorized infantry and artillery were in close support. Panzer divisions were all-arms teams, not tanks alone; they were backed by infantry divisions depending in part on animal transportation. Germany had only six Panzer divisions against Poland, and won against France, Britain, Belgium and the Netherlands with but ten. France alone had more and better tanks, about 2,460 to 2,439, but did not employ them efficiently. The German combat teams in all their early WW II campaigns disrupted enemy armies and cut them off from their bases, or from each other; they were disorganized and forced to surrender rather than destroyed.

At the risk of over-simplification, a few words about the use of tanks in French, British and German armies may be in order. The French still assigned their machines largely to infantry forces to serve as mobile support weapons. British tank tactics were limited, of course, by scarcity of machines; there were only five mechanized cavalry regiments with 171 (mostly light) British tanks in the Battle of France. British tanks were committed, however, largely independent of infantry support. The Germans neither supported infantry with their tanks nor had their tanks operate independently. The Panzer divisions of two units had one predominantly tank regiment (brigade), but the other contained infantry, artillery and combat engineers, all motorized and to some extent mechanized even in 1940.

German ground-air teamwork for Blitzkrieg war was such that Panzer divisions could advance as quickly as their tanks could roll with constant air cover. If the tanks were held, dive-bombers came in immediately; infantry, artillery and engineers were well up and prepared to take over within minutes. The Panzer divisions never operated alone, however, because they sometimes needed even more infantry and artillery than they had in their own organization. The German overall success was due to the joint efforts of all, including a command system which was flexible and took advantage of initiative from squad to corps level. War always involves killing, but German casualties in the entire Battle of France amounted to only 150,000, less than a third of the British casualties in the inconclusive Battle of the Somme in 1915. Even the losers were comparatively unscathed, save in prisoners.

The German victories in Russia in the summer and autumn of 1941 were the largest ever won until that time. The exploits of Rommel and his Africa Corps in Libya and Egypt in 1941 and early 1942 were spectacular to the point of genius. German human casualties continued to be light compared to WW I. But the first Russian winter counter-attack, and the fighting in North Africa in 1942, changed this; Germany began to feel the combined weight of her enemies acting together. The Allied economy and industrial potential produced war *matériel* as never before in history; divisions fully equipped for war sprang into being. Further, the enemies of Germany were copying her organization, weapons and tactics intelligently and with imagination. The Western Allies and the Russians were using what the Wehrmacht had pioneered.

WW II GERMAN INFANTRY ORGANIZATION

German organization throughout WW II was flexible and changed too rapdily to follow in detail. As mentioned briefly, Panzer divisions in which shock predominated over fire and movement were usually square, two regiments of two subordinate teams each—total personnel about 10,000. Standard infantry divisions were larger and triangular, three regiments of three battalions of three rifle companies with support units at each level, but TO&Es changed at least once in each year from 1933 to 1945. There was often more than one type in being at the same time, even before attrition forced economies of manpower and critical weapons.

On the other hand, the German infantry maintained a continuity in organic principles throughout. The basic fighting unit was the rifle squad with one LMG. The Einheit concept was that all larger military units would be made up of multiples of the simplest team which could perform basic missions. Squad rifle-LMG teams were combined to form platoons and larger units, but these were subject to the operation of another principle by which support weapons needed by infantry at various levels were made organic to infantry at these levels. Since platoon commanders often needed a light mortar, a 50-mm. mortar squad was made a part of his command along with three rifle-LMG squads.

With these two principles in mind, plus the original triangular infantry concept, the German infantry organization becomes simple. A company was three rifle platoons plus supporting arms. There were three rifle companies plus a support weapons company in each battalion. The infantry regiments, the main combat elements of an infantry division, were composed of three battalions each and remained fairly constant save for the elimination of the third battalion in some cases late in the war. Each regiment had 14 consecutively numbered companies consisting of three rifle companies and one support weapons company repeated three times; the thirteenth was an AT and AA company, and the fourteenth a cannon company. The AT and AA company in 1939 had towed 37-mm. AT guns and motorized dual 7·92-mm. AA MGs. Later these were appropriate changes for more effective weapons. The cannon company in 1939 had six 75-mm. infantry howitzers (880 lb. with 13-lb. projectiles fired to a maximum range of 3,800 yards) and two 150-mm. infantry howitzers (85-lb. projectiles with a maximum range of 5,200 yards). These weapons were horse-drawn. Later, they were towed and the 150s were sometimes, but not always, replaced by 120-mm. mortars in larger quantities.

The support company of each battalion (MG company in German nomenclature) had three MG platoons (four MMGs each) and one mortar platoon (six 81-mm. mortars). A German rifle company had no weapons platoon, but there was an AT squad in company HQ; as mentioned, each rifle platoon had in 1939 a mortar squad armed with one 50-mm. mortar. At first the AT squad had three Cal 7·92 high-velocity AT rifles, but was later armed with the far more powerful Panzerfaust, a shaped charge recoilless device, and the Panzerschreck which used the rocket principle. The MMGs of the MG companies were the LMGs of the rifle squads, save for a tripod mount; the MG34 was supposed to be standard in all units in 1939, but there were others. The MG42 took its place and was a better weapon.

A rifle company contained 180 to 200 men until attrition set in; the 50-mm. mortar squad was abolished and replaced with a rifle-LMG squad about 1940. Squads contained ten men originally, but were reduced to nine about 1943; the fourth squad in each rifle platoon disappeared earlier. An infantry division contained more than 15,000 men in 1939, even without assigned armour and other support, but shrank theoretically to 9,069 in 1944— and to much less in actual combat.

Throughout WW II, the small units of German infantry retained a remarkable mobility and independence. Leaders were encouraged to use their intiative and imagination rather than to rely on manuals. Fire from all weapons was always advocated, but the individual squads were often allowed more freedom in the execution of offensive missions than was normal in other armies. The presence of a belt-fed high cyclic rate LMG in each squad gave it great firepower to cover manoeuvre. The emphasis was always on getting a lot of bullets headed in the general direction of the enemy, rather than hitting an individual target with one well-aimed shot. On offence, German infantry always employed speed, vigour and dash. Combat engineers using shaped and other demoliton charges, and flame-throwers, were frequently of great value against prepared defences.

German small units, when composed of good troops, were also well trained in the proper use of organic support weapons in defence. The squad LMGs were particularly suited to defence where adequate ammo for their high cyclic rate could be more easily available; these could shift to the long belts of ammo like those used by the MMGs. When all these automatic weapons were supported by organic mortars, AT weapons and howitzers, even a small unit had a considerable defensive potential.

German infantry of all types and at all levels showed astonishing ability and speed in consolidating a position they had won and could defend it well almost immediately. They were also remarkably fast in launching couter-attacks to regain positions lost, with a full employment of every German support arm in the area.

THE NEW WEST GERMAN ARMY AND ITS WEAPONS

West Germany was admitted to NATO on 9 May 1955; soldiers first enlisted on 12 November of that year. But the Bundeswehr did not really begin to function until 1957 and was only 182,000 men strong in February 1961. In the autumn of 1964, however, it is regaining not only the efficiency of the Wehrmacht, but some of its strength. No other national army is so completely integrated with NATO; West German divisions have all been assigned to NATO command as soon as they approach full strength. The West can match Russia and her Satellites only if the reborn West German economy and industry produce proportionate armed force. The new army will eventually be complete, but we are interested most in its infantry, its best developed component at the present time.

Before discussing the weapons and tactics of this new force, let us review briefly what has happened as regards small arms in Germany in the last forty years. By losing WW I, the Germans lost also their obsolete weapons. They were not allowed to produce new arms for about fifteen years. When they finally ignored this restriction, they had new models ready, in part developed in Switzerland. Every German infantry support arm of WW II was post-WW I in design; many similar arms of Britain, the U.S. and their allies were of WW I origin as late as 1962.

The Germans retained from WW I, however, the 7·92-mm. Mauser cartridge and the basic infantry rifle—the Model 1898 bolt-action Mauser—although those manufactured for WW II had shorter barrels. They retained from WW I the 9-mm. Parabellum pistol cartridge and many Model 1908 Luger pistols which fired it, but issued also newly manufactured Walther P-38 pistols which used the same ammo. Both these cartridges were about as close to perfection as anything can be in life; and they are still used more widely than any others throughout the world.

The German WW I heavy, water-cooled Maxim Model 1908 MG and its modifications did not fit into the new type of war; the LMGs of WW I were not outstanding. Both were replaced with a series of air-cooled MGs designed and produced to give mobility and firepower. As mentioned, the MG34, and later the MG42, could function as either LMGs or MMGs according to mount and feed devices. Both weighed about 25 lb. and had high cyclic rates of fire. The MG42 occupied a unique place in the affections of the German army. It was used everywhere, always with complete success. Its most unusual characteristic was a cyclic rate of above 1,000 r.p.m. which meant extreme inaccuracy from a bipod mount, but Germans feel that this is not a disadvantage in combat.

During the years when Germans were not allowed to produce new weapons in their own country, they appear to have worked on SMGs abroad. The best of these was probably the wooden-stock Model 1928 Schmeisser which performed well in the Spanish Civil War, but was nearly as long as a rifle, and heavier. Early in WW II, Germany began to issue this basic weapon with a folding stock and made mostly of stampings; it is generally referred to as the MP40 and was probably the best SMG of WW II. By 1944 German infantry was almost as dependent upon it as on their standard rifles. It can still be fired more accurately in bursts than most other SMGs because it is heavy (10·6 lb.), has a low cyclic (about 475 r.p.m.), and has close to an 'in line' conformation when the wire stock is unfolded.

Germany manufactured and used a lot of other rifles, MGs, SMGs and pistols during WW II. The arsenals of occupied countries mostly continued to produce their own weapons, but for German use. These were all emergency arms of no permanent interest. There were, however, two types of AR designed by the Germans and produced and used in fair quantity in WW II which are still of extreme interest.

One of these was the antecedent of the modern Russian AK. The mass attacks against the Germans in the East during WW II caused them to rely more than ever on burst fire, even from personal arms. But none was available in 1942 which gave entire satisfaction. MGs used full-power rifle ammo and had so much recoil that they were inaccurate; no man could use one as a shoulder rifle. The SMGs, including the fine MP40 series, were accurate and efficient, but lacked range and power because they fired a pistol cartridge.

The Germans began to use experimentally in Russia in 1943 a cartridge which was intermediate in power between their rifle and pistol ammos. This round, the 7·92 Kurtz, used a bullet of the same diameter as the rifle, but weighed only 120 grains and had a velocity of only 2,300 f.p.s. The fine German assault rifle, MP44, fired this intermediate power round—it resembles an SMG in appearance and was produced largely of stampings. It was short, had a moderately low cyclic rate (500 r.p.m.), and an 'in line' stock, but weighed more than 11 lb. The weapon proved itself in combat; the ammo was sufficiently powerful for most missions and gave good burst fire accuracy. The Germans and the Russians who had experience with these new arms were well impressed by them.

The other principal German WW II AR development may be considered to be the antecedent of NATO assault rifles. The revolutionary FG42, which could fire bursts fairly accurately, weighed only 10·5 lb. unloaded; it was made of stampings and had an ultra-modern look. It had many features of the CETME and the FN, but was not produced in quantity during WW II. It was used in the invasion of Crete by the German paratroopers as a substitute for bolt rifles and squad LMGs, but was not trouble-free and used up ammo quickly.

When the new German army began to take shape in 1957, they could again assemble a complete new family of small arms, although they were equipped for some months with British and U.S. weapons. Characteristically, the first weapon chosen was the MG; these had been the backbone of the Wehrmacht. After trying out all models then available, the Ordnance Department preferred the old German MG42. This decision was based essentially on high cyclic rate, simplicity, reliability and a quick barrel-change capability not matched by any other MG at that time. At first, captured weapons were bought back from France, but new weapons were soon being manufactured. These were slightly redesigned and chambered for the NATO round. The MG42-59 can deliver more bullets over any given period of time than any other ground automatic weapon in the world, but as a bipod mounted squad LMG it is still inaccurate.

The Germans selected the FN rifle as their temporary standard. All that were delivered were capable of full automatic fire if desired for assault roles. Some of the early German FNs weighed less than 8 lb. and had no bipods. Only the first shot of a burst could be kept on a silhouette target at 25 metres. Some minor adjustments were then made, but the FNs firing fully automatic from the shoulder or hip essentially just squirt bullets garden-hose fashion.

A team of small-arms designers working in Spain for the Spanish government, but composed in part of former Germans, had produced by 1960 a new assault rifle known as the CETME. This weapon is new, but has obvious similarities to the FG42 and MP44. It fired the NATO round, but as produced in Spain was not entirely satisfactory. The shortcomings were eliminated, however, by Heckler and Koch of Oberndorf, the home of the old Mauser works. The CETME as now produced by this firm is called the G3 and is a fine, relatively heavy infantry rifle which can deliver bursts, if these are necessary. But for accuracy, fast sustained single-shot fire is better. The G3 is said to be simpler and cheaper to produce than the FN.

The Germans experimented in the late 1950s with many SMGs including their old MP40s, but finally chose the Uzi as produced by FN and others. This weapon has all the usual advantages of modern SMGs, but the characteristic that told most in its favour in the German trials was its compactness. It is the shortest and least bulky SMG in NATO. Since the introduction of the G3, SMGs are not considered to be important weapons for primary infantry combat. Men who have them should be inconvenienced as little as possible, particularly while getting in and out of vehicles and while carrying heavy weapons and ammo.

The new West German army was created to stop an avalanche of heavy Bloc divisions coming from the east. They want to do this with air power, armour and artillery as well as infantry firepower. They do not want to assume a static defence and are doing all in their power to protect their soldiers by armour when possible. The German infantry relies today even more on mobility and co-ordination of all arms than they did in the early stages of WW II. Infantry is still indispensable, but the Germans hope that if it must fight, it can do so protected at least in part by armour.

They go a step further than other armies and want their infantry not only carried in APCs, but able to fight from them if the situation makes this possible.

At platoon level, this means that the West Germans require four Swiss-made Hispano Suiza APCs (Model 30) which allow every man save the driver to fire from the vehicle. There are again three rifle squads, plus an HQ sections, in each rifle platoon; all four units consist of eight men each and have one LMG, one light powerful AT weapon, and several G3 assault rifles or SMGs. Each of the APCs has also a 20-mm. Hispano Suiza HMG manned by one of the squad.

A rifle company contains four rifle platoons, plus an HQ; there are no heavy elements in the HQ other than the APC weapons of an AR, the AT weapon and the 20-mm. HMG on each vehicle. But modern German infantry battalions which contain three rifle companies also have a heavy weapons company which has mortars of two sizes (81 mm. and 120 mm.) which can be fired from their carriers, self-propelled 90-mm. guns, and an AT platoon with 48 wire-directed AT missiles. This Panzer Grenadier infantry is not yet universal; the APCs and the 90-mm. self-propelled guns are still present in inadequate numbers. But the aim is in that direction; motorized and marching infantry will eventually be replaced with these mechanized units.

The Bundeswehr does not want to fight by companies. Their primary mission will require the co-ordinated effort of many corps consisting of several nationalities. Complicated and extremely expensive weapons far beyond our scope would be employed. But wars have a way of ultimately pitting men with their personal weapons against others similarly armed. This might happen on nuclear battlefields even more often than in the past.

The new German infantry battalions have all support arms thought to be required for such combat. They fulfil the old German organic support weapon principle of providing each CO with all the organic arms he needs. But at rifle company level, tactics will be limited by the lack of organic support arms. Discounting platoon AT weapons which are desperation weapons, a rifle company now has only direct fire MGs and rifles. These are the only weapons which could be used efficiently from APCs on the move.

The Germans realize, of course, the great importance of support weapons in all types of infantry combat, but also appreciate the advantages of simplicity and specialization. Battalion level weapons can always be assigned, but mobility and dash of the type which early in WW II probed for a weak spot even on a platoon front and then exploited it to the utmost, will be best retained by keeping rifle companies light. The platoons, either in APCs or dismounted, can move and communicate; their direct-fire capability is unimpaired even though the battalion must now supply support fire. The Germans desire in the future to fight on foot as little as possible.

The German emphasis on area fire is the most pronounced in Europe today. Their MGs and G3s can put down a lot of it. The Germans feel that really accurate AR fire is of little tactical consequence; enemy soldiers are seldom seen on modern battlefields. The G3 rifle is the equal of many squad ARs including the U.S. M14 Modified. Squirted bullets may be as likey to score hits as carefully aimed shots; high cyclic rate fire makes an awe-inspiring sound. Even though the MG42–59s hit nothing, they contribute to fire superiority which is said in some circumstances to be more important than causing enemy casualties.

Defensively, the real firepower of each rifle company will also come from its MG42–59s. There will probably be extra weapons of this type available in each platoon taken from APCs, as well as tripod mounts to convert them to MMGs. When cleverly concealed and arranged to give interlocking fields of fire over a considerable depth, these MGs are tough to beat.

XIV

Russia and the Satellites

THE Russian army is the most powerful ground force in the world today. Other nations within the Soviet sphere of influence enhance even further the Communist Bloc military potential. There are 100 modern and powerful Bloc divisions in Central Europe which could be in action within forty-eight hours; this number could be doubled or tripled within six weeks, but quality would fall off. The Russians have made great progress since WW II in their organization, training and tactical practice in gigantic war games. They have a new family of small arms as well as other modern *matériel* of many types.

The Russians, in the spring of 1941, had more armour and motor transport than any other army in the world, twice as much as the Germans. They had startlingly new infantry weapons, such as the Tokarev semi-automatic rifle equipped with telescope sights. The Germans in a few weeks smashed Russian armour and captured tens of thousands of vehicles; Germans used the new rifles until they jammed because of the cold.

After being defeated and pushed back hundreds of miles, the Russians scrapped their ultra-modern ideas, their political Commissars and the Communist Party requirements for advancement in the army. The slogans which stopped Napoleon in 1812 appeared again; 'Holy Russia' of 1812 became 'Mother Russia' of 1942. The stubborn, inarticulate resistance of Borodino appeared again at Stalingrad. Patriotism and bolt rifles replaced Communism and the Tokarevs; divisions reverted to animal transport. Modern sophisticated weapons and new ways of using them were given up for the tactics and strategy of Peter the Great and Kutuzov. The people who were a poor match for the Germans when fighting in the modern way, won when they returned to simplicity, mass attack and stubborn primitive defence.

Final conclusions, even for WW II now twenty years old, should include, however, consideration of four additional factors. Hitler rather absurdly insisted on defending every foot of captured territory. The Germans alienated the Russian civilian population which was at first friendly. The very heart of Germany was being bombed severely during the period of Russia's greatest success. Finally, an enormous tonnage of the best weapons and *mat riel* in the world was being delivered to Russia by the U.S. and Britain.

In 1945 Russian infantry divisions contained 9,619 men and consisted of three infantry regiments of 2,474 each, plus artillery and other support elements. Each regiment had three rifle battalions and an HQ which included a mortar company (seven 120-mm. mortars), an AT battery (six 45-mm. guns), and AT rifle company (twenty-seven 14·5 AT rifles), and an SMG company with 100 men each armed with an SMG.

Each rifle battalion consisted of about 600 men divided into three rifle companies (143 each), an MG company (58) with nine water-cooled Cal ·30 MMGs, a mortar company (61) with nine 82-mm. mortars, and an AT rifle platoon (23) with nine 14·5-mm. AT rifles. Each rifle company had three rifle platoons and a weapons platoon; these had together two MMGs, eighteen LMGs, and two 50-mm. mortars besides rifles, SMGs, and infantry AT devices of several types.

After the 1945 victory, the Communist Party lost no time in reclaiming the army. The officers who had risen quickly in the crucible of combat were re-educated both politically and in regard to military theory; some men were in school for three years. Many were downgraded or retired; those who remained were politically acceptable and academically efficient. During this period, the Soviet army again became ultra-modern, but on a more practical basis. Their support *matériel* is again elaborate and numerous. They have more heavy tanks and large mortars and a greater diversity of artillery than any other high command desires today.

The Russian army is divided into Fronts, Armies and Corps, all of which are large and vary in accordance with requirements. Divisions are still triangular with support elements at each level.

A rifle division continues to have three rifle regiments, each of three battalions plus some other elements. The basis of power in the Soviet army is still their infantry; they feel it may be more important now than before the advent of atomic weapons. The Russian infantry will fight on its feet, even though motorized or mechanized for travelling and manoeuvre.

The Russian army makes no effort to conceal the organization, weapons and tactics of its infantry battalions. A rifle battalion now contains 550 men, 55 of whom are not primary combatants. The remainder constitute four HQ support units and three rifle companies. The support units employ respectively, (*a*) six 82-mm. mortars, (*b*) six quad-mounted 14·5-mm. HMGs, which are towed, (*c*) four RRs and two self-propelled assault guns, and (*d*) six Cal·30 MMGs.

The battalion heavy weapons are not greatly different from most of those employed in the West. The Russian 82-mm. mortars are substantially the same as the 81-mm. pieces common in NATO and will function with that ammo. Their quad 14·5-mm. HMGs are similar to U.S. quad Cal·50s, save that the individual guns are slightly more powerful (about Cal·60), and not self-propelled. The so-called RRs, however, are smooth-bore and fin-stabilized. The self-propelled assault guns do not have Western counterparts, for they are neither armoured nor even enclosed; they have skeleton carriages and an auxiliary motor by means of which they can travel slowly for short distances. For strategic moves, they are towed behind trucks. The RRs were until recently 82 mm., and the assault guns 57 mm., but both are now being replaced with similar arms of a larger size.

Each rifle company of 105 men has an HQ (5), an MG platoon (10) with three Cal·30 MMGs, and three rifle platoons (30 each). Each platoon consists of three nine-man squads and a three-man HQ. Before discussing personal weapons details, some historical background is required.

In 1945 the Russian infantry was using surviving Tokarev rifles and many short bolt-action weapons based on the original Mosin-Nagant Model 1891; they had also a squad LMG, and several progressively heavier MGs all firing the 7·62-mm. Russian rimmed cartridge. All these were sturdy and effective, but not modern, save for the Tokarevs; the AR and the MGs were heavier than those found in other countries and fired slower. Together

A small task force of eight US Marines going ashore—showing M14 rifles, an M3 SMG, and a US 1911 A1 pistol in its holster

US soldier in a one-man flying machine

US marines leaving a helicopter fast during manoeuvres at Camp LeJeune in North Carolina

US MC equipment transported by helicopters

A Greek MMG team with the Model 1919A4 weapon; the squad leader to the rear has the US M1 SMG

Training in the Greek army with the 57-mm. RR

A Canadian regimental serjeant major with the A2E3 SMG. The C2AR is shown to the right

A Canadian crew fires an 81-mm. mortar

A Canadian rifle squad in front of their APC. The squad leader on the extreme left has an SMG; the rest have SLRs (C1s) save for the man on the extreme right who has a Canadian AR (C2)

with these rifle cartridge weapons there was a semi-automatic pistol (also called the Tokarev after its designer) and two SMGs (the PPSH and the PPS) firing the powerful 7·63-mm. Mauser pistol cartridge, called the 7·62-mm. in Russia.

Soon after WW II, the Russians began as part of their modernization programme to experiment with both rifle and pistol cartridges of reduced power. An intermediate power rifle cartridge, similar in ballistics to the German 7·92 Kurtz, was introduced which retained the old 7·62-mm. bore (Cal ·30). The new round was slightly longer, but thinner than that of the Germans. Both fire a bullet of approximately 120-grains at about 2,300 f.p.s.

Three new weapons have been issued in quantity to fire the 7·62 Intermediate ammo; they are a semi-automatic infantry carbine (the SKS), a powerful SMG (the AK), and a squad AR (the RPD). These three weapons were intended to replace all rifles, carbines, SMGs, ARs and MGs used by line infantry throughout Bloc armies. Obviously, such a family of small arms would lack power, but the Russians had two support HMGs, one something like the U.S. Cal ·50 and the other like the Cal ·60, which would in theory give them even more powerful flat trajectory fire at longer ranges than any Cal ·30 MMG.

The SKS was a well-made weapon which weighed 8·8 lb. loaded with ten rounds of ammo in a detachable box magazine. The standard model could not be fired full-automatic and had a permanently attached bayonet. Tests of this weapon indicate that its accuracy was entirely adequate to 300 yards and its killing power in direct fire satisfactory to 500. Because of low recoil, the weapon was pleasant to shoot; its issue sights were generally well adjusted.

The new AK weighs 10·5 lb. loaded with a 30-round staggered box magazine. It is capable of both full- and semi-automatic fire. It resembles, both in operation and in appearance, the German MP44 and has a cyclic rate of 600 r.p.m., or a little less. The standard issue model has a wooden stock; there is a folding metal stock model of approximately the same weight. Both models take a bayonet which is not permanently attached.

The RPD weighs 14·5 lb. without any magazine. As first issued, there was a drum-type magazine which held 100 rounds; a 250-round double-drum arrangement was also provided. This high ammo capacity was not considered necessary, so a 50-round drum was introduced. The latest change is to have the RPD capable of handling all the drums and the 30-round AK magazines also.

Pistolwise, the Russians concluded that nobody ever did much damage with a handgun and evolved a 25-oz., double-action semi-automatic (the PM) that looks like a slightly enlarged German Walther PK of WW II. The cartridge is a 9-mm. short (not the ·380) firing a 93-grain round-nosed bullet at about 1,100 f.p.s., considerably below the 7·63 Mauser or the 9-mm. Parabellum in power.

These three new shoulder weapons and the new pistol were modern, reliable and reasonably simple to supply, even though stampings are not used as liberally as in some Western arms. If one admits that real rifle power is not needed in battle, because of the numerous support weapons organic in the Russian battalions, regiments and divisions, the four new arms are certainly a great improvement on the multitude of the WW II weapons which they were supposed to replace. The idea was hard to fault in theory.

The using services, however, gave it a fit. The most crushing blow fell first. The old 7·62-mm. Russian rimmed cartridge was retained for company and battalion MMGs and for use by snipers. The RPD, although an accurate arm at short range because of its intermediate power ammo and its low cyclic rate, was adjudged inadequate for MG missions at above platoon level. The rather large group of Russian competitive riflemen and snipers did not like the SKS. This weapon is supposed to have developed faults in the Hungarian fighting and has been replaced by the AK.

On the other extreme, the AK was found to be too heavy and bulky for many uses, particularly in vehicles. A beefed-up version of the PM pistol with holster stock, full-automatic fire, and a 20-round clip was developed. This weapon (the APS) is a fine piece of engineering and an advantageous substitute for an SMG for men who will not be in combat. But for SMG use, it is as much under-powered as the AK is over-powered. Nine years after the PPS was supposed to be gone (1964), there were still a lot of them in the hands of troops, although perhaps not line infantry.

The Russians have not achieved their original aims by introducing their two new cartridges and weapons designed for them. They have now accepted the indefinite continuation of their nineteenth-century 7·62-mm. rimmed cartridge and have not eliminated the old pistol and SMG round either. Old weapons have been replaced by new ones which have advantages in rapidity of fire, weight and reliability. But their new arms are inferior to the old beyond 300 yards; neither the AK nor the APS is really an effective SMG.

To return to infantry organization, the Russian rifle company with a full strength of 105 men is small. It is lightly armed and mobile on foot or in vehicles. The only weapons in the company firing a full-power rifle cartridge are the three MMGs in the weapons platoon. Platoons appear not so definitely separated into squads as in some armies. Squads have often been combined after casualties, but each nine Russian infantrymen have now an RPD, seven AKs, and one AT weapon, a Panzerfaust-type recoilless device, the APG2, with a bore of 40 mm., but a warhead of 82 mm. which projects beyond the muzzle. It has an accurate range of about 100 yards and is both light and powerful.

Russian field manuals stress the offence. Large movements on wide fronts are more important in their strategic thinking than smaller battles for limited objectives. Specifically, if a 'hot war' should come, they plan to penetrate to and across the Rhine in one great sustained push in which all opposition will be kept off balance by continuous thrusts from Soviet units of various sizes.

Initially in a major Russian offensive, they will try to execute two or more break-throughs on wide fronts. The spots will be chosen carefully after air and ground reconnaissance and espionage; they will conceal their intentions and the exact areas to be attacked both before and during the early stages of the action. They will bring a tremendous amount of relatively short-range artillery to bear on the fronts selected and search out the rear areas with more powerful stuff, perhaps with low-yield atomic weapons. The barrage on the enemy's front line will be similar to the WW I type both in intensity and its rolling movement in front of the attacking ground forces.

A Russian assault would be delivered in waves; they desire to keep up momentum at all costs. They know that they are going to lose a lot of men, but if a complete break-through can be achieved, enemy casualties will be even greater. When one wave is spent, another will take its place. They will push around strong-points that cannot be taken immediately; a succeeding echelon, better armed for such missions, will handle the job minutes or hours later. They want to keep the attack rolling once it is started, even though it may appear to degenerate into infiltrations. They feel that if they have a numerical superiority of three to one in the sectors they attack in earnest, there is no need to fear having any considerable portion of the attacking force cut off.

The training for these offensives begins early, both with recruits and in staff schools, and permeates thought *and* action. A newly inducted soldier spends dozens of hours in bayonet practice. He learns how to get through an opponent's guard and stick him with a bayonet. He has to continue this work until his instructor is convinced that he really has confidence in his ability to kill with cold steel. The Russians are not fools; they realize that not many enemies will actually die this way. But the training is good for developing the offensive spirit in a nation that has been more noted in the past for their stubborn defences than for brilliant offensives.

Once individuals have assimilated this offensive spirit, units of progressive size begin to practise attacks not only in summer, but in Russian winters also. Their armies have unique facilities for actual live-fire exercises of the largest type. Groups of divisions will be kept rolling for days over hundreds of miles. Damage to a few privately owned trees in some NATO countries leads to reprimands for the COs responsible. Thousands of acres are torn up in Russian war games, and even a few soldiers and civilians killed, but all is dismissed as necessary for realistic training.

Let us try to visualize what it would be like to be in front of one of the Russian attacks. Perhaps half an hour before the infantry-tank thrust began, there would be a barrage. The mere arrival of the barrage would not necessarily mean that we were to receive an attack, for some artillery fire of this general type would probably be delivered over a wide area. A barrage could be used as a feint and to conceal as long as possible the point to be attacked in earnest. If it were particularly severe in our area, however, it would be probable that we were in the path of the main attack. We might not be able to get an effective counter-barrage; our communications might be broken and impossible to re-establish. Our entire territory, front and rear, would be receiving a thorough going over from Soviet artillery and tactical aircraft. Our supporting weapons would have serious difficulties; the Russians now have both sound and flash equipment for their counter-battery fire. If they had managed to achieve their concentration, mature their plans, and launch their attack before we took counter-action, they would be tough to stop.

As their initial barrage lifted, we should come out of our bunkers and sit up in our foxholes. Some of us would soon see in the darkness, rain or fog individual Russian soldiers armed with AKs probably firing single shots from the hip as they came forward; we would open on them, or in their general direction. This would attract the Russian tanks which have the mission of attacking immediately any force which holds up their infantry. If we had surviving RRs, or other long-range weapons suitable for AT work, we would use them now. These might win time to consolidate the friendly troops that had survived in our area into the best defensive situation available.

But AT weapons of the larger sort are hard to conceal once they fire, particularly big RRs. We would probably not have them long, unless we retained the ability to move them around, or withdraw them underground. A retreat would already be impossible; our best course might be to counter-attack into the flank of the Soviet advance. If we continued to survive, we would become an isolated strong-point and as such would receive attention from specialized enemy teams with successively heavier weapons. We would want to take advantage of every favourable factor, conserve ammunition and any support weapons we still had, and spread out as much as our strength would allow. It would be necessary to take all the cover possible, but suicidal to go deep into bunkers again.

We would be subjected to periods of heavy concentrations of fire from many support weapons as well as the Cal · 30 MMGs and the new small arms. We would then receive infantry-tank assaults assisted by Russian engineers with explosives and flame. Our chances for ultimate survival would depend upon our fighting efficiency and many factors beyond our control. There are few Bastognes, but the defeating of one of these Russian attacks depends largely on the cumulative casualties inflicted by groups such as ours. The longer we resisted, the greater the odds would be against us. But our opportunities for causing loss to the enemy would also increase. So long as we retained some flexibility, our situation would not be hopeless.

The Russian theory of defence, although played down in their textbooks, is carefully thought out and practised. Again they consider first a theatre of war stretching for hundreds of miles, and visualize a situation where their defences can be up to forty miles in thickness. This depth would be broken down roughly into four different zones. The Security Zone is closest to the enemy and consists first of outposts and patrols to a thickness of as much as ten miles. The front of this zone would be occupied by the reconnaissance battalion (300 men specially equipped) of each infantry regiment. There would probably be one of these units supported by appropriate armour approximately every four miles of front. Behind this open area, there would be a Combat Security Line held by infantry battalions with their organic heavy weapons, but little or no additional support.

About 1,500 yards to the rear of this nearly continuous line would be the Main Zone of Resistance with a depth of six to eight miles. Depending on time, terrain, and the importance of the sector, this area would be full of concealed strong-points, some occupied and others not. It would be tough going, particularly for armour. The Russians do not advocate, however, the use of their own medium tanks against the armour of an enemy, since they believe that their losses would make such actions unprofitable. They would prefer to stop enemy tanks with their AT artillery and heavy assault guns. The latter, in Russia, are really super gun-tanks, except that they have no wide traverse turrets.

To the rear again, there would be an Intermediate Zone of Resistance of about ten miles, not so heavily held as that immediately to the front and occupied principally in order to ambush, or channel into killing lanes, the advancing enemy. There would be positions held by skeleton forces, or not held at all, so that an attack on them would leave the enemy open to counteraction from Russians occupying less obvious positions. Finally, the fourth zone is known as the Second Defence Zone and is normally from six to eight miles thick. Although not strongly held initially, this area would abound, according to present theory, in bunkers reasonably proof against even nuclear weapons.

A Russian infantry battalion, regardless of where it was in this mass of defences, would plan to use strong-points rather than continuous lines of trenches. On defence, the infantry would strive to survive an initial bombardment and then come up fighting with their crew-served weapons, particularly with their MMGs firing the old 7·62 rimmed ammo. They would mount numerous counter-attacks, however, in platoon, company and battalion strength in which their AKs and RPDs would be effective.

Russian strategy and tactics include more than enormous attacks and defences in great depth just described, but the other things are secondary and special adaptions of the same general principles. Defences against counter-attacks delivered by the Russians are only miniature versions of their larger actions. In a chance meeting, the Russian idea is to attack as soon as possible with everything available rather than wait for complete organization. Russian regiments and battalions are to some extent ready to fight independent actions, but their companies and platoons are not nearly as able to do so as their British and U.S. counterparts.

The Russians have no well-developed plan for fighting retreats. They do, however, practise disengaging actions. Rather than retreat in the face of the enemy, Bloc armies would endeavour to break off all contact completely, either by an artillery barrage or counter-attacks, and then move to the rear. Normally, such action would be taken in poor weather or at night. If atomic weapons were being used, they would certainly be employed in such a situation.

It would be a mistake to underrate the Russian infantry. The individual Russians do not lack initiative, bravery, brains, or professional efficiency just because they live under a dictatorship. The natural fatalistic stubbornness of the Russian character will certainly be apparent in any action they fight, but many squad, platoon and company commanders know their jobs and have fine units with an unequalled amount of practice in large-scale manoeuvres. The squads and platoons sometimes have a family feeling which transcends life itself.

On the other hand, the Russian army is not composed entirely of Russians. The conscripts from other racial groups within the vast Soviet land mass are not such good soldiers, nor so patriotic. In spite of all the training, indoctrination and preferential treatment, many soldiers are admittedly untrustworthy; disgruntled individuals who for one reason or another have run foul of the system are more numerous than in any Western army. In spite of considerable recent improvement, their logistics in a long war would probably be about up to the WW I level for the West. There is a lot of fatalism rather than enthusiasm and initiative in high places. The West Germans, who certainly know them better than any of the rest of us, have far less fear of the Russians than some armies that have never met them in combat.

The Satellite nations of Central Europe all have armies which follow the Russian lead in organization, weapons and tactics, but there are variations. The Czechs had a 7·62-mm. short rimless round similar to, but not interchangeable with, the new Russian 7·62 mm. The Czech weapons are still not identical with those of the Russians, but they are said now to use the Russian cartridge. The weapons chambered for the old Czech cartridge are said to have been sold outside the Bloc, in part to Cuba.

Throughout Bloc armies there is now an emphasis on accurate sniper fire, based on the three pairs of marksmen with scope-sighted rifles organic to Russian WW II rifle companies. This type of fire was also important from guerrillas. All Bloc armies have carefully trained marksmen with fine weapons ready for this type of special combat, but now they are usually organic to regimental HQ.

Some of the Satellites, particularly East Germany, are still using weapons of national origin. German MP44 firing the 7·92 Kurtz is still frequently photographed, but other older weapons are in the hands of reserves only and may soon be replaced entirely. National characteristics still persist in organization and small unit tactics. The military spirit of Prussia is now apparent in Communist East German units.

XV
Red China

CHINA achieved a high level of civilization and military power more than 2,000 years ago. During the nineteenth century, however, European trading nations took over small areas of the country and were dictating to all Chinese governments. In the Boxer Rebellion of 1900, a small international army with modern weapons marched easily anywhere and stormed Peking with only a few casualties.

In the 1920s, the sleeping giant began to stir. Fighting occurred between various factions over large areas; war lord armies were numerous. The Nationalists under Chiang Kai-Shek finally won, but were replaced by the Japanese throughout much of the country. During WW II, the Nationalists and the Communists were allies against the Japanese, but fought each other thereafter. The Communists finally won all the mainland (1949).

Red China is immense in area, population and ultimate military power. The population of over 700 million could lead to the largest army in the history of the world. In the immediate future, however, their economy appears unable to support such a force. They have about two and a half million men on active duty, but use them periodically for agriculture and construction. Efficiency is limited by *matériel* deficiencies which still extend right down into infantry squads. The average Chinese soldier is poorly armed by Western standards.

We should not forget, however, that war is made by men, not weapons. The Chinese showed in Korea that they can be tough, daring and effective opponents. They adopted a type of offence and defence which minimized their disadvantages and emphasized their strengths. We must guard against over-confidence based on Western weapons superiorities. In a shooting and marching war, the Chinese infantry will be better than their equipment. About seven million men have been in the army for varying periods; many more millions are in their partially trained Public Security Forces.

The Chinese army today is essentially the Red army of 1926 improved by a dozen years of guerrilla fighting in the chaotic pre-WW II period, six years of war as the allies of the Nationalists against the Japanese invaders, and a final four years of combat against the Nationalists. The Korean War followed; in 1953 the Red Chinese commanders had more combat experience than the Russians and Germans combined. The last twelve years of comparative peace have been utilized to improve organization, training and equipment.

Throughout their long period of conflict, the Chinese Communists were fighting mostly guerrilla-type actions. Only towards the end of their Civil War and for a part of the Korean conflict were they operating as a regular force with solid fronts, lines of communication and definite objectives. Even today, strategy and tactics are influenced by the guerrilla techniques which the older Chinese officers know so well. Younger men have been formally trained both in Russia and in modern Chinese staff colleges.

The organization of Chinese armed forces are in part beyond the comprehension of most Western minds. The army blends indistinguishably into the Communist Party. The top military commanders are also the rulers of China. The army is all-powerful and seems at some levels to include both navy and air force. Rank and insignia were only made definite in 1955; even today, generals spend part of each year as enlisted men.

On the other hand, there is no mystery as to actual units, weapons and general constitution of their forces. Horse cavalry divisions are still in existence; there are also some armoured divisions. Artillery and engineering units, some of divisional size, are known to exist. The Russian organizational influence was strong, but not all-important, and is beginning to wane.

The Chinese army is essentially an infantry force. Their real power comes from triangular infantry divisions (TO&E strengths 17,600) with fairly thin supporting elements at each level. The organization of their infantry regiments (4,150) seems now to be standardized after a good deal of experimentation following the Korean War and is theoretically similar to that of the Russian army. The scarcity of armour, self-propelled and conventional artillery and motor transport, however, makes a considerable difference in the actual composition.

There are three rifle battalions (840 each) and one weapons battalion (590 men) in each regiment. The weapons battalion consists of an artillery company, a mortar company, an RR company, and an AA company. Many artillery companies still have four 70-mm. howitzers which fire a 9-lb. shell at a muzzle velocity of 675 f.p.s., but are gradually receiving modern Russian-type 76-mm. guns. The mortar company has four 120-mm., and some smaller, mortars. There are usually six 57-mm. or 75-mm. U.S.-type RRs in the RR company, but these are being replaced with similar Soviet-type weapons which are smooth-bore and fin-stabilized. Many AA companies still have 12·7-mm. Russian HMGs, but some have the newer quad-mounted Soviet 14·5-mm. ZPUs.

A Chinese regimental HQ is larger than usual and contains, in addition to support units, a reconnaissance section and a security company. This last organization is unusual, and appears to be a development from the guerrilla origin of the Chinese army. It is essentially an elite unit of about 300 well-armed men; their principal function is to protect the regimental commander and his immediate military family and also accomplish critical missions of short duration. This security company has been to some extent downgraded theoretically, but appears to be still fully operational.

Each rifle battalion has an HQ (55), three rifle companies (200 men each), a mortar company (75), and an MMG company (110). There are in theory nine 82-mm. mortars and nine MMGs in the two support companies, but many battalions still have only four mortars and six MMGs. The mortars are the simple reliable type used in all Bloc armies; the MMGs are also mostly of Russian origin and heavy. The latter appear old-fashioned with their low two-wheeled carriages, long trails and armour shield. These were, however, the most effective weapons that the Chinese had in Korea and are still good. Their low cyclic rate and considerable weight (about 150 lb.) allow continuous and stable operation. The Chinese appear to choose their best soldiers for handling these weapons and know how to deliver accurate indirect as well as direct fire.

Each rifle company contains three rifle platoons and a weapons platoon provided with three 60-mm. mortars and two U.S.-type 3·5-in. RLs. The number of the latter may have been increased slightly recently. The rifle platoons consist of an AR squad and three other squads. The designation rifle is used here in a loose sense; weapons that we would call rifles are not issued at all in many platoons. More of this presently.

There are three categories of small arms in China today. The most numerous class includes Japanese, U.S., British, old Russian, and War Lord Chinese weapons of WW II and before. Some of their bolt Mauser rifles are more than sixty years old; many Chinese copies of foreign ARs, SMGs, and the like are of poor quality. But these weapons are now mostly in the hands of Public Security Forces, not the Chinese army.

The second most numerous class of small arms came from Russia during the Korean War. These were mainly the weapons produced in the U.S.S.R. after the beginning of WW II. The Mosin–Nagant carbine (M1944) is probably the most widely carried arm in the Chinese army today, but the two Russian WW II SMGs, the M1941 (PPSH) and M1943 (PPS), are also numerous. So are Russian MGs of several models. All these weapons fire the old 7·62-mm. Russian rimmed rifle ammo or the 7·63-mm. Mauser pistol cartridge.

Since 1956, the Chinese have been rearming with the new Soviet intermediate power carbines (SKS), SMGs (AK), and ARs (RPD). The Chinese at present have more SKS carbines than AKs. All are presently being produced in Chinese factories. But the replacement rate from home manufacture is low; Russian imports are said to have stopped. Besides, the Chinese appear to have no intention of eliminating SMGs firing pistol cartridges. The Chinese copy of the PPS M1943 is still being produced.

Throughout the mobile phase of the Korean War, the Chinese were sending into action platoons armed only with a bag full of grenades; other platoons would have SMGs only. These weapons are now issued to the same men, and an AR squad added to each platoon. The assault potential of men so armed is considerable at short range. Other platoons have more conventional rifle and AR distribution.

Pistols are important in the Chinese army and were used in Korea as a kind of insignia of rank; the better the pistol, the higher the officer. There are still many makes and models, but the two new Russian reduced-power weapons (PN and APS) are rare. Anything that will shoot is kept in service, for arms are not as common as in Western armies. Many members of crew-served weapons teams and grenadiers have no personal arms at all. In the event of a major war in which reserves were used, some Chinese soldiers would again go into action intending either to pick up the arms of their own casualties, or to take weapons from the enemy.

The Chinese leaders are capable military men with a lot of actual combat experience. Why do they allow conditions that appear to us to be so undesirable to continue, while giving away millions in the form of international aid and spending even more in trying to develop a nuclear military potential? There are probably several reasons, the most important of which is the guerrilla origin of the Chinese army itself. The fact that there were more men than small arms did not hurt greatly the efficiency of the old Communist forces.

The scarcity of weapons applies equally to ammo for personal arms. Chinese soldiers are not carefully trained marksmen, but they have been taught to conserve their cartridges. When the Chinese crossed the Yalu in November 1950, they received 40 rounds per rifle and about 80 rounds per SMG. They could expect no resupply for weeks. To a lesser extent, this same thinking applied to AR gunners. In a nation with poor logistics and a weak economy, this approach has advantages. On the other hand, the Chinese MMGs in Korea had relatively abundant ammo; these are a privileged class of arms in China.

In their guerrilla days, the Chinese specialized in ambush and surprise, particularly at night. Where possible, they will still attack only where they think they are sure of winning and try to exterminate their enemies quickly. Their best defence in their guerrilla days was a fighting withdrawal followed by a disappearance. These tactics were still apparent in Korea and probably will continue to be used by the Chinese, although they now have a regular modern army trained in conventional warfare.

Much was written of Chinese 'human sea' assaults in Korea. Chinese grenadiers of poor quality did attack in masses early in the mobile operations period of the war, but even then there were better units taking advantage of these operations to infiltrate U.S. lines and attack rear echelons. Heavy frontal attacks by

Chinese infantry, variously armed, will continue in their future wars, but they won't do this thoughtlessly or inefficiently. There are sure to be other less obvious attacks co-ordinated with them.

Their more dangerous offensive manoeuvres will continue to be tactical surprises in which Chinese units succeed in getting within yards of enemy lines undetected, and in passing through or between fortified positions to attack rear elements. They will continue to try to encircle and annihilate, or at least envelop one flank and attack from unexpected angles. Darkness and poor weather not only limit enemy tactical air activity, but conceal Chinese movements; they take full advantage of their closer-to-nature background to terrorize their enemies at night and in poor weather. Relatively, they fight better under these conditions than more civilized armies. Their plans will be simple, but well co-ordinated. At almost every level, there will be two thrusts rather than one; the one in front is not as dangerous as that from the flank or rear. Even though they now have a great deal more heavy equipment than in Korea, their infantry will have limited organic support by Western standards.

Defensively, the Chinese in Korea showed two different tendencies. In mobile operations, they left such a wide belt of no man's land that they scarcely held anything at all. They would prepare a kind of ambush zone in which they were so well concealed that U.S. patrols could move right over them without realizing their presence. The Chinese would not disclose one of their ambush positions just to cause a few casualties, but would spring to life when a more profitable target approached unwarily.

In the static phase of the Korean War, the Chinese adapted U.S. defensive tactics to their own requirements. As mentioned earlier, they constructed underground fortifications of extreme power, size and complication. Their mortar and artillery barrages were not up to Western standards, but they were able to do much better than they had earlier. Their mortars were well handled; Russian guns of medium size and fine accuracy were fired a couple of times at important targets and then pulled back into caves, only to appear an hour later for two more shots from a different opening. The U.S. artillery continued, however, to be more effective.

Infantrywise, the Chinese finally co-ordinated fire teams of rifles, SMGs and ARs and supported them with MMGs and light mortars. Defensively, they learned to use their excellent MMGs in well-chosen positions with interlocking fields of fire, as well as having their mortars zeroed in for close support. They were still deficient, however, in arranging a real concentration by several weapons on a single objective and in manipulating support fire in defensive situations.

CONCLUSIONS

The Chinese army has a sobering ultimate potential. At present, however, and for a generation to come, China will not be able to maintain as many soldiers as a Western nation of one-tenth her size. Their lack of an effective system of support means that they can operate only within walking distance of China. Even the narrow Formosa strait has been an effective barrier so far. But the Chinese within areas which they can reach will be extremely formidable.

Chinese infantry in combat can move, fight and communicate, although their moving is mainly on foot and at night when opposed to superior air power. Their fighting qualities are unquestioned; stamina and fatalistic bravery go far to make up for their weapons disadvantages. They have a discipline that conquers the natural fear of death; their top leaders know combat from long practical experience. Communications were weak, but are improving. Their type of fighting does not require as much continuous interchange of information and orders as in the Western armies.

XVI
Canada

THE Canadian army was intimately connected with that of Britain through WW I and WW II. Even today, higher echelon organization and equipment tend towards Britain or the U.S. There is still a complete understanding and interchanging of ideas between these three countries at all levels, but the Canadian army is now entirely independent.

Canadian infantry battalions have begun to assume an individual form. In some ways, they are the most modern in the world; there are more organic support weapons, radios and motor vehicles per soldier than anywhere else. Canadian rifle companies differ in personnel, training, organization and equipment from those of any other country. Their weapons, tactics and basic concepts of war are uniquely Canadian.

Canadians have thought about atomic realities even in regard to rifle companies and platoons, but their basic offence and defence has not been radically changed. Organic vehicles and support weapons will be available, but Canadian infantry is prepared to fight primarily with the personal arms that each man carries. The most important of these are the rifle and the squad AR; for Canada, these are the C1 and the C2 respectively. They are basically the NATO round FN, known in Britain as the SLR, modified in accordance with Canadian requirements and manufactured in Canada.

The C1 rifle cannot be made full-automatic under any circumstances, not even by exchanging a selector lever from a C2. The C1 has a solid fore-end which cannot be used as a bipod. A separate launcher is required to fire any form of rifle grenade. This rifle is both rugged and accurate. It has the best and simplest rearsight that I have seen on any military rifle. Once zeroed, a

A British Vickers ·303 MMG and crew. This weapon is being replaced by the GPMG with tripod firing the 7·62 NATO round

British demonstration team with a 120-mm. RR

The modern West German AT weapon. This is a recoilless device and not a rocket launcher

A West German G3 rifle being fired off-hand

A West German soldier and the Uzi SMG

Greek infantry armed predominantly with British weapons, one BREN and several rifle No. 4s are easily picked out, but two men on the extreme left have US M1 rifles

The five Italian soldiers who form the assault section of their seven-man rifle squad. They are armed with four Beretta SMGs and one M1. The other two men in the squad have a BAR and another M1

The Spanish ALFA model 1955 MMG

The new French Model 1952 GMPG in two different conformations

A special night-illuminating device mounted on a US Model 1919 A4 MMG

soldier merely turns a large dial with clearly marked white numerals to elevation for additional range. Both the weapon itself and the standard Canadian ammo are accurate and reliable. The Canadian-made C1 is at least the equal of any other military rifle presently issued.

The C2 AR is similar to the C1, but has a heavier barrel, a fore-end that can be converted to a bipod, a hook on the butt-plate and a switch that allows full-automatic fire. The Canadians have introduced a 30-round magazine which is interchangeable with standard 20-round magazines, but is intended primarily for the C2. This rifle with a loaded 30-round magazine attached weighs 15·4 lb., more than the U.S. M14 Modified, but much less than the BAR or the old Canadian BREN. The C2 is more reliable than the BREN in really cold weather.

How accurate is the C2 in bursts? Canadian officers and NCOs with many years of small arms experience do not claim that the C2 is a match for the BREN in long bursts. But it can shoot better full-automatic than the U.S. M14 Modified because of its greater weight, its straight line of recoil into the shoulder, and its slightly lower cyclic rate of fire. The Canadian Le Clerc team won in 1962 and was second to the Netherlands in 1963 and 1964 mainly because of the accuracy of the Canadian C2 teams.

The Canadians who do well in competition with their C2 have an astonishing ability to manipulate the trigger. They appear to fire irregular bursts, but are actually firing only one or two rounds at a time. They get good target accuracy this way. But the C2 fires from a closed bolt and is essentially a squad AR of the lightest type and not really an LMG. Because of it, the Canadian army has introduced more medium and heavy automatic weapons at company and battalion level than is usual.

The Canadian infantry has, in addition to rifles and ARs, a limited number of SMGs and pistols. They have adopted the British L2A3 SMG, and the FN Browning 1935 pistol. Like the C1 and C2, both are manufactured in Canada by Crown companies which are in part privately owned. The Canadian SMG differs slightly from the British version, but can still take a bayonet. The L2A3 is in several ways the best in the world. It weighs only 6 lb. unloaded and is only 19 in. long with the stock folded. It can be used for single shots or bursts, has a 34-round magazine, and fires at the relatively low cyclic rate of 550 r.p.m. It can be carried with stock folded and the magazine out as easily as a telescope, even in vehicles.

The L2A3 has also been issued experimentally, after the British fashion, to rifle squad leaders and others who direct rather than fight themselves on a primary basis. This is particularly desirable where there is a good deal of getting in and out of vehicles.

A Canadian rifle company consists of five officers and 149 other ranks, and contains three rifle platoons (35 each), a support section (24), and an HQ (25). The support section has two 81-mm. mortars, two 106-mm. RRs, and two Cal ·30 MMGs. Each rifle platoon consists of three rifle sections of ten each and an HQ of five.

Everyone in the company has a personal weapon except the medical orderly at company HQ who is unarmed. The five officers have their pistols. The six men primarily responsible for the support section mortars, RRs and MMGs, plus the three men who carry the 3·5-in. RLs, one in each rifle platoon HQ, have SMGs. There is one C2 in each rifle squad, one with the RR section, and two with the mortars. All the rest now have C1s. This makes a total of five pistols, nine normally issued SMGs, twelve C2s, and 127 C1s. There are in addition the eight to fifteen spare L2A3s at company HQ for temporary issue to men going on night patrols and the like.

Each rifle company has 22 motor vehicles; there may soon be one more. These are organic within the company and remain under company control at all times under any foreseeable conditions, except where terrain would make them totally inappropriate. These vehicles carry petrol, food, water and ammo for a minimum period of three full, active days. Under normal conditions, these supplies are held in reserve for emergencies and not used up and replenished.

Some Canadian rifle companies are presently supplied with all unarmoured vehicles which operate on wheels. Other companies have tracked APCs for each rifle squad and for the mortar section. Eventually, all infantry will have APCs, but the Canadians are now in the process of standardizing their design for these vehicles. The two principal problems are whether riflemen in an APC should be able to fight with their personal weapons without leaving it, and whether the machine needs a dual travelling capacity, tracks for cross-country and wheels for roads. The new Canadian

APC will surely be fully enclosed, of low silhouette, and armed with at least one automatic weapon for its own protection.

Communication in a Canadian rifle company involves a lot of equipment. Even though orders can be oral or by signals as in other armies, they are prepared to dispense with these entirely. Foreseeable conditions in a big war, the type that Canadians are primarily prepared to fight, may make dispersion imperative; distances are likely to be too great for old means of command. Under static conditions, Canadian signallers would lay telephone lines within both company and battalion areas. Telephones are more efficient than wireless, but they do not expect to use telephones often in combat.

Canadians will rely on three different types of radios for battalion communications, each with progressively longer range. A platoon has a four-unit system interconnecting the CO and his three squad leaders. Each platoon CO is also connected, but on a more powerful system and a different frequency, with his company CO, the support fire control centre, the other platoon commanders and the company motor pool. The company commander is in turn connected on a still more powerful system with his battalion CO, battalion fire control HQ and other company COs. These elaborate systems require considerable maintenance, but the company has this skill, ample spare parts, and even spare units right in its own organization.

In addition to the two 81-mm. mortars in each of the four battalion rifle companies, there are four 4·2-in. mortars at battalion level. The battalion mortar commander has responsibility for training the company mortar sections and will have authority to use them in his support fire programmes, subject only to range and emergency use of one or more sections by their own company commanders.

There are four more 106-mm. RRs at battalion level to supplement the eight in the rifle companies. All these are individually jeep mounted and primarily for AT use. The battalion RRs may be assigned to company commanders or kept in reserve as required by terrain and circumstances.

The medium and heavy MG situation in a Canadian battalion is presently confused; the weapons in use are not ideal for their tactical roles. The U.S. Cal ·30 air-cooled tripod-mounted Brownings (Model 1919A4) at company level require ·30-'06 ammo. These will be replaced soon with 7·62 NATO weapons, probably a Canadian version of the British GPMG, although the U.S. M60 is still being considered. A company commander may assign his two MMGs either together or separately to his platoons, or keep them under his own control.

There are eight HMGs at battalion level, individually jeep mounted. The primary mission of these weapons is to attack enemy APCs and other thin-skinned armoured vehicles. Anti-personnel use is secondary; a heavy, extra-high-velocity bullet is not required to kill a man. The weapons actually in use are U.S. Cal ·50 air-cooled Brownings. Recent changes in design and thickness of enemy APC armour has reduced the range at which one of these weapons will penetrate to as little as 200 yards. There will probably be a more modern HMG issued soon to replace the Cal ·50s; a high-velocity 20-mm. similar to the West German Hispano-Suiza, mounted in a lightly armoured vehicle, would be ideal.

The Canadians are thinking about fighting, if they do have to fight, in the most modern manner possible. Their radios, vehicles and powerful support weapons are only part of this picture. They have faced squarely the problem of nuclear weapons and decided to prepare for the worst. Canada is as ready as humanly possible to fight in the devastation of an atomic battlefield. All infantry, to be effective, must fire, move and communicate. The Canadians are ready to do these on a scale never achieved before at comparable levels.

Terrain is extremely important to mechanized infantry. The Canadians are primarily organized and equipped to fight the Russians on the North German plains. Secondarily, they have a good capacity with some vehicular adjustments for operation in northern Canada, either winter or summer. They are not immediately ready for guerrilla warfare anywhere, nor for fighting in Cuban jungles or Greek mountains. But well-trained soldiers can adapt themselves to new conditions quickly.

At company level, there are two Canadian concepts of offence. An attack which is part of a general movement against a major opponent would be made in close co-operation with armour and supported by modern heavy weapons and tactical air power. Such an effort would call for fast and continuous infantry movement possible only in vehicles. A company commander might have tanks co-operating with him; all would move forward as fast as it was practical to do so, taking full advantage of terrain and higher echelon support. This attack would be made in conjunction with other infantry and armour units all advancing in the same general direction, but there would be no broad front, only probing columns.

I saw a demonstration of such a manoeuvre. An infantry company in APCs, reinforced by ten Centurion tanks, had been advancing supposedly for miles without serious opposition. Finally, there was solid resistance which the tanks could not brush aside unassisted. The rifle squads still did not get out of their APC, but the entire small command delivered an all-out attack.

The tanks pinned down the enemy with their high-velocity 24-pounders; each would fire three or four rounds from a hull-down position just behind a crest, and then move to a new place. The 81-mm. mortars had been dismounted, ranged and had opened fire; the 106 RRs were also dismounted from their jeeps and firing from advantageous positions on each flank. Suddenly, every tank and two of the three rifle platoons still in their APCs moved forward more or less in line. The third rifle platoon APCs were in close support. The idea was to have armour, not flash, take the long-range fire of the defence. But when the APCs and tanks came close to their objective, the riflemen tumbled out fast to protect the tanks at ranges where enemy RLs, flame-throwers and Energa rifle grenades would be effective.

This infantry-armour collaboration is of extreme importance in Canadian infantry thinking; a company of tanks may be permanently added to each infantry battalion soon. Infantry on foot, or even in thin-skinned APCs, is vulnerable to automatic weapons of the enemy which cannot hurt tanks. But the tanks cannot really protect themselves against courageous enemy infantry equipped with modern tank-killing devices at below 300 yards. Friendly riflemen can prevent the defence from employing these.

Now we come to the second type of company offensive, one made on its own, save for perhaps some assigned battalion support weapons. Attacks of this type may be required on atomic battlefields where larger units cannot operate. A company would still move forward in its vehicles and dismount only when forced to do so and as close as possible to their objective. The company

CO would arrange for supporting fire from his 81-mm. mortars, assign his MMGs and 106-mm. RRs a series of objectives or routes of attack, and then send forward two dismounted rifle platoons with the third in support. Normally, each of the leading platoons would have two sections in a rough line and the third close behind. These rifle squads would have unusual mobility because their ARs—the C2—are only a little heavier and no more bulky than a standard rifle. They would be able to advance by fire and manoeuvre supported by organic and assigned heavy weapons. Their three 3·5-in. RLs would give some close-in AT and bunker opening capability.

On defence, Canadian rifle companies will endeavour to make the best possible use of their mobility. They do not want to dig in, or stay in one place. Even in a more or less static situation, they would like to move forward and backward and avoid revealing their intentions. The Canadians realize, however, that even in nuclear war, it may be necessary to hold something definite; they would prepare the best defensive position possible in the time available, but would stress concealment.

Mortars are of particular importance on defence. Standard procedure is to have the 4·2-in. battalion mortars, as well as the company 81s zeroed in and actually laid on routes over which the enemy might attack. In an emergency, a company CO can call for fire and have mortar shells in the air within a minute or so. The RRs of each company would be positioned so as to defeat enemy tanks. The four additional RR at battalion level might be assigned to individual companies as required. The battalion HMGs would also be placed where they would be likely to be needed against APCs.

In the last analysis, defence depends upon men armed with rifles and ARs. Other weapons are necessary, but do not produce the ultimate decision. If training has been proper, the weapons and ammo sound, and the will to win stronger than that of the opposition, the defence can cause so many casualties that a counter-attack will be decisive. The Canadians have confidence in their riflemen and their ability to hit combat targets. A C1 or C2 rifle in the hands of a veteran hunter who has 30 rounds in his magazine would be bad medicine for the enemy when soldiers meet face to face at intermediate to short range, either on defence or in a counter-attack.

The officers and men of the Canadian infantry are fine physically and mentally; they are superbly trained and well equipped for the type of war they are most likely to fight. They have dared to think of all possibilities, no matter how unpleasant. Properly supported, their infantry will be tough and efficient anywhere.

XVII
France

SOME units of the French army today are well-armed, well-trained and well-organized for modern missions of all types. French infantry in Bastille Day Parades puts on remarkably fine shows; French teams have won international shooting competitions in recent years. It would be illogical to believe, however, that France and the French army can forget a century of military disappointment.

French soldiers began WW I with high hopes for a new series of Napoleonic type victories; their cry was 'on to Berlin'. Throughout the awful conflict which followed, some French units fought heroically, but the enormous casualties, the continuing strain of trench warfare and the lack of success undermined the morale of others. In 1917 some French divisions actually mutinied, but the ultimate WW I victory did a good deal for the spirit of the French army. It appeared in the 1930s to be the strongest in the world, but morale was probably still low.

France built the Maginot Line at a cost of many millions to protect not only her borders, but also her soldiers. This project was useless operationally and weakened the infantry in spirit. The swift German victory in the Battle of France (May and June 1940) indicated that some French units had no desire to fight in the open. France was beaten before her army as a whole had lost one per cent in casualties. The Germans were numerically inferior in men, in armour and in other weapons, but won because of better organization, direction and military spirit.

A sense of shame permeated the French army; this was removed only in part by the fine fighting done later in WW II. Frenchmen both in her organized military forces and in the Resistance made a real contribution to the freeing of their own country and the ultimate defeat of Germany, but the memory of defeat lived on. France had more severe military problems after WW II than any other Western nation. The Indo-Chinese war was larger than many of us realize and the final defeat more conclusive. The war in Algeria was even worse. Frenchmen could win small battles, but not finish off the native opposition in the old way. Casualties mounted; neither the allies of France nor even many French soldiers were really interested. Some of both had sympathies for the other side. A real victory could have been achieved only by tremendous outlays of men, money and munitions, and by a change in the combat attitude of the average French soldier. When de Gaulle came to power, he had the prestige to conclude an intolerable war and undoubtedly did what was best for France.

The French army, however, had deep roots in Algeria. The loss of another war which involved the abandoning of many Frenchmen was hard to take. The Gallic military spirit is still strong, but has to look back to the days of Napoleon for an entirely satisfactory pattern of victory. Even then they find their triumphs terminated by Waterloo.

The French army today has been completely reorganized and partially re-equipped. President de Gaulle's efforts have not only achieved the production of atomic weapons, but also a modern army capable of conducting with reasonable efficiency a war of any size or type. The reorganization of 1962 embodied, of course, what the French armies had learned in Indo-China and Algeria as well as their WW II experience. It may also have been affected by the mysticism and faith in things French of de Gaulle himself.

There are three general types of French divisions. First, there are front-line units of the NATO type which are usually composed of three brigades each. There are also some independent brigades. These NATO forces are entirely mechanized, with their motor transport organic within the structure of each unit down to and including the rifle squad.

The second type of French divisions are for territorial defence in depth. The mountain of words which questions produce in regard to this part of the French military force leaves an outsider confused as to organization and composition. There appear to be regiments as well as brigades; battle groups are thrown into the conversation at random. These are triangular military formations at the present time, but could be reconstituted to resemble

WW II Resistance forces. The French have tried to orient these defence divisions secondarily towards maximum usefulness in the event of the country being hit by nuclear weapons, or occupied by an enemy.

The third type of French division—actually considerably smaller than a standard division—is a Strike Force essentially for airborne and amphibious operations. A unit of this type is similar in concept to a USMC battalion landing team, or a large British carrier-based force. Their training centres indicate, however, less professional knowledge and personal dedication.

The organization and equipment of all three of these divisions are to some extent the same, but the French have endeavoured to tailor all units to fit their probable operational environment. The territorial defence forces are lighter than either of the other two and capable of taking full advantage of their intimate knowledge of the home areas where they will probably fight. The Strike Forces will have great strategic and fair tactical mobility and instant light firepower; they would endeavour to take advantage of air and naval support to make up for their own deficiency in organic heavy weapons. French NATO divisions cannot, of course, conform to any non-French pattern, but appear to be Pentomic in concept. The French have more armoured cars in their NATO forces than any other member nation.

A French rifle company usually consists of the normal three rifle platoons, a support weapons platoon, and a company HQ. The weapons company is currently equipped with 81-mm. mortars and light RRs. This structure is not constant, however, throughout the French army and varies radically in territorial defence units.

According to the 1962 changes, a NATO rifle platoon has four units of ten men each in an APC. There are three rifle squads and one platoon HQ section. Each rifle squad has one AR, and nine rifles or SMGs. The exact proportions between rifles and SMGs have not been standardized, but appear to be about even. The French emphasize that more rifles or SMGs can be issued as circumstances require.

A rifle platoon CO has no organic mortars, MMGs, or RRs in the usual sense. He does have, however, three extra MMGs and four RLs in his vehicles as well as one Cal · 50 HMG in his own APC. All can be manhandled into combat; platoon HQ personnel do practise with the Cal ·50 HMG against ground targets, but this weapon would limit marching mobility.

France developed, almost unaided by Britain and the U.S., an atomic capability. French aircraft, armoured cars and tanks have achieved international recognition for fine quality and performance. In spite of France's recent superb economic recovery, the money spent on sophisticated weapons appears to have delayed the production and distribution of a sufficient quantity of modern small arms throughout all French units. Recent Bastille Day Parades continue to reveal an assortment of infantry weapons requiring more different ammos than in any other major army.

This diversity of small arms has been caused by the military history of France over the past fifty years. The nation had her own rather numerous family of weapons designed and made in France both before and during WW I chambered for the 8-mm. Lebel cartridge, the first small-bore smokeless powder military round. Somehow, these rifles in several lengths and types are the most aesthetically pleasing of any military weapons, not only to Frenchmen but to others. They are still used for many purposes.

In the 1930s, France developed new pistols, rifles and SMGs which required three new ammos, two of them unique to the French service. During the later stages of WW II, French forces were armed with both British and U.S. small arms. Most of these are still in reserve; U.S. personal infantry arms requiring three American ammos were still in the hands of active-duty French units as late as 1964. Similarly, the Foreign Legion was armed with WW II German small arms.

The disadvantages of this multiplicity of weapons was and is obvious to all in the French army. A new rifle, pistol, SMG and GPMG were developed by 1952. All were completely French; although the pistol and SMG fired the 9-mm. Parabellum. The rifle and MG were at first chambered for the new round introduced into the French army in 1936, a 7·5-mm. rimless cartridge.

The post-war French rifle (MAS 1949) is a semi-automatic that weighs only 8·5 lb. It is well designed and has an ammo capacity and magazine system superior to the U.S. M1 Garand, but it does not physically fit most Anglo-Saxons. It was converted to fire the 7·62 NATO round in 1956, but many arms chambered for 7·5-mm. French ammo are still in the hands of troops.

Through the late 1950s France had the same unfortunate variety of ARs and LMGs as in rifles. But the Model 1952 GPMG has, at least in theory, replaced all these; the same actions can be equipped with the heavy barrels and tripod mounts so they can function in the manner of MMGs for both direct and indirect fire. The light version of this weapon, the same action equipped with a bipod mount, a light barrel, and folding butt stock, is the French Squad AR; it is belt-fed (disintegrating clips), but is provided with an efficient pouch to contain 50 rounds—so loaded it weighs between 17 and 18 lb. Barrels for both the LMG and the MMG can be changed quickly.

France had the dubious distinction of being the only nation in WW II, and later, to use in combat SMGs requiring three different ammos. The MAS, brought out right after the end of WW I, was chambered for the 9-mm. Parabellum, now the standard SMG cartridge of NATO. A few years later, however, the French introduced a fine SMG which fired the 7·65-mm. long Browning cartridge, also used in the French 1935-A semi-automatic pistol. The Free French in WW II used U.S. SMGs chambered for the Cal ·45 ACP, as well as British Stens, and German Schmeissers chambered for the 9-mm. Parabellum. All these SMGs, except the post-WW I MAS, were used in Indo-China and Algeria; some may still have an active reserve status. The MAT 1949 SMG is now standard; it is a first-rate SMG of medium weight, reasonable cyclic rate and fine combat potential.

In the last thirty years, the French have officially adopted five semi-automatic pistols and used several dozen other handguns including obsolete revolvers. The only weapon of real importance is now their Model 1950. This weapon appears somewhat crude, but is an up-to-date copy of John Browning's last design, the FN Model 1935.

Many French professional soldiers are competent, dedicated and practical. Their Infantry School at St. Maxient is one of the best in the world. Those responsible for the instruction there have faced squarely an unpleasant situation and have analysed their recent mistakes. In the Battle of France, some units not under fire did nothing. Others which were fired upon by Germans were pinned down mainly by noise. In extreme cases, French infantry and artillery withdrew or surrendered to inferior forces. Units of all sizes were all too confident that the vast sums expended for concrete and steel fortifications would not only stop the Germans but save French lives as well; in consequence, firepower was neglected.

Small-unit fighting in Indo-China and Algeria was also sometimes disappointing. Some companies were efficient, courageous and anxious to meet their enemies face to face. Others were ripe for defeat before they fired a shot. Once an action started, they sat down in the best fortifications available and sent bullets, mortar shells and even medium artillery projectiles in the general direction of their enemies. French units sometimes voluntarily gave up the hours of darkness to their opponents. Individually and collectively, some French soldiers were more interested in the expiration of their term of service than in going out and finding an elusive, vicious enemy.

The new French tactical training emphasizes the correction of these mistakes. Their major infantry aim appears to be the developing of small-unit *esprit de corps* and the ability to react immediately to any local situation with positive, well-directed action. Today, they want every infantryman to be confident of his ability with his personal arm and anxious to use it. The French are keeping their companies and platoon organically light and the assignment of even personal weapons flexible not only because of their own experience, but also because no one really knows the requirements for small units in nuclear war.

The new aim appears to be the creation of French units which will use all weapons and even employ aimed fire. The Maginot Line complex must go. Even foxholes, bunkers and trenches are being de-emphasized; under certain circumstances armoured cars and tracked APCs can do a better job defensively, for they allow mobility. The French teach each man that nothing can replace tough infantry willing to meet the enemy on foot in the open with personal and organic weapons.

Military Anglo-Saxons may say that lip service to this principle is cheap; the French have always given it. It is easy to be critical, but the French were not alone when the Battle of France began. The magnificent effort at Dunkirk in which some of them joined heroically did not help France in her darkest hour. The U.S. was not the most thoughtful of allies in WW II, nor always friendly in small matters since. We are finding, in spite of our considerable *matériel* advantages, that an Indo-Chinese war is difficult to wage and perhaps impossible to win. Some U.S. units have also suffered from bunkeritis.

The Free World must have France; NATO without the French army and territory is unthinkable. Since de Gaulle came to power, difficulties have multipled, but France has more troops in NATO groups in West Germany today than Britain and is spending a larger percentage of her magnificent new national income to preserve Western ideals and institutions throughout the world than the U.S. French soldiers may be a trifle volatile at times, but they have been magnificent fighters and will be again.

XVIII

Italy, Greece and Turkey

ITALY joined NATO in 1949; Greece and Turkey became members on 18 February 1952. These three countries extend what was once an alliance of countries bordering on the North Atlantic into the eastern Mediterranean and even the Black Sea. This area, far to the south-east of Russia and her Satellites, is of great strategic value, but also has to be defended. The principal ground forces for this defence, if war should come, are the Italian, Greek and Turkish armies.

All three are stronger now than ever before in history. In spite of local frictions mainly over Cyprus, they realize fully the importance of unity and the great value of their position to the Free World; the extended Black Sea flank may be NATOs greatest strategic asset. Can Russia risk sending hundreds of Bloc divisions west so long as the Soviet homeland is open to attack from the south? Turkey and Greece stretch for 1,300 miles below Russia-in-Europe. Moscow is only 1,100 miles north of the centre of Turkey.

These three countries also effectively seal the outlet from the Black Sea into the Mediterranean; the Dardanelles are firmly under Turkish control. Sea lanes to the west thread Greek islands and pass Italy and Sicily. Russia, both Czarist and Communist, has tried for at least joint control of this area for centuries, but still lacks a single warm-water port with access to the oceans of the world in time of war.

The U.S. has spent billions in the eastern Mediterranean; all three countries are now economically and politically much improved. The hatreds for Communism and Russia are real in Greece and Turkey. The situation in Italy, where the Communists are a powerful, recognized political party, is not clear, but there is no question of the loyalty of the Italian armed forces to their government and of that government to NATO.

The strategic offensive threat from NATO in this area comes from major installations of a secret nature. The Turkish newspapers reveal, however, that powerful missile bases exist within their borders. Many of the controversial U-2 flights originated in Turkey; NATO knowledge of profitable targets to the north is probably complete.

Defence of the area is complicated; should war come, Bloc forces would undoubtedly launch strong, swift attacks. The Turkish bases and the Dardanelles are a long way from Communist frontiers, but the right flank of NATO, which stretches from the Adriatic almost to the Caspian, is vulnerable in many places. Serious penetrations by Communists from the north could cause trouble.

The Land South-east NATO command in Izmir (formerly Smyrna) on the western coast of Turkey is responsible for the co-ordinated and unified operation of all friendly forces in the area and for defending these borders. The military strength of NATO would be enhanced by difficult terrain and British and U.S. air and naval forces throughout the Mediterranean, but the Greek and Turkish ground forces would probably be totally engaged before disposable portions of the Italian army could come to their aid. British and U.S. Army and Marine units have taken part in recent NATO manoeuvres here. An entire division can now be flown from America to this area in a few hours. But if war comes, Anglo-American aid will be limited by other commitments.

The NATO right flank is naturally strong. The Black Sea covers more than half the front; rugged mountains lie close behind most of the coastline and along the Turkey-in-Europe and Greek boundaries with Communist nations to the north. To the east, the area between the Black and Caspian Seas is also mountainous and mostly unfavourable for armour. Throughout most of this front, infantry is of primary importance. Companies and battalions will be operating frequently in country so rugged that even their organic support weapons will have trouble moving; tanks would be defeated by terrain alone, or slowed to a crawl.

The Turkish and Greek armies have carefully prepared them-

French rifle instruction with the Model 1949-56

Netherlands rifle training with instructor and two recruits

A Canadian APC which is actually a converted tank—in the background, a centurion tank

The US M113 APC and M60 tank

The US M113 APC

The author firing the Russian Model 1943 PPS SMG. The Russian Model 1941 PPSH SMG can be seen on the table to the left

Now he fires the Russian DP AR or LMG

The Russian SKS carbine. This weapon uses the 7·62 intermediate power round and can be fired semi-automatically only

The upper three weapons are semi-military or military shotguns. In the middle is the US model which saw service in both World Wars. The other two are being used in Vietnam; they are made respectively by High Standard and Remington. The bottom weapon is a British military musketoon of the late 17th century

These three weapons were all captured from the Viet Cong. Top, the Chinese Model 1950 SMG which is a copy of the Russian PPSH Model 1941; bottom, the French MAT Model 1949 SMG. The weapon in the middle is of local village manufacture

selves for the defence of their areas and are ready to begin at a moment's notice. Surprise is virtually impossible, even across the Black Sea, because of modern electronic equipment manned by NATO personnel. The Turks and Greeks have the necessary aircraft, artillery and mechanized forces to defend the narrow avenues suitable for armour. Elsewhere, supported infantry is more important. Let us look carefully at these troops, particularly at the weapons, organization and tactics of infantry battalions and companies. They differ from each other widely, but have been built up after careful review of terrain, national capacities and previous military experience within each country.

First, Greece. In the event of war, a Bloc theatre commander would undoubtedly consider an attack on that country where it is narrowest. A penetration through the mainland into the Greek islands would seriously compromise the whole NATO position. But this border is one of the most rugged in the world. The Greeks won their Bandit War (1946-9) against Communist enemies in this area. They know it well and are prepared both materially and spiritually to defend it. The Hellenic army realizes that it may have to face formal attacks from across the border and guerrilla action in rear areas where long-absent Greek Communists might be air-dropped with weapons and supplies. The Greeks are confident, however, that they can hold the border and again beat their old Communist enemies behind it.

This army has done more than just accept British and U.S. arms, motor transport, and other munitions. They have chosen carefully those pieces of equipment which fit their needs and then assimilated them into their own organizations. With unusual forbearance, they have resisted the temptation to over-arm and become immobile. They preferred to receive from the U.S., during the Bandit War, natural mules from Missouri—they call them Trumans—rather than the mechanical mules which are small trucks of great manoeuvrability.

Greek infantry organization, weapons and tactics are essentially those which worked best in their Bandit War. Only the British in Malaya have done so well since 1945. A Greek infantry division follows the triangular concept with a support unit at each level. There are three rifle regiments per division and three rifle battalions per regiment. A rifle battalion is composed of 750 men divided into an HQ, a weapons company, and three rifle com-

panies. Companies, platoons and even squads can operate independently when required, but the Greek battalion is the smallest
unit that would be continuously employed semi-independently.

The weapons company has four 57-mm. RRs, six 81-mm.
mortars, four U.S. Cal ·30 MMGs (M1919A4s), and nine 3·5-in.
RLs. The presence of this last weapon at battalion level is unusual
in NATO, but a sound decision for the Greek army. The RL is,
of course, basically an AT weapon; battalion COs know well the
terrain over which they will fight and are the best judges of
where these weapons will be needed.

Each rifle company is composed of 154 men divided into an
HQ, three rifle platoons and a weapons platoon which is armed
with three U.S. Cal ·30 LMGs (M1919A6s), and three 60-mm.
mortars. Each rifle platoon consists of 36 men divided into three
rifle squads plus a lightly armed HQ section. The rifle squads
are composed of ten men and occasionally have two BARs, but
one per squad is more common and is about all that a really
mobile platoon can carry with it and supply with ammo.

Until 1948, the Greek army used British weapons. The navy
and air force are still supplied with British small arms; even the
army is using them in part for training purposes, because of the
enormous stocks of ·303 British cartridges on hand. But the active
army now has mainly U.S. arms. Experienced officers did not
mind losing British 2-in. and 3-in. mortars which were relatively
inaccurate, but the Vickres MMG and the BREN LMG, which
both fired the ·303 British cartridge, were harder to give up.
These weapons were heavy for their types, but accurate and
reliable. All active duty units now have U.S. M1 rifles and U.S.
BAR ARs; U.S. M1 SMGs are carried by squad leaders and some
other men in each rifle company. Pistols are more popular in the
Greek army than in others because of the personal nature of
much of the Bandit War; a variety of British and U.S. models
are presently in use.

Greek officers and NCOs are taught that the most important
factor in all operations is terrain. In both offence and defence,
they must first know every foot of their fighting area. Because
of Greek terrain, organic mortars are not concentrated so often
on a single point as in other services. Each mortar usually has an
individual target, or a series of them. The MGs are placed in

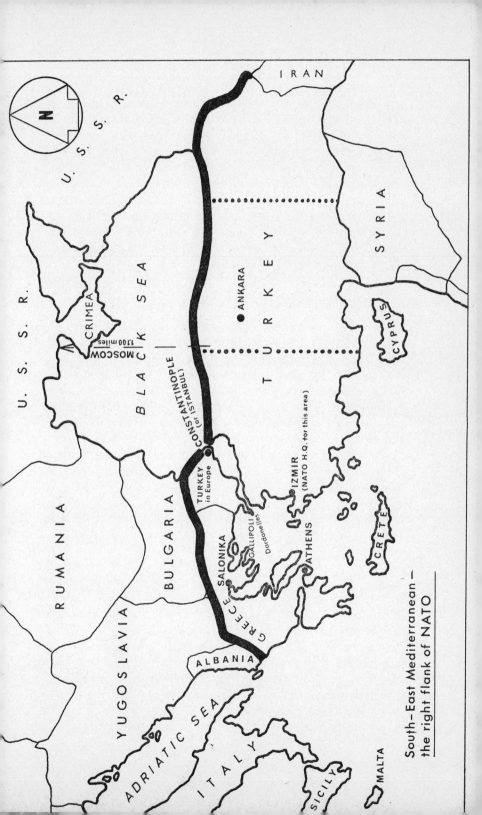

South–East Mediterranean —
the right flank of NATO

accordance with terrain, but with particular emphasis on criss-crossing fields of fire from unit flanks.

A company would normally begin its assault with two rifle platoons in line and the third in support. The two assaulting platoons would like to have all three squads in line. The fire tactics of the individual squads would depend on whether there were one or two BARs in the unit. The two-BAR squads would leapfrog forward with their two separate fire teams moving alternately. In the more frequently encountered one-BAR squad, this weapon would cover the advance of the riflemen who would then all fire so that the BAR could get forward.

On defence, a company would normally assume a six rifle squad line and have three in reserve (one from each platoon, or a complete platoon according to circumstances). The company CO would pay particular attention to fields of fire for his MGs and BARs which would interlock so as to cover as thoroughly as possible the entire front. Support weapons of battalion level and above would be zeroed in for a defensive barrage as soon as a front line was definitely established. At night, all these arms would be left so that fire could be called down in a few seconds.

Greek infantry can operate along guerrilla lines, as they did in their Bandit War. They appreciated thoroughly the advantages of small offensive victories which depend upon proper intelligence, aggressive planning and speedy execution. Most important of all, almost every battalion CO and many other officers and NCOs are veterans of a victorious war of this type.

Now for Turkey. The Turks would defend their Bulgarian border in much the same manner as the Greeks would theirs; both are mountainous and rugged. Greece and Turkey would co-operate effectively in joint operations in Europe in spite of their Cyprus antagonisms, because of their mutual hatreds and fears in connection with Russia and her allies.

The defence of Turkey in Asia is a much larger problem. The Black Sea coast, and the common border with Russia far to the east, stretch for more than 1,000 miles. Both are essentially the same type of terrain, however, because actually defending a beach under modern concentrations of bombs, missiles, rockets and artillery projectiles may be next to impossible. The real fighting would probably occur in rugged mountains south of the coast.

Turkish armour, heavy artillery, guided missiles and mine fields are adequate for the portion of the border country where tanks can operate effectively, but efficient supported infantry is more necessary over 95 per cent of this border. Turkish divisions have been reconstituted on a Pentomic plan, but details of their organization differ from the recently abandoned U.S. pattern in that assignment of tanks and light artillery to the five battle groups is not so definite. Each regiment, the Turkish equivalent of a battle group, may include a company of tanks (17) and a battery of six 105-mm. howitzers. But a lot of border terrain is unsuitable for them. Unless the country is fairly open, division commanders will keep these units for general support.

The combat elements of a Turkish regiment are five rifle companies, one weapons company, and a reconnaissance platoon. Total personnel runs to about 1,500 men. The weapons company has twelve jeep-mounted 106-mm. RRs and six motorized 4·2-in. mortars. The reconnaissance platoon has two 75-mm. RRs, one 81-mm. mortar, and, if terrain permits, some lightly armoured vehicles.

A rifle company consists of 189 officers and men in an HQ (10), a weapons platoon (41), and three rifle platoons (46 each). The HQ has four 3·5-in. RLs and the weapons platoon three 57-mm. RRs and three 81-mm. mortars. Each rifle platoon is composed of three rifle squads and a weapons squad. The weapons squad of eleven men is armed with two Cal·30 LMGs (M1919A6), one 3·5-in. RL, six rifles and five pistols. Each rifle squad of eleven men includes a squad leader and two fire teams of five men each armed with one AR and four rifles. The squad leaders on the border have rifles, although some in Ankara carry SMGs. Each fire team includes one rifle equipped with a grenade launcher.

The Turkish rifle company is one of the most powerful direct-fire units in NATO; their squad is the only standard two-AR squad in NATO other than that of the U.S. The two LMGs in each infantry platoon, backing up six ARs, give a real advantage against, for instance, a Russian platoon which has nothing but intermediate-power small arms. The Turkish platoon arms and ammunition are heavier, of course, but will not have to be carried so far.

All weapons in the Turkish army, from the platoon LMGs up, are standard U.S. arms. ARs and below, however, are predominantly Turkish. They have chosen to continue to make and use their own rifles chambered for the 7·92-mm. Mauser cartridge, because they found that the Turkish version of the bolt Mauser was both sturdier and more accurate than the used U.S. M1 rifles available to the Turks for comparison purposes.

Squad ARs in Turkey are of two types. The Hotchkiss is French-designed, but Turkish made; these are more common. There are also some Czech Brno ARs similar to the British BREN. Both types are relatively heavy, 25 lb.-plus loaded, but deliver accurate bursts with great reliability. Disassembling and cleaning, almost a fetish in the Turkish army, are simple and easy.

The Turks feel that SMGs are valuable for some special operations and for personal defence, but not for regular infantry combat. The British Sten firing the 9-mm. Parabellum and the U.S. M1 chambering the ·45 ACP are available in sufficient quantities to meet all requirements. Another personal defence weapon is the Turkish semi-automatic pistol similar to the German Walther police model (PP); all I saw were chambered for the ·380 ACP, called the 9-mm. Browning in Europe. This weapon is light, compact and well made. The Turks say that no pistol is satisfactory for infantry combat, but point out that some members of heavy weapons crews can carry more ammunition, if they are not burdened with a rifle.

In the larger sense, Turkish armies will be on the defensive if a shooting war starts; their NATO mission is to keep Bloc forces out of Turkey. An overall defensive does not preclude regiment, division and corps attacks. The Turkish infantry, with its love of cold steel at close quarters, is well qualified for this type of combat. Their organic mortars, RRs, MGs and RLs give their numerous fire teams ample cover in the usual leapfrog daylight-attack patterns. Night, bad weather and difficult terrain hold no terrors for Turks. They can and will take advantage of concealment to launch concentrated offensives.

The tactical thinking of the Turkish army indicates, however, a slight preference for defence based, no doubt, on their national character. As Britain and France found out when they were the allies of Russia in WW I, no soldiers anywhere could fight more stubbornly than the Turks did in Gallipoli, even in the face of apparently impossible logistic disadvantages. In Korea, they just would not give up a foot.

The Turks prefer to occupy a series of strong-points rather

than a continuous line of trenches. In such a defensive alignment they rely, until an enemy approaches within relatively close range, on indirect fire from their mortars and howitzers controlled by forward observers using the latest type U.S. communications equipment and direct fire from their RRs, MGs and ARs. Their RRs would normally be held for targets of considerable value because their blast to the rear gives away their position with the first shot. At aimed fire range, the Turkish riflemen would exert an enormous effect upon the outcome. They have always been fine blood-and-guts soldiers and know how to shoot.

As for Italy, the Italian army is better constituted to come quickly to the assistance of the primary defenders of the NATO right flank than any other in Europe. Its ability to do this in real force would depend, however, on whether there were attacks on Italy. If Yugoslavia and Austria were allowed to remain neutral, NATO commanders would be able to use a substantial part of the Italian army in Greece and/or Turkey.

An Italian infantry division now has the usual triangular structure, three regiments consisting of three battalions with supporting elements at each level. A battalion is composed of three companies plus a heavy weapons company with six 81-mm. mortars and four 106 RRs, all motorized. A rifle company consists of 124 men divided into an HQ, three rifle platoons, and a heavy weapons platoon with two Breda MMGs, two 57-mm. RRs, and two 60-mm. mortars.

The Beretta SMG is the most numerous weapon in the Italian army. Their rifle squad consists of seven men armed with four SMGs, two U.S. M1 rifles, and one U.S. BAR. This unique small-arms distribution leads to changes in tactics and effectiveness. Offensively, the SMGs and liberally issued hand-grenades give a considerable assault potential. Defensively, the BAR and the two M1s will need the support of crew-served heavy weapons available at company and battalion level. The SMG in Italy is effective only at the shortest ranges because of the power of the cartridge, the difficulty of directing the weapon precisely, and the fact that their training emphasizes instinctive pointing at below eye-level rather than aiming.

The Beretta SMG is not often seen outside Italy. There are several different but essentially similar models, all easily identified by the two separate triggers. All are straight blow-back actions and fire the 9-mm. Parabellum cartridge. They have permanently attached wooden stocks, but do not now take bayonets. Loaded they weigh between 9 and 10 lb. and are usually 31 in. long; the cyclic rate is about 700 r.p.m.

I fired several Berettas extensively; the two-trigger arrangement has definite advantages. Fast single shots at 100 yards can be delivered with considerable accuracy with the front trigger, if one aims the weapon like a hunting rifle. This is not, however, the standard way of firing the weapon in the Italian army.

The rear trigger fires bursts. Because of their weight and good muzzle brakes, Berettas hold well in full-automatic fire. I was able to place every shot of a single 30-round burst on a life-sized silhouette at 20 metres. The weapon could be improved, however, by lowering its cyclic rate. Young soldiers who have little experience with firearms would benefit particularly from such a change, although their fire would be still more efficient if they fired single shots only. All recruits prefer squirt fire, although targets even at close range never have as many holes in them as they expect.

The Italian army prefers its Breda MMG to all others for the weapons platoon of each rifle company, even though an additional type of ammo (7·92 mm.) is required. This weapon is effective in long bursts and accurate because of its weight (about 85 lb.) and relatively low cyclic rate (about 450 r.p.m.), but foreigners usually fail to see how its advantages could outweight the obvious ammo problem.

The standard pistol in the Italian army is now the well-known Beretta semi-automatic, first made before WW II. These are chambered for the ·380 ACP, and are light (weight, loaded, 25 oz.), compact weapons, well made and nicely finished. Because of the forward projection on the bottom of the magazine, they feel good in the hand.

The Italian army may be called on to fight anywhere in Europe; they are more flexible than either the Greeks or the Turks. Their relatively small, lightly armed platoons and companies suggest, however, a preoccupation with the type of combat in which they were engaged from 1943 through the end of WW II. This fighting was usually in the mountains and not against heavy enemy formations. But they are capable today of both anti-guerrilla missions and conventional combat. Their mobility and offensive capacity would be most welcome on NATOs eastern flank; if Greece and Turkey brought their assailants to a stand, the Italian army would surely roll them back.

XIX

The Benelux Countries

M<small>ORE</small> important battles have been fought in the Netherlands, Belgium and Luxembourg, or close to their
borders, than in all the rest of Europe. All three nations
have produced good soldiers and fine generals in the past and are
charter members of NATO. All now have strong economies and
are staunch in their desire to remain in the Free World. The
Luxembourg army is too small—less than a brigade—to be of
much consequence, but the Netherlands and Belgium could now
make a real contribution to the defence of Western Europe.

The Netherlands was the first country to sign the North
Atlantic Treaty. No member of this organization is more dedicated
to the general purpose of protecting themselves through common
action against Communist aggression. Their monarchy is as
democratic as that of Britain. The country today is more pros-
perous than at any other time in its long history. One is impressed
by the thriving condition of shipping, agriculture and industry.
Even the loss of much of their colonial empire has not greatly
hurt the parent country.

The present Dutch military contribution to NATO is considerable. There is a full army corps of two divisions with additional tank and artillery support on active duty and combat-
ready; it is integrated into the North German NATO command.
It would move out from eastern Holland immediately in the
event of an emergency, to defend the great plain which stretches
from the Rhine into Poland.

The Netherlands also supplies a formation of fighter-bomber
aircraft at present based in West Germany and immediately
capable of taking defensive action against aggression. The Dutch
naval units forming part of the present NATO fleet include one

modern aircraft carrier. In the reserve behind these forces already integrated into the NATO organization, there are two more divisions which would be ready in weeks, another air wing, and several more modern naval vessels.

A Netherlands division is similar to the old U.S. Pentomic unit; it has five combat groups, each composed of infantry, artillery and tanks. Complete mechanization was achieved early in 1962 for all active duty units, although armoured cars are used instead of APCs for some infantry. This is not a handicap because of the system of hard-surface roads in the most likely theatre of operations. Soviet units are similarly equipped.

A rifle company is the same whether it walks, is carried in armoured vehicles, or transported by air. It consists of 172 of all ranks divided into an HQ (22), a weapons platoon (27), and three rifle platoons (41 each). The weapons platoon has three 81-mm. mortars plus personal arms. Each rifle platoon has three rifle squads (nine each), a weapons squad (nine) and an HQ (five). The weapons squad has two 84-mm. RRs (Gustav) and personal arms.

NETHERLANDS SMALL ARMS

Colonel Cornelis de Ruiter entered his army in 1939 at the age of eighteen. He was evacuated to Britain in May 1940 and has commanded troops in combat in Europe and the Indies. He has several fighting decorations and has been the head coach of all three Dutch teams which have won the Le Clerc Infantry Weapons Trophy. He is a fine shot himself and knows his weapons and tactics. He has conducted extensive tests with all available small arms in order to choose the best possible infantry rifle, squad AR and SMG for his country. He explained in detail what their problems have been and their hopes for the future.

The Netherlands lost virtually all their old family of small arms during the German occupation in WW II. Most of the weapons used by the Free Dutch forces in Europe were supplied by Britain and the U.S. Even as late as 1963, the major portion of the Dutch infantry was still armed with the U.S. M1 rifle. Some reserve units still have British rifles. The new FN NATO rifle already described has become the new standard service rifle and will eventually supersede all others.

The Netherlands squad AR was the British BREN. These originally fired the ·303 British rimmed cartridge, but were partially converted to the NATO round. The Dutch still have confidence in the BRENs, but were faced with the problem of finding a substitute for them. Since Britain was giving them up, the Netherland army does not want to retain them. They do have a small arms manufactory (Hembrug), but producing a few ARs from time to time would not be economically sound. After extensive trials, they have chosen the FN GPMG, already adopted by Britain over the German MG42-59. Many units still have BRENs, however, including the again victorious 1964 Le Clerc Trophy team from the Netherlands.

These new MGs are extremely important in the Netherlands. Each squad has an extra GPMG in its APC which can be used dismounted. There are six extra GPMGs and tripods carried in company HQ vehicles. If a Netherlands company took a semi-permanent defensive position, all would be distributed in accordance with terrain. A total of 24 MGs in a 172-man company is high; no other NATO nation uses so many.

SMGs presented a problem similar to infantry rifles in the Netherlands army. There were a lot of weapons of several different types using two ammos. The most numerous were the U.S. Thompsons and British Stens. The Dutch preferred the latter largely because of the superiority of the cartridge (9-mm. Parabellum) for SMG use and attempted to standardize on it. But when Britain abandoned the Sten in favour of the L2A3, the Dutch had no source of new Stens. Rather than manufacture replacement parts for the Sten and a few new weapons each year, the Netherlands decided to replace eventually all their SMGs with a new weapon. They chose the Uzi—designed and produced for them in Israel. There are 58 SMGs in each rifle company issued to men who will be directing others, or carrying equipment and ammo.

The Netherlands army is using the 1935 FN Browning semi-automatic pistol. The Dutch, perhaps because of their Indonesian experience, place more faith than usual in pistols and have chosen a powerful one with maximum ammo capacity, 13 rounds. There are 16 pistols in each rifle company.

Dutch battle groups have all the support weapons of modern war including tanks, artillery both conventional and recoilless, and missiles of various types. Companies are relatively light. The three 81-mm. mortars at company level are to give some organic indirect fire and are of the standard NATO type. The two RRs in each platoon weapons squad are for accurate direct fire and are the same type recently adopted by Britain. The MMG is the squad AR (FN GPMG) with a tripod mount added.

According to the new grenade theory common on the Continent, riflemen will furnish some of their own AT support. There are six or seven standard rifles in each rifle squad; another one is equipped with a telescope sight for use by the sniper. In units still equipped with M1 rifles, three men per squad are equipped with a GL attachment for their rifles and carry two AT (Energa) rifle grenades each. Where a squad has the new FN rifles, all riflemen can fire both AA and AP grenades without any change in the rifle itself, save for the use of a blank cartridge. AP rifle grenades can be projected to a full 400 yards; each is roughly the equal of a defensive hand-grenade in power. Accuracy was so difficult to attain quickly and without interrupting normal direct fire that this entire idea has been downgraded.

There is another attachment to rifles that is most important in the Netherlands, the bayonet. Colonel de Ruiter and other infantry officers with combat experience told me that this primitive weapon is the final arbiter of infantry combat. Even though only a small percentage of total casualties are caused by it in modern wars, a willingness to close and fight hand-to-hand gives small units a real advantage in morale.

The Netherlands is a small country with a population of only a bit over twelve million. Its land frontiers are about as naturally indefensible against modern attack as can well be imagined. The Dutch army collapsed quickly when hit by Hitler's war machine. Their numerical inferiority in men, aircraft and armour was so great they just did not have a chance. They learned, however, the folly of small-nation neutrality in modern struggles.

Holland today has an entirely different plan. Within the NATO framework, they can make a real contribution to joint security. The morale of their fighting soldiers is high. Their officers and NCOs are professionals; many have a lot of combat experience. The Dutch infantry is well armed and beautifully trained; its tactics will be suited to terrain and similar to those of Britain. Their high proportion of ARs and MMGs gives real firepower both on attack and in defence. Even under combat conditions, their riflemen deliver aimed fire and can use grenades and bayonets too.

BELGIUM

On 1 July 1960 the entire Belgian NATO army was fully mechanized; all 40,000 men can climb into combat vehicles and be off. No man has to walk; no combat soldier is carried in a truck. The weapons of this army are equally modern. All small arms use either 7·62-mm. NATO or 9-mm. Parabellum ammo. These soldiers are trained for today's type of warfare.

The importance of the Belgian NATO army in their national thinking may be judged by the fact that its C-in-C usually outranks the Chief-of-Staff at home. This Belgian corps is completely committed to NATO and is deployed ready for immediate action in West Germany. Even its logistics are in large part autonomous, rather than dependent upon Brussels.

The Belgians are good allies; they sent to Korea more fighting men than any other nation except the U.S. and Britain. Their rotation of officers was sufficient so that a large percentage of those on active duty at that time served in combat alongside British and U.S. troops. Since Korea, many Belgian officers and NCOs have attended schools in other NATO nations, particularly those of Britain and the U.S. Some battalion-sized Belgian units have been trained for long periods with British and U.S. units in West Germany.

The Belgians have a lot of new equipment, but rely on infantry of the old type. They feel that nuclear war would emphasize the value of small units who fight with arms that they carry in their hands when moving and fighting on foot. Neither atomic explosives nor armour can hold territory; a man with a rifle can.

The Belgians lost all their old weapons in 1940, but were rearmed with those of Britain and the U.S. later on. They adopted the U.S. ·30-'06 cartridge as stanadrd for their rifles and MGs at the end of WW II, and set out to rearm themselves. They had the advantage of the firm of Fabrique Nationale d'Armes de Guerre of Herstal located near Liege and popularly known as FN. This organization has had a remarkable influence on military firearms throughout the world. Their production facilities and their research and development department are outstanding. John

Moses Browning, America's greatest firearms inventor, had a long and close personal relationship with FN. They manufactured more Browning-designed firearms than were ever made in America. He died in Liege just as he was completing work on his fine semi-automatic military pistol, later known as the FN Browning Model 1935.

The first Belgian small arms need was for a new rifle. FN designed and began to produce a new semi-automatic infantry weapon along with Belgian BARs. Both were used satisfactorily by the Belgian forces in Korea; the interchangeability of ·30-'06 ammo was convenient. This FN semi-automatic rifle was produced in fairly large quantities for the Belgian army and also sold internationally, usually chambered for the 7·92-mm. Mauser cartridge.

Beginning about 1948, the FN designers worked closely with the British government to produce an entirely new infantry rifle now known as the FN or SLR; this chambers the 7·62 NATO cartridge. As mentioned, the entire Belgian Intervention Force is presently armed with it, but the earlier ·30-'06 FN is still used by Belgian forces at home.

The British SLR and the Canadian C1 can fire single shots only. When the same basic rifle was issued in West Germany, however, everyone had a switch which allowed either full-automatic or semi-automatic fire, at the discretion of the user. The Belgian army has decided on an intermediate course. Of the eight FN rifles issued in each squad, five can fire semi-automatic only. Three can deliver either type of fire according to the position of a small lever on the left of the receiver.

One FN in each infantry squad is equipped with a telescope sight and issued to the sniper. The Belgians feel that under ordinary battlefield conditions, observations and fire at ranges longer than about 200 yards are difficult when a man has to use his unaided eye. They realize, of course, the capacity of the FN rifle for hitting men at a great deal longer range, but believe that a scope is necessary to pick out an indistinct, distant and perhaps camouflaged target.

The Belgian squad AR in their NATO force is the FN rifle with a heavy barrel and bipod similar to the Canadian C-2; this weapon is known in Belgium as the FALO. These have replaced all BARs in the NATO forces and will do the same at some future time when ·30–'06 ammo ceases to be used by the army organizations at home.

Belgian organization has followed U.S. changes to some extent, but has at present a variable arrangement in which there are usually three groupments to a division. Each groupment is composed of mechanized infantry, self-propelled artillery, and tanks, and is capable of fighting unsupported. There are usually two mechanized battalions of infantry in each.

An individual infantry battalion, whether mechanized as in the Intervention Force, motorized in the Base Force, or functioning on foot in the Interior Force, is approximately the same. A battalion has three rifle companies, a support weapons company, and an HQ. The support company has four Lloyd self-propelled 90-mm. anti-tank guns, four 4·2-in. mortars, six 83-mm. RLs, six MMGs and one Cal ·50 HMG.

A rifle company with a total strength of 168 is divided into an HQ (36) and three rifle platoons (44 each). There are two 81-mm. mortars in a mortar section of company HQ, and one Cal ·50 HMG for AA defence. Individual weapons in the whole company are 15 pistols, 42 SMGs, 111 FNs (9 with scopes and 27 capable of bursts), and 8 FALOs (heavy barrelled bipod FNs).

Each rifle platoon consists of a platoon HQ of eleven men and three rifle sections or squads of eleven men each. The platoon HQ has one 83-mm. RL, two MMGs, and one 60-mm. mortar as well as two FN rifles, four SMG and five pistols. Each rifle section has an MMG on the APC which can be dismounted, two ARs, and eight rifles, one with a telescope sight and three capable of burst fire.

The new Belgian infantry will function as a team; no single weapon overshadows the others. They have, however, unusual flexibility. As might be expected from the fact that the Belgian army is the first to be completely mechanized, their infantry tactics are based on movement. Speed and lightness seem to be important everywhere. The entire infantry weapons team can arrive quickly and go into action. The only difficulty is with the rather heavy load of support weapons and ammo at platoon HQ, but these would be carried either in an APC or by some smaller vehicle.

The full-automatic potential of a Belgian platoon is high, especially if the FNs that can fire bursts do so. Various systems of

A Norwegian soldier and the folding stock Schmeisser (MP40) SMG

The present family of US NATO round small arms consisting of M14 Modified AR, the M60 MMG and the M14 rifle

Top left. An Irish soldier with the new 84-mm. Carl Gustav light RR and the three types of ammunition normally employed. Above: the Carl Gustav SMG. Left: an SLR. Below: a ·303 BREN

*A West German customs guard with a US M2 carbine within
touching distance of the wall between East and West Berlin*

*Two US Model M48A2 tanks with bulldozer attachments at Checkpoint Charlie, thirty yards
from the wall between East and West Berlin*

US army adviser oversees weapons inspection carried on by a Vietnamese officer and infantry-
man. The two weapons in the foreground are M1 Thompson SMGs; in the background, is an
M1 or M2 carbine

Vietnamese soldiers crossing a stream. Note the US walkie-talkie radio, and the M1 or M2
carbines

covering fire for offensive movement have been carefully worked out; the MMGs and FALOs would normally fire alternately at various suspected targets all along the platoon front while the FNs concentrated on an area just ahead. Support would be provided by platoon and company mortars as well as higher echelon weapons. Assaults through populated areas have been carefully rehearsed.

On defence, the Belgians would, of course, rely greatly on battalion and higher support arms; the groupment tanks and battalion self-propelled high-velocity guns would be necessary against a BLOC offensive. At company and platoon level, the Belgians would like to remain mobile even on defence; APCs are good protection against radioactive fallout. They realize, however, that infantry holds best even today when dug in. Their burst-fire weapons properly emplaced would produce a lot of defensive small-arms fire.

The Belgians have confidence in their infantry weapons and in their other equipment. Their morale is high and their will to fight unquestioned. If the individual soldiers do as well as they did in Korea and as their fathers did in World War I, the nation can make a real contribution to NATO defence. The Belgians do not want war, but if it should come in West Europe, they may be effective when needed most. The combat readiness of the Belgian corps in West Germany is second to none.

XX

Guerrilla War

LARGE parts of the world are now cursed with guerrilla warfare. It is cruel, brutal, and directed in part against the most defenceless of civilians. The areas where guerrillas are most likely to operate are already relatively poor in food, education, transportation and medical facilities. Irregular combat in such places destroys what few aspects of civilization there are; both sides frequently behave like beasts.

Even though guerrilla war is relatively more important today than ever before, we must realize that it has occurred for thousands of years. A poorer armed and organized force has generally made terrain and a friendly civilian population into allies by disappearing into them when convenient. Jungle, mountain and desert fighting has taken place whenever belligerents had to fight in areas where there were these kinds of terrain. West European nations met this sort of thing in gaining and maintaining their colonies. An organized professional army under a sensible commander has frequently used favourable elements in a civilian population against another professional army which was occupying an alien area. Wellington utilized the partisans of Portugal and Spain almost perfectly against the French during the Napoleonic period. The word guerrilla—small war—comes from this conflict.

These conflicts in the past have usually had their emotional basis in patriotism; the local people were fighting foreign invaders and perhaps their local collaborators. This was still true in Russia, Norway and France during WW II. More recently, the spiritual differences between the two sides have been political and economic rather than national. Communist propaganda has stressed class prejudice and jealousy, the unity of those who have little against those who have a lot.

Perhaps the most outstanding characteristic of twentieth-century guerrilla warfare is its interdependent dualism of combat areas. The fighting is only in part with weapons in battle; it is also in the minds of the mass of the people. Once the people are won over, the war is nearly won. But the guerrillas must demonstrate time after time that they can win small shooting conflicts before they can control the minds of the local inhabitants; even 'have nots' won't support a movement unless they are convinced that it will win.

Since the end of WW II, we have seen several of these dual-type conflicts. As already mentioned, Mao Tse-Tung beat the Nationalists in China in both areas. Castro in Cuba won quickly when the Cuban peasants started to rally to him; so did Giap in Indo-China. The fighting in Algeria was similar and had the same ending, although racial patriotism was probably more important than Communism.

Another aspect of guerrilla war in this century has been the help for guerrilla forces from friendly Communist nations. Relatively small amounts of material foreign aid have become increasingly important in final guerrilla victories, but cannot accomplish a victory alone. Conversely, anti-Communist aid to governments fighting guerrillas can also be decisive. The Greek Communists definitely lost their Bandit War (1946–9) in spite of massive assistance through Bulgaria, Jugoslavia and Albania just beyond the border, because of U.S. and British aid. The Malayan Communists were finally beaten by British soldiers and local Malay police and militia, even though support from the Communist world continued. The struggle in South Vietnam still goes on; complete victory for one side or the other seems a long way off, but both sides are being sustained by cold-war opponents from beyond their borders.

A pattern has emerged in these Communist take-over guerrilla wars; the Communists themselves have written about them in detail. At the outset, guerrillas may have the sympathy and backing of only a small part of the civilian population. They must find an area where they are popular with the people, or can use inaccessible terrain. If the local civilians co-operate freely with the government, guerrillas would never get a start. But if they can find a place to operate among a few friends, all is well. Once the guerrillas have some sort of base area, they can enlarge it by terror and by good works. The political tactics of guerrilla movements are of extreme importance, but beyond the scope of this study. Military and political tactics must be co-ordinated, however, at every stage. Only by political and military gains can one side or the other obtain the additional popular support which will ultimately snowball into complete victory.

During the first stage of a modern Communist take-over war, the guerrillas live within the body of the civilian population. They have no more than platoon- and company-sized concentrations located in difficult terrain; even these dissolve as necessary. For propaganda purposes, the guerrillas must not be defeated, but they can retreat, disperse and disappear. They can manage to preserve the idea of final victory with a series of the most inconsequential triumphs, but they must not be beaten, and they must retain a dominance in intelligence. It can be as important to make the other side seem impotent and ridiculous as to win a battle. But final success depends upon killing the enemy, taking his weapons, and keeping the initiative.

The essentials of successful guerrilla tactics are speed, surprise and power to accomplish a limited objective quickly. Military intelligence is absolutely necessary, but it is really only common sense. Guerrilla leaders must know more of government forces than those forces know of the guerrillas, but friendly civilians can provide most of this information.

The better handled guerrilla movements in recent years have made physical training, discipline and careful planning and rehearsing the means by which they have won action after action. Their great danger is that their over-confidence will lead them into attempting something too big too soon. The Communist image can be shattered by even small defeats, such as the Bandits suffered in Greece. Once this happens, a complete government victory can be achieved quickly.

If a guerrilla movement is not crushed, it will begin to control some sectors of a country and can soon deny government forces easy access to them. This is their second stage. The organization and tactics of the guerrillas now change; they will still retreat, but ambush their enemies rather than dissolve. They must be able to create diversions, such as other attacks on the government flank and rear, cutting government communications, and taking the offensive in other areas. Guerrillas will always be less well armed and organized, but can be more audaciously led, more numerous and better informed.

The final stage of Communist guerrilla war is after they have gained sufficient strength, organization and heavy weapons to fight a conventional war. Giap and Mao won actual battles of considerable size. Castro appeared about ready to embark on them when Batista fled Cuba. The Greek Communists undertook the third stage when they realized that they were losing the second, in the hope that the heavy support they were receiving from across the border might swing the tide of war to them.

Guerrilla organization is as variable as terrain, but leadership at all levels is of extreme importance. Squads should be no larger than in regular armies and must have at least an adequate commander; platoon-sized units must always be able to function independently. Companies of normal size or under are usually the largest units that can act together continuously in the first and early second stages. Late in the second stage battalions can take shape, but must be broken down quickly without loss of efficiency for operations which require it. In the third stage irregular forces really cease to be guerrillas.

The weapons used by guerrillas will be influenced by the physical and economic condition of the country where they are operating, and by outside aid. Logistic support from across international boundaries is easier today than ever before. But as long as the cold war remains cold, the weapons that come in from outside will be limited. World opinion as well as transport difficulties probably will not allow regular sustained deliveries of complicated munitions, advisors and technicians over a long period.

Throughout the history of partisan warfare, personal weapons and ammo have assumed great importance. The letters of Francis Marion, the Carolina Swamp Fox of the American Revolution, are as emphatic about this as the more recent writings of Che Guevara. Wellington took care to provide his Spanish partisans with good British muskets and powder when this was possible. But in guerrilla operations, local leaders must take primary responsibility for their arms. Guerrillas have always been able to live off the country, but weapons and ammo have been a more difficult problem.

Guerrillas cannot pick and choose their equipment, or only to a limited degree. Most countries suitable for guerrilla conflict are already poor; they will get poorer with the attrition of civil war. Guerrillas must use any military *matériel* which is available. Even today, in the era of air drops and submarine shipments, successful irregulars must collect and maintain every firearm in their areas and capture as many as possible from their enemies.

The twentieth century has emphasized motor transport, but most guerrillas must use it sparingly until after they have entered the third phase of their war and started to operate on conventional lines. Vehicles are hard to obtain and harder to conceal; even worse, they require virtually unobtainable quantities of petrol, oil, tyres and spare parts. Communications equipment has also been difficult to get and maintain. Conceivably, future guerrilla bands may have a few jeeps and transistor radios, but logistics simplicity and concealability have always been their greatest early advantages.

A guerrilla force must provide its members with the minimum essentials of life according to the previous civilian experience of the group. Some dedicated leaders, once accustomed to linen sheets, have slept on bare wet ground for months, but the rank and file must be fairly well maintained. Most modern guerrilla bands live better and have better medical attention and education facilities than they had before they joined the movement.

When people go to war against constituted authority, strange arms will be pressed into service including clubs, spears and home-made firearms. Local artisans throughout the world seem to have the capacity of producing more effective arms than most engineers think possible. The Viet Cong has a nucleus of modern military arms either captured, or brought in from outside, but has augmented them with cannibalized weapons and astonishing village manufacturing. Everything must be used. U.S. ammo for the new M79 GL was stolen or captured in 1964, but no weapons were available. A local artisan fabricated an arm to handle these cartridges from parts of a shotgun, some scrap-iron, and a piece of pipe.

Ideally, weapons should be light. Guerrillas must be able to move long distances on foot and carry everything they need. If an arm complete with ammo interferes with mobility, it may prove a fatal handicap. The support weapons of conventional infantry at battalion and even company level are usually too heavy. Most men will be armed with a personal shoulder weapon or a pistol. The best types will depend upon the terrain in which they are used. In tropical jungles, shotguns are particularly effective. In the bare Greek mountains, rifles capable of precise shooting at long range were important on both sides.

Ammo always presents a serious problem; guerrillas cannot just buy it at hardware stores in any country suitable for irregular warfare. More ammo is always desired than can be obtained. Individual rounds must be rationed, according to Guevara, like water in a desert. Most recruits are not good shots, but target practice must be held to a minimum. The main source for ammo resupply may be the regular forces the guerrillas are fighting. Operations in which the capture of ammo is the main objective are often undertaken.

Pistols have been popular with guerrillas, particularly in Eastern Asia. They are light and do not consume a great weight of cartridges. Their inherent disadvantages are minimized because ranges are short and combat is of a personal nature. Where pistols cannot be obtained, knives and machetes are often used.

Hand-grenades are useful in guerrilla fighting. The conventional type would be best if available, but others can be made from commercial explosives. The dramatic Molotov Cocktails—glass bottles of paraffin and motor oil covered with flaming, petrol-soaked waste—are simple and effective against armoured vehicles and buildings. The Cubans adapted a 16-gauge shotgun to throw these mortarwise to ranges of 100 yards.

If guerrilla movements progress, their leaders can be more selective in regard to the arms for some of their better units. Lightness and ammunition economy, as well as simplicity and ruggedness, are still important, but an LMG has advantages both psychologically and in firepower. They can usually be obtained from the enemy, but should be handled by a team of six to twelve men rather than the normal two assigned to them in regular infantry. When the weight of an LMG and its ammo is divided between a number of men, it can be moved quickly, particularly when the individual guerrillas have little else to carry.

With further growth, heavier weapons can be added; MMGs, RLs, and small mortars are all useful, but the wise commander will not load his band down with arms that impair mobility. Conventional and RR artillery and big mortars could be used, if captured with ammo, but should be abandoned without regret when necessary.

Regardless of how much *matériel* is captured or received from friends across the border, ultimate victory will depend upon keeping the weapons firing. A few men capable of simple repair are vitally needed. Spare parts, if available, are fine, but baling wire and nails can often serve the same purpose. An efficient commander will not sacrifice a single weapon under any circumstances, even though inoperative. At worst, it can be cannibalized with a second defective arm to produce one good one and some extra pieces.

Every successful guerrilla movement in the recent past has recharged at least some of its expended cartridge cases. If bullets, primers and smokeless powder are available, this is easy. These components are not so complicated to produce as they appear; fair substitutes for smokeless powder have been made under primitive conditions.

Regular forces operating against guerrillas have practically unlimited supplies of weapons of all types, but they must avoid employing too many and too heavy weapons. The French operating in Algeria loaded themselves down with arms and armour so that even infantry became road-bound. They spent the hours of darkness behind static defences or in concrete pillboxes. They would fire tons of ammunition wildly in the general direction of their enemies.

On the other hand, the British infantry operating in Malaya was finally successful, in part because of their judicious use of wheeled APCs. The Greeks used 60-mm. mortars effectively even in their toughest mountain terrain. Other and heavier modern support weapons can be employed under favourable circumstances. The USMC is developing helicopter delivery techniques for powerful support weapons including light armoured vehicles. With dynamic, aggressive leadership based on good and timely intelligence and proper planning of operations, heavy weapons should be effective where they can be transported with speed and surprise.

The danger in counter-guerrilla operations is that the regular force will try to substitute weapons for initiative and courage. If soldiers will not meet their opposition man to man, they will lose regardless of their arms. Infantry must always move, fight and communicate. The wise regular CO will take full advantage of his weapons, so long as they do not make him immobile, but he must also guard against the tendency for men to rely on weapons alone. Regular infantry squads are more powerful than any guerrillas because of their superior equipment, training and discipline. ARs, rifles, SMGs and grenades will be more effectively handled by regular soldiers who have been thoroughly trained and have plenty of ammo. They can also use RLs, MMGs, mortars and RRs, if circumstances are right. But weapons are only tools; they must be used properly. Audacity is more important than firepower.

Counter-guerrilla commanders must appreciate the dualism of the war they are fighting; the conflict is also in the minds of the people. Heavy weapons and fortifications which appear to prevent defeat may be politically dangerous; when David and Goliath fight, the crowd is always with David. Guerrillas must be beaten both militarily and politically. The best way for a regular force to do this is to go out and catch the enemy as the Greeks did in their Bandit War. They took the fight to the Communists and won over their civilian population at the same time.

Government forces operating against guerrillas must also realize the importance of not supplying the enemy with arms and ammunition. A single rifle, even a handful of cartridges, means little to regular soldiers, but can do a lot of damage in the hands of a dedicated opponent. The well-meant efforts of the U.S. in several parts of the world have supplied our enemies with a lot of fine equipment. Mao took shiploads of U.S. *matériel* from Chiang Kai-Shek and his Nationalists. The Cuban Communists cleared the anti-Castro air cover from their invasion beach in April 1961 with three U.S. jets originally sold to the Batista government.

The success of recent guerrilla operations has made a deep impression on everyone who thinks about war. For a variety of reasons, some groups behind the Iron Curtain and in the West are discontented. If a 'hot war' came, both sides would encourage insurrections and give direction, training and logistic support to any movement of the guerrilla type so formed. The U.S. Special Forces have been carefully chosen from double volunteers, organized, and trained to work with antagonistic ethnic groups who live under or near Communist domination. Russia probably has similar plans for Italian, Spanish and Greek Communists.

In the event of an all-out, perhaps non-nuclear war, both sides might find themselves aiding guerrilla activities in their opponents' territory and also fighting counter-guerrilla campaigns in their own. Weapons are of extreme importance in all such operations, but they must be used intelligently.

If a hot war does not come, we will probably have years more of intermittent Communist guerrilla activities in various parts of the world. We must supply our friends with arms and equipment to combat enemies within their borders. We should also supply the technical, strategic and tactical assistance to make these weapons effective. Total victory in the field may take a long time to achieve, but if the regular forces of our allies equal the guerrillas in intelligence and audacity and surpass them in firepower based on our weapons and advisors, the rest of the world may be gaining months of relative peace.

XXI

The Future

WHAT lies ahead in infantry weapons and tactics? Never in the history of war has this question been so hard to answer. The major problem is, of course, nuclear war. Missile-delivered nuclear warheads of the largest sizes could so devastate the cities and towns of major belligerents that logistic support for field armies as it has existed so far would be impossible. The armies themselves might sustain so many casualties that they could operate only in relatively small units. Complicated weapons requiring special fuel, ammo and maintenance could disappear.

On the other hand, complete destruction of one or both sides appears to be unlikely now or for several years to come. Even total use of these new weapons probably won't lead to an immediate decision. Both sides would undoubtedly suffer terribly, but neither might be able to wage sophisticated war appreciably better than the other. Even after hydrogen bombs, there could be small-scale infantry fighting over wide areas, perhaps waged with savage intensity.

Another possibility is, of course, limited war in which homelands are not attacked with nuclear weapons. Smaller size warheads might, or might not, be used tactically; the rest of the fighting might resemble WW II. Almost surely, however, the fighting forces engaged would be more spread out by atomic casualties, or by threat of them. Regiments, brigades, divisions and larger units could cease to exist in their WW II concentrations. There could be more man-to-man fighting with battalions, companies and platoons the only operational units. Quick concentration, speedy action, and almost immediate redeployment could be the aims of offensive commanders.

Best of all, the prospect of nuclear war could be such a deterrent in itself that major nations may maintain the present precarious peace for years. But small wars waged in primitive nations appear to be inevitable. Even though one or both fighting forces may receive logistic support from nations with sophisticated weapons capability, arms used may be simple. Combat in Vietnam could be typical; U.S. and Vietnamese combat troops are being transported in helicopters and receiving some support fire from the most modern light weapons, including air-borne 105 mm. pack howitzers. But the actual fighting bears some resemblance to wars fought earlier in the century in banana republics.

Major total war, major limited war, and most backward-country armed conflicts will probably place a premium on infantry-type units. In the immediate future, weapons and tactics at battalion level and below will surely continue to be important. But there will be changes in these, perhaps of unprecedented magnitude. War in the year 2000 is in the province of forecasters using crystal balls, but the next few years will undoubtedly be influenced most by projects and developments presently in various stages of maturity. We can evaluate these in some detail.

The problem of how best to protect infantry against atomic and nuclear casualties is being studied intensively. Major armies will have a fair ability to defend themselves against radioactive fallout and some other harmful features of these weapons. Most of this is classified and extremely tentative, but the officers responsible believe that they are making progress. There are definite plans and training procedures. Protective clothing, dispersion, bunkers and air-conditioned vehicles all have good potentialities.

Strategic and tactical transportation will undoubtedly change even for infantry in the immediate future. British and U.S. bases throughout the world will probably continue to shrink. British combined forces with Royal Marine carrier-based Commandos capable of going into action anywhere on short notice have decreased the need for local garrisons. U.S. Marine battalion landing teams which are in part air-transportable can accomplish similar tasks. The 1958 USMC descent on Lebanon was accomplished in part with Marines from thousands of miles away. The 1961 British landing at Kuwait started with 600 Royal Marine

Commandos being flown ashore from H.M.S. Bulwark and backed up by other air- and sea-transported units from as far away as the United Kingdom. Within a week, 7,000 men were brought in who certainly prevented serious trouble. British action in Brunei began in December 1962 with a similar concentration from distant bases. Early shows of force such as these have prevented the beginning of fighting which might later have developed into real war.

Another tendency towards decreasing the need for dispersed forces is the growing employment of massive air transport. The U.S. has on order 58 transport aircraft capable of handling 500 to 700 battle-equipped soldiers. These planes are not complicated save for their size, and will not need enormous runways. They will be able to carry divisions anywhere on short notice, but not their heavy weapons and support inventories at above battalion level. Logistic support entirely by air for large forces is still impossible.

New small aircraft are appearing throughout the world with astonishing rapidity. Helicopters will undoubtedly improve in speed and load capacity, but cannot rival in the immediate future fixed-wing level-flight planes in ruggedness and efficiency. Compromise designs already show promise for troop transport and combat.

One-man flying machines are in operation. Tactical air support is of extreme future importance, but high-speed jet aircraft have several disadvantages in this connection. We may expect a partial return to propeller-driven planes at speeds common in WW II in the immediate future. They can bomb and strafe more precisely and remain in target areas for longer periods with the same amount of fuel. Their greater use in anti-guerrilla war is probable.

Land transport for rifle squads is presently a reality; all modern armies have APCs available for at least part of their infantry. But there is an unsolved problem in relation to terrain and efficiency. Almost any type of terrain can be mastered by an appropriate vehicle, but no one has yet invented anything that is efficient for transport over all types of combat territory. Wheels, tracks, and perhaps even air cushions, have advantages and disadvantages. Wheeled vehicles are in general most efficient, reliable, easiest to maintain, and fastest. Full tracks are best where roads are scarce, but have many disadvantages. Snow, swamp and water require specialized capabilities not compatible with strength, low cost and ruggedness.

A second problem with regard to tactical transport for infantry is whether soldiers shall have full fighting capability while in their vehicle. The Germans desire this and have an APC in which the entire squad can fire from the vehicle even while moving, but the top must be open. Only actual combat can prove whether infantry fighting inside a 'buttoned-up' APC can be efficient. The odds appear to be against it; fire while in motion will not be accurate, and visibility will be comparatively poor. But in nuclear war it may be necessary. APCs give their crews almost as much radiation protection as heavy tanks, so long as both are properly air-conditioned.

The future of armour (tanks, assault guns and the like) does not vitally concern us, but the amount of infantry-armour co-operation does. The tank, in some form, appears to be necessary for proper support of some infantry operations, but the increasing power of AT weapons of types not readily spotted and destroyed by the tanks themselves means that tanks must be protected by infantry. APC mounted riflemen probably cannot give this protection, but they can as soon as they emerge. Sharp and complete vision are vital in spotting and destroying hostile AT weapons.

The trend towards heavier organic infantry support weapons at low level may continue. RRs and similar devices may be added to rifle squads. New, more effective, and lighter mortars will undoubtedly be evolved and placed as far down as rifle companies. Infantrymen will have a greater missile capacity than ever before. The new U.S. heat-seeking AA rocket—the Redeye —can be launched by a single infantryman and knock out any low-flying enemy aircraft in the immediate vicinity. Various wire-directed AT missiles, such as the British Vigilant, are common at battalion level; they will undoubtedly improve. At present, their greatest handicaps are that they normally have a minimum range of about 350 metres and are limited in regard to maximum range by both visibility and wire-carrying capacity. A similar U.S. device known as the shillelagh can launch a beam-guided missile from a large-bore light howitzer so that it has no minimum range and may be directed by an observer in a helicopter.

If infantry is able to fight efficiently from vehicles, weapons weight ceases to be so important. Cal ·50, 20-mm., and even larger HMGs may become common. This would accelerate the decline of the old MMG (heavy in weight, but of rifle calibre). Mechanical improvements have increased the efficiency of LMGs and ARs; the need for long-range, indirect fire from MMGs seems to have disappeared. Mortars and rockets can do these jobs better, because they are more powerful and require less training to be used efficiently.

New heavy infantry support weapons could be of extreme value if major armies fight each other in normal terrain. If other factors are equal, the army with the greater direct firepower and the greater HE capability will win. If dispersion is required—and it surely will be required—maximum firepower and HE capability must be well down in infantry organizations to be available when needed. Infantry support weapons of even more power and complexity seem to be indicated.

On the other hand, guerrilla fighting which is at present going on in several parts of the world, and will undoubtedly continue in the years ahead, may tend to simplify organic arms at battalion level and below. AT missiles with a range of thousands of yards are obviously useless where the enemy has no tanks and combat conditions are usually such that even if he had them, they could not be seen at a range beyond that of the usual man portable RL. For guerrilla conflict at least, infantry units must remain light. APCs have been used in anti-guerrilla operations, but tanks are normally a handicap. Light mortars and MGs are more useful than RRs.

Night fighting in future will probably be at least as important as that in daylight. The Dutch have evolved a light infra-red system for an infantryman so that he can hit an enemy with his rifle at 150 yards in total darkness. The West Germans and others have tank-mounted white and infra-red searchlights of great power and penetration. U.S. Special Forces do about 75 per cent of their training manoeuvres in darkness.

The personal arms of the individual infantrymen of the future are probably going to be changed radically. A new U.S. weapon known as the SPIW (Special Purpose Infantry Weapon), which has the capabilities of a rifle, a controlled pattern shotgun and a light mortar, has been under development for some time. It is said to resemble an over-and-under shotgun and fires a single medium-sized dart, a cluster of small ones, or an HE bomb. There have been delays in this development and only experimental issue through August 1965. The U.S. discontinued production of M14 rifles and ARs presumably because of the SPIW, but now may adopt something else for the time being at least.

The U.S. Army and Air Force have bought more than 100,000 AR15s (now known as M16) a light, burst-firing assault rifle chambered for the Cal ·223 cartridge. This weapon has some advantages over all military shoulder arms issued at present, particularly in regard to weight and lethal wounds under some conditions. Its principal disadvantages are its power, its length—it cannot be folded—and its lack of AR or LMG capability.

Because of the delay in adopting something radically new, the USMC conducted a long series of tests to evaluate an entire system of small arms built around the Cal ·223 cartridge evolved in 1963 by the brilliant Gene Stoner. His system includes a carbine or SMG, a standard rifle, an AR, an LMG, and an MMG. All are essentially the same; any weapon can be changed into any other by substituting components. This arrangement has great advantages in manufacture, training and supply of spare parts.

The USMC tests, which were competitive in each class, indicate that the Stoner rifle can be fired more accurately with less training than the M14 or M1 on known distance ranges, and much more effectively than either on combat type pop-up targets. The Stoner AR (BREN magazine configuration) and LMG (belt-fed) outshot the M14 Modified by a wide margin and were substantially ahead of the BAR and the M60 with bipod only. These new weapons were not only better in all tests, but saved approximately 50 per cent in weight.

The big question in the minds of Marine experts is the future of the Stoner tripod-mounted MMG which fires, of course, the same Cal ·223 ammo. This cartridge has about the power of the new Russian intermediate round, but the Russians found they still needed a full rifle power MMG. Some USMC thinking, only partially confirmed at present by actual field tests, indicates that direct-fire fighting by infantry will extend no further than a belt about 500 yards wide in front of the approximate firing line. Diagonal fire from MMGs would need, however, to reach effectively the back of this area at normal enfilade angles, say a maximum range of 1,100 metres. The Cal ·223 bullets will not penetrate a steel helmet at this range, but will still go through any modern body armour. NATO round bullets from M60s will not penetrate the helmet either, but they do have more energy remaining.

Grazing fire from Stoner MMGs will certainly be efficient for most requirements out to 800 yards and perhaps beyond. These weapons are more accurate and stable, and have the priceless advantage that there are two rounds rather than one for the same weight. At greater ranges, MMGs of any type are probably less effective than mortars and other support weapons organic to USMC rifle battalions. But we should not ignore the Russian experience; an efficient heavy Cal ·30 MMG may still be needed.

Another small-arms development already well started is in connection with close-range multiple projectile discharges of particular importance to armies operating against guerrillas. A maximum of close-in firepower is sometimes required quickly. Two bullets from each rifle cartridge are already being provided for special use, but each has only about half the power of a normal bullet.

We of the Free World should not be led to believe that new small arms are our exclusive future privilege. The shotgun type ammo principle used in the SPIW and the M79 GL is undoubtedly being developed by our potential enemies also. They are known to have rebarrelled some of their new intermediate power family of small arms to take the same cartridge necked down for Cal ·22 (5·56-mm.) bullets. These weapons may not yet be standard issue, but have appeared on the black market in West Berlin.

In any survey of the future, one must consider the unpleasant possibility of poison gas and harmful bacteria. The gases of WW I were uncertain and often did damage to those who set them free. Improvements have undoubtedly been made and new substances added. There is supposed to be a liquid which will temporarily reduce a strong man to a gibbering idiot, and a nerve gas which induces paralysis. Germs are even worse. There is no way to guard against all these at the same time and fight too. Modern armies have gas masks, but keep them mostly in storage. The effective types do not last long after issue. Some training is given in gas and germ defence along with that in connection with radiation, but total protection even from the presently known chemical agents is not possible. Protective clothing and other equipment necessary to defend individuals against them, even if available, would greatly reduce combat efficiency and morale. The future here is confused; perhaps if the world must fight at all, public opinion and fear of retaliation will prevent the introduction of these weapons into war at all levels.

What will happen to the infantry soldier and small rifle units because of all these changes? Can equipment and *matériel* replace men? For thousands of years, men have dominated war. Wars have always been won by men with weapons in their hands. The nations which have survived in the past have done so because of the courage, skill and weapons efficiency of their fighting men. If modern science is unleashed in all its frightfulness in a future war, the odds still seem to favour the nations which have better fighters individually and in small units. Weapons have changed over the centuries, but the basic principles of firepower and shock have not. Leadership, organization, discipline and the ability to fight, move and communicate will remain paramount. Common sense at all levels and among civilians is also necessary.

Country	MMG	ARs	Rifles	SMGs	Pistols	Ammo required
Belgium	FN GPMG¹ & Brownings	FN (FALO) BAR	FN (NATO)	Vigneron	1935 FN Browning	7·62 NATO, 30-'06, 9-mm. Parabellum
Britain	Vickers, FN GPMG (Tripod)	BREN, FN GPMG (Bipod)	FN (Old) SLR (FN)	L2A3 (Sterling)	1935 FN Browning	7·62 NATO, ·303 British, 9-mm. Parabellum
Canada	M1919A4	C2 (FN-FALO)	C1 (FN)	L2A3 (Sterling)	1935 FN Browning	7·62 NATO, ·30-'06, 9-mm. Parabellum
Denmark	MG42/59 (Tripod)	Madsen	M1	Hovea (M49)	SIG (Neuhausen)	·30-'06, 7·62 NATO, 9-mm. Parabellum
France²	SIG (Neuhausen) M1952 (Tripod)	MG42/59 (Bipod) M1952 (Bipod)	M1949/56	MAT1949	M1950	7·5 French, 7·62 NATO, 9-mm. Parabellum
Germany	MG42/59 (Tripod)	MG42/59 (Bipod)	G3 (CETME)	Uzi	P38	7·62 NATO, 9-mm. Parabellum
Greece³	M1919A4	BAR	M1	Thompson (M1) Beretta	Several Beretta	·30-'06, ·45 ACP
Italy	Breda	BAR	M1	Beretta	Beretta	·30-'06, 7·92 mm, 9-mm. Parabellum
Netherlands	BREN (Tripod) FN GPMG (Tripod)	BREN, Normal MG42/59 (Bipod)	M1, G3	Sten, Uzi	1935 FN Browning	·30-'06, 7·62 NATO, ·303 British, 9-mm. Parabellum
Norway	M1917, M1919A4	BAR	M1	MP40 (Schmeisser)	Luger (M1908)	·30-'06, 9-mm. Parabellum
Portugal	Breda	Dreyse M38 MG34 (Borsig)	M98/37 and others	FBP, Uzi	Luger (M1908)	7·92 Mauser, 9-mm. Parabellum
Russia	DP, DPM	RPD (Degtyrev)	AK (Kalashikov)	APS (Stechkia)⁴	PM (Maharov)	7·62 Russian, 7·62 Intermediate (M1943), 9-mm. short pistol
Spain	Alpha	FAO	CETME, M98/37	Parinco III Star Z 45	Several	·30-'06, 9-mm. Parabellum
Turkey	M1919A6	Hotchkiss	Bolt Mauser	Thompson, Sten	Copy of Walther PP	7·92 Mauser, ·30-'06, ·45 ACP, 9-mm. Parabellum, ·380 ACP
U.S.	M60	M14 Modified	M14, M1, M16	M3, M2 Carbine	M1911A1	7·62 NATO, ·30-'06, Cal ·30 Carbine, ·45 ACP, Cal ·223
USMC⁵	M60	M14 Modified	M14	M3 (Special issue only)	M1911A1	7·62 NATO, ·45 ACP

¹ The FN GPMG is known as the M.A.G. (Mitrailleuse à Gaz) on the Continent.
² The French armies in various places have dozens of additional small arms in use or in reserve, chambering for at least ten more ammos.
³ The Greek army has also the entire WW II family of British small arms.
⁴ The WW II PPS SMG firing the 7·62 Russian pistol cartridge is also sometimes still in use.
⁵ The USMC appears to be adopting a Cal ·223 family of small arms.

TABLE II. Details of MMGs

Country	Weapon	Weight[1] in pounds	Cyclic[2] rate r.p.m.	Type of Action	Cooling	Type of Belts[3]	Ammo
Belgium	GPMG (FN)	46	700 or 1,000	Gas	Air	Disintegrating links	7·62 NATO
Britain	Browning	45 (?)	400–600	Recoil	Air	Fabric	·30–'06
	GPMG (FN)	46	700 or 1,000	Gas	Air	Disintegrating links	7·62 NATO
	Vickers	95	500	Recoil[4]	Water	Fabric	·303 British
Canada	M1919A4 (U.S.)	45·0	500	Recoil	Air	Fabric	·30–'06
Denmark	MG42/59	50 (?)	1,200	Recoil	Air	Metal	7·62 NATO
France	M1952 (Tripod)	45 (?)	700	Delayed Blow-back	Air	Metal	7·5 French, 7·62 NATO
Germany	MG42/59	50 (?)	1,200	Recoil	Air	Metal	7·62 NATO
Greece	M1919A4 (U.S.)	45	500	Recoil	Air	Fabric	·30–'06
Italy	Breda	about 75	500	Gas	Air	Fabric	7·92 mm.
Netherlands	GPMG (Tripod)	46	700 or 1,000	Gas	Air	Disintegrating links	7·62 NATO
	BREN (Tripod)	40	500	Gas	Air	Box magazine	·303 British
Norway	M1919A4 (U.S.)	45	500	Recoil	Air	Fabric	·30–'06
	M1917 (U.S.)	86	400	Recoil	Water	Fabric	·30–'06
Portugal	Breda	about 75	500	Gas	Air	Fabric	7·92 mm.
Russia[5]	DP, DPM, RP46	27–30	600	Gas	Air	Pan magazine and metal	7·62-mm. rimmed[5]
	DS (Model 1939)	72	550 (low 1,100 (high)	Gas	Air	Fabric	7·62-mm. rimmed[5]
Spain	Alfa M44	88	780	Gas	Air	Metal	7·92 mm.
	Alfa M55	88	780	Gas	Air	Metal	7·62 NATO
Turkey	M1919A6 (U.S.)	32·5	600	Recoil	Air	Fabric	·30–'06
U.S. Army	M60	36·4	550	Gas	Air	Disintegrating links	7·62 NATO
USMC	M60	36·4	550	Gas	Air	Disintegrating links	7·62 NATO

[1] Includes normal mount; many MMGs listed can be used with more than one mount, and some have other variables. No ammo or ammo box included.

[2] Cyclic rate varies from specimen to specimen; those given are approximate only. The U.S. Browning series is particularly subject to intentional and unintentional variations; the M1919 can be made to fire extremely slowly, if desired.

[3] All weapons in this class are belt fed, save the BREN used in the Netherlands army and the Russian DP and DPMs.

[4] Assisted by gases at muzzle.

[5] The Russian army has three LMGs in each rifle company and six MMGs in each rifle battalion firing the full power 7·62-mm. Russian rimmed cartridge, not the 7·62-mm. Intermediate.

TABLE III. *Details of ARs*[1]

Country	Name of AR	Weight loaded in pounds	Cyclic Rate r.p.m.	Length in inches	Type of Action	Magazine or Feed	Ammo
Belgium	FN (FALO)	13·4	700	41·5	Gas	20-round box below	7·62 NATO
	BAR (Belgian)	21·0	550	45·1	Gas	20-round box below	·30-·06
Britain	GPMG (Bipod)	24·0	700 or 1,000	49·2	Gas	50-round belt	7·62 NATO
Canada	C2 (FALO)	14·5	600	41·5	Gas	30-round box below	7·62 NATO
Denmark	Madsen	23·1	450	45·0	Recoil	30-round box on top	·30-·06
	MG42/59	25·0 (No ammo)	1,200	48·0	Recoil	Belt of 50	7·62 NATO
France[2]	M1952	Varies	700	46·0	Delayed Blow-back	Belt of 50	7·62 NATO, 7·5 French
		18–23 (No ammo)					
Germany	MG42/59	25·0 (No ammo)	1,200	48·0	Recoil	Belt of 50	7·62 NATO
Greece	BAR (U.S.)	21·5	340 or 600	47·0	Gas	20-round box below	·30-·06
Italy	BAR (U.S.)	21·5	340 or 600	47·0	Gas	20-round box below	·30-·06
Netherlands	BREN	25·0	500	45·6	Gas	30-round box	·303 British
	GPMG (Bipod)	24·0	700 or 1,000	49·2	Gas	50-round belt	7·62 NATO
Norway	BAR (U.S.)	21·5	340 or 600	47·0	Gas	20-round box on top	·30-·06
Portugal[3]	Dreyse	24·0	750	47·0	Recoil	Boxes from side or drums	7·92 Mauser
	MG34 (Borsig)	26·5 (No ammo)	850	48·0	Recoil	Box from side or drums	7·92 Mauser
Russia	RPD (Degtyrdev)	19·4	650	40·8	Gas	100-round belt[5]	7·62 Intermediate
Spain[4]	FAO	23·6	600	45·5	Gas	20-round box on top	7·62 NATO, 7·92 Mauser
Turkey	Hotchkiss or Brno	26–28	500–600	about 47	Gas	Boxes below and on top	7·92 Mauser
U.S.	M14 Modified[6]	44·6	750	10·5	Gas	20-round box below	7·62 NATO
USMC	M14 Modified	44·6	750	10·5	Gas	20-round box below	7·62 NATO

[1] Barrel lengths and flash hiders vary, so lengths given above are overall and weights are not constant. Cyclic rates vary somewhat from gun to gun of the same model.

[2] France has only a few ARs of type shown above in active service; the rest are of at least six different types.

[3] Portugal also uses Madsen ARs.

[4] In Spain, all CETMEs have bipods and are about as effective in bursts as the FN FALO.

[5] There are other feed arrangements, including 250-round drums and provision for using the AK 30-round magazines.

[6] The U.S. Army is replacing their standard M14 Modified by basically the same weapon with a new stock; the new type weighs about 1·25 lb. more.

TABLE IV. *Details of Rifles*

Country	Weapon	Weight loaded in pounds	Cyclic Rate[1]	Length in inches: no bayonet	Type of Action	Magazine Capacity
Belgium	FN (NATO)	10·4	650 r.p.m.[2]	41·4	Gas	20
Britain	FN (Old)	10·0	Single shots only	43·7	Gas	10
	SLR (FN)	10·4	Single shots only	41·4	Gas	20
Canda	C1 (FN)	10·4	Single shots only	41·4	Gas	20
Denmark	M1	10·5	Single shots only	43·0	Gas	8
France	M1949/56	10·0	Single shots only	43·4	Gas	10
Germany	G3 (CETME)	12·5	550 r.p.m.	38·1	Delayed Blow-back	20
Greece	M1	10·5	Single shots only	43·0	Gas	8
Italy	M1	10·5	Single shots only	43·0	Gas	8
Netherlands	M1	10·5	Single shots only	43·0	Gas	8
	FN	10·4	Single shots only	41·4	Gas	20
Norway	M1	10·5	Single shots only	43·0	Gas	8
Portugal	M98/37 Mauser and others	9·3	Single shots only	43·	Bolt	5
Russia	AK	11·7	600 r.p.m.	34·3	Gas	30
Spain	CETME	12·5	550 r.p.m.	38·1	Delayed Blow-back	20 or 32
Turkey	M98/37 Mauser	9·3	Single shots only	43·5	Bolt	5
U.S.	Bolt Mauser	9·7	Single shots only	about 46	Bolt	5
	U.S. M14	9·2	Single shots only	44·1	Gas	20
	U.S. M16 (AR-15)	6·8	750 r.p.m.	37·5	Gas	20
USMC	U.S. M14	9·2	Single shots only	44·1	Gas	20

[1] Where a cyclic rate is shown, the rifles can fire either single shots or bursts.
[2] Nine of the 35 standard FN rifles in each rifle platoon have a selector switch which allows burst fire; the other 26 can fire single shots only.

TABLE V. Details of SMGs

Country	Name of SMG	Weight loaded in pounds	Cyclic Rate r.p.m.	Minimum Length in inches	Ammo[1]	No. of Rounds in Magazine	Finish
Belgium	Vigneron	8·74	600	24	9 mm.	32	Medium
Britain	L2A3	7·80	550	19	9 mm.	34	Good
Canada	L2A3	7·80	550	19	9 mm.	34	Good
Denmark	Hovea (M49)	9·25	550	20·8	9 mm.	36	Medium
France	MAT 1949	9·41	600	18·3	9 mm.	32	Medium
Germany	Uzi	8·9	650	25·2 or 17·9	9 mm.	25	Good
Greece	U.S. M1 Thompson	11·0	650	31·0	·45 ACP	20 or 30	Good
Italy	Beretta	9·0	600	37·0	9 mm.	40	Medium
Netherlands	Sten	9·3	525	35	9 mm.	32	Poor
	Uzi	8·9	650	25·2 or 17·9	9 mm.	25	Good
Norway	MP 40 (Schmeisser)	10·6	475	25	9 mm.	32	Medium
Portugal	FBP M48[2]	8·9	500	22	9 mm.	32	Medium
	Uzi	8·9	650	25·2 or 17·9	9 mm.	25	Good
Russia	PPS[3]	8·0	650	24·3	7·62 Russian	25	Fair
	APS	4·0	750	12·3	9 mm. Short	20	Good
Spain	Parinco III	7·2	600	25	9 mm.	32	Good
	Star Z45	9·95	515	23	9 mm.	30	Medium
Turkey	U.S. M1	11·0	650	31·0	·45 ACP	20	Good
	Sten	9·3	525	35	9 mm.	30	Poor
U.S. &	M3	9·9	450	22	·45 ACP	30	Poor
USMC[5]	M2 Carbine	5·5+	700	36	·30 Carbine	15[4]	Good

[1] The '9-mm.' ammo is all 9-mm. Parabellum unless otherwise noted.

[2] These weapons normally issued with bayonets.

[3] This and other SMGs firing this cartridge are supposed to have been abandoned in Russia, but appear still to be in use. The AK is sometimes also considered to be an SMG.

[4] Or more, depending upon model of magazine.

[5] The USMC does not normally use the M1 and M2 Carbine; the SMGs (the M3 mainly) are special issue.

TABLE VI. *Rifle Company Organization*

Country	Personnel in Co. HQ	Personnel in H.W. Platoon[1]	No. of Rifle Platoons	Personnel in each Rifle Platoon	Total Personnel in Rifle Platoons	Total Personnel in Company
Belgium	36	Nil	3	44	132	168
Britain	12	24	3	32	96	132
Canada	25	24	3	35	105	154
Denmark	23	13	3	29	87	123
France	CLASSIFIED AND VARIABLE		3	40	120	VARIABLE[2]
Germany	16	Nil	4	32	128	144[2]
Greece	10	36	3	36	108	154
Italy	13	24	3	29	87	124
Netherlands	22	27	3	41	123	172
Norway	24	40	3	41	123	187
Portugal	25	58	3	34	102	185
Russia	5	10	3	30	90	105
Spain	36	31	4	45	180	247
Turkey	10	41	3	46	138	189
U.S. Army	12	36	3	44	132	180
USMC	9	53	3	47	141	203

[1] In some armies, Company HQ will include a section responsible for handling crew-served arms; in other cases, they will be in a separate platoon. Occasionally, heavy weapons will be in Company HQ and in a separate platoon also.
[2] There appears to be a difference between Panzer Grenadier and standard infantry; this is for the former.

TABLE VII. *Rifle Company Individual Weapons*

Country	Total Personnel	ARs[1]	Rifles	SMGs[1]	Pistols	Total[2] Weapons
Belgium	168	18	93	42	15	168
Britain	132	9	122	Nil	1	132
Canada	154	12	118	18	5	153
Denmark	123	9	72	37	5	123
France			CLASSIFIED and VARIABLE			

Table VII. (contd.)

Country	Total Personnel	ARs	Rifles	SMGs[1]	Pistols	Total[2] Weapons
Germany	144	18	109	13	22	162
Greece	154	9	126	10	9	154
Italy	124	12	25	78	9	124
Netherlands	172	9[3]	98	58	16	181
Norway	187	9	109	45	24	187
Portugal	185	9	105	45	35	194
Russia	105	10	81[4]	Nil	14	105
Spain	247	14	148	57	42	261
Turkey	189	18	129	Nil	36	183
U.S. Army	180	18	104	Nil	58	180
USMC	203	27	150	Nil	26	203

[1] SMGs can often be issued in place of rifles to squad leaders and special patrols.

[2] Total Weapons is often not the same as Total Personnel, usually because AR gunners also have pistols. In Canadian rifle companies, the medical orderly is unarmed; in Turkey the MMG gunners have only their primary weapons.

[3] This does not include the three extra GPMGs in each rifle platoon or the six extra carried in company HQ vehicles.

[4] These are AK assault rifles with burst fire capability.

Table VIII. Rifle Company Support Weapons

Country	In H.W. Platoon	In Rifle Platoons	In Company Headquarters
Belgium	Nil	3—60-mm. Mortars 6—Cal ·30 MGs 3—81-mm. RLs	2—81-mm. Mortars 1 Cal ·50 HMG
Britain	2—84-mm. RRs 2—81-mm. Mortars 2—MMGs	3—84-mm. RRs 3—2-in. Mortars 3—3·5-in. RLs	None Permanently Assigned
Canada	2—81-mm. Mortars 2—106-mm. RRs		Several AA MGs on vehicles
Denmark	3—60-mm. Mortars 2—3·5-in. RLs 5—ARs with tripods	3—3·5-in. RLs	2—Cal ·50 HMGs
France	CLASSIFIED		
Germany	Nil	Several RLs and MGs About 16 AT weapons, one in each APC	Variable More Panzerfausts in each vehicle, also tripods and extra MG42/59s

TABLE VIII (*contd.*)

Country	In H.W. Platoon	In Rifle Platoons	In Company Headquarters
Greece	3—MMGs 3—60-mm. Mortars	Nil	Nil
Italy	2—MMGs 2—57-mm. RRs 2—60-mm. Mortars	3—3·5-in. RLs	Nil
Netherlands	3—81-mm. Mortars 2—Light AT weapons	6—84-mm. RRs	1—Cal ·50 HMG 6—Extra GPMGs Several light AT weapons
Norway	3—57-mm. RRs 3—60-mm. Mortars 1—3·5-in. RL	3—MMGs 3—3·5-in. RLs	1—Cal ·50 HMG 1—3·5-in. RL
Portugal	3—60-mm. Mortars 3—MMGs (MG34s w/tripods)	3—3·5-in. RLs	2—Cal ·50 HMGs 2—3·5-in. RLs Sometimes AT and AA weapons
Russia	3—MMGs 1—AT weapon	9—AT weapons	No standards set
Spain	3—81-mm. Mortars 2—106-mm. RRs 2—3·5-in. RLs	8—MMGs 8—3·5-in. RLs	
Turkey	3—81-mm. Mortars 3—57-mm. RRs	6—MMGs 3—3·5-in. RLs	4—3·5-in. RLs
U.S. Army	3—81-mm. Mortars 2—106-mm. RRs	6—MMGs 6—90-mm. RRs	2—3·5-in. RLs Several Cal ·50 HMGs
USMC	1—3·5-in. RL 6—MMGs 6—3·5-in. RLs	Nil	Nil

NOTE: ARs, GLs, and personal weapons are not included. Company HQ weapons are subject to some variation in many services. Some have extra ARs and kits to transform them into MMGs.

Tables

TABLE IX. Rifle Platoon Organization

Country	Personnel in Pl. HQ[1]	Personnel in H.W. Squad	No. of Rifle Squads	Personnel in each Rifle Squad	Total Personnel in Rifle Squads	Total Personnel in Rifle Platoon
Belgium	11	Nil	3	11	33	44
Britain	8	Nil	3	8	24	32
Canada	5	Nil	3	10	30	35
Denmark	5	Nil	3	8	24	29
France[2]	10	Nil	3	10	30	40
Germany[3]	8	Nil	3	8	24	32
Greece	6	Nil	3	10	30	36
Italy	8	Nil	3	7	21	29
Netherlands	5	9	3	9	27	41
Norway	5	9	3	9	27	41
Portugal	7	Nil	3	9	27	34
Russia	3	Nil	3	9	27	30
Spain	3	9	3	11	33	45
Turkey	2	11	3	11	33	46
U.S.	3	11	3	10	30	44
USMC	5	Nil	3	14	42	47

[1] Sometimes Platoon HG personnel handle heavy weapons where there is no separate H.W. squad.

[2] French organization variable; this one is sometimes encountered.

[3] This appears to be the new Panzer Grenadier organization; an older infantry organization of four 8-man squads plus an 8-man Company HQ also existed until recently.

TABLE X. *Rifle Platoon Weapons*

Country	Total Personnel	ARs	Rifles	SMGs	Pistols	Heavy Weapons[1]	Total Weapons[2]
Belgium	44	6	26	7	5	2 MMGs 1 83-mm. RL	48[2]
Britain	32	3	29	Nil[3]	Nil	1 60-mm. Mortar 1 84-mm. RR 1 2-in. Mortar	34
Canada	35	3	30	1	1	1 3·5-in. RL	36
Denmark	29	3	18	7	1	1 3·5-in. RL	30
France[4]	40	3	18	18	4	4 RLs 3 MMGs 1 Cal ·50 HMG	51
Germany	32	4	26	2	4	4 AT Weapons[5]	40
Greece	36	3	29	3	1	Nil	36
Italy	29	4	8	16	1	1 3·5-in. RL	30
Netherlands	41	3[6]	29	8	4	2 84-mm. RRs	46
Norway	41	3	27	6	5	1 3·5-in. RL 1 MMG	43
Portugal	34	3	21	8	5	1 3·5-in. RL	38
Russia	30	3	26[7]	1	3	3 AT Weapons[8]	33
Spain	45	3	34	8	3	2 3·5-in. RLs 2 MMGs	52
Turkey	46	6	32	Nil	6	1 3·5-in. RL 2 MMGs	47
U.S.	44	6	28	Nil	10	2 90-mm. RRs 2 Cal ·30 MMGs 6 GLs[9]	54
USMC	47	9	33	Nil	5	3 GLs[8]	50

1 Sometimes these are carried in APCs but not taken on foot.
2 Does not include the four MMGs from the platoon APCs.
3 SMGs can be issued for special duty.
4 French organization is not standardized; this is one possible combination. The heavy weapons include those mounted in their APCs and not really foot mobile.
5 These are German Panzerfausts with the warhead larger than the bore; they are about equivalent to the 3·5-in. RLs used throughout the rest of NATO.
6 There are three more GPMGs in the APCs which can be dismounted and employed for ground use as necessary.
7 These are AK assault rifles with burst fire capability.
8 These are organic to rifle squads, one to each.
9 These GLs are organic to rifle squads, two to each.

TABLE XI. *Rifle Squad or Section*

Country	Number of Personnel	Weapons
Belgium	11	One MMG,[1] two ARs (FALO), eight rifles (one with scope and three capable of bursts), and one SMG.
Britain	8	One GPMG, six or seven SLRs, tentatively one 84-mm. RR.
Canada	10	One AR, nine SLRs.
Denmark	8	One AR (Madsen or MG42/59), five M1 rifles, and two SMGs.
France	10	One AR, nine rifles and SMGs combined,[2] one AT weapon.[1]
Germany	8	One MG42/59, seven G3 rifles, one AT weapon.[1]
Greece	10	One or two BARs, seven or eight M1 rifles, one SMG.
Italy	7	One BAR, two M1 rifles, four SMGs.
Netherlands	9	One AR either an FN GPMG or a BREN, eight rifles either FNs or M1, or seven rifles and one SMG.
Norway	9	One BAR, eight rifles.
Portugal	9	One AR, eight rifles.
Russia	9	One AR (RPD), seven AKs, one AT weapon, one pistol.
Spain	11	Eleven CETMEs or one AR and ten rifles (CETMEs or bolt Mausers).
Turkey	11	Two ARs, nine rifles.
U.S. Army	10	Two ARs, six rifles, two GLs, two pistols.
USMC	14	Three ARs, ten rifles, one GL, one pistol.

[1] These are carried in the APC and assigned to dismounted personnel as required.
[2] The proportion of rifles to SMGs is variable.

General Note: Several armies have extra SMGs for issue instead of rifles to squad leaders and others.

TABLE XII. Modern Military Cartridge Data

Name of Cartridge	Bullet Weight in grains	Muzzle Velocity in feet per second	Muzzle Energy in foot pounds	Remarks
7·62 NATO	150	2,800	2,150	Full Rifle Power
·30-·06	150	2,800	2,150	Full Rifle Power
·303 British	180	2,540	2,580	Full Rifle Power
7·92 Mauser	198	2,625	3,030	Full Rifle Power
7·62 Rimmed Russian	165	2,750	2,700	Full Rifle Power
7·5 French	139	2,700	2,250	Full Rifle Power
7·62 Intermediate Russian	122	2,400	1,550	Intermediate Rifle Power
Cal ·223	55	3,300	1,328	Intermediate Rifle Power
9-mm. Parabellum	115	1,140	332	Pistols and SMGs
·45 ACP	230	830	340	Pistols and SMGs
7·62 Russian Pistol	87	1,400	375	For obsolescent Bloc SMGs and pistols
9-mm. Short Russian	94	1,100	225	New Russian low power for pistols and SMG
Cal ·30 Carbine	110	1,970	948	For low power U.S. Carbines
·380 ACP	95	950	190	For pistols

NOTE: Ballistic details can vary widely even in the same country; those shown are normal.

Bibliography

THE usual list of a few dozen books referring to specific aspects of a general subject cannot be furnished in this case. There are several problems. First, hundreds of books have been written in English alone about military history. So much has been produced in regard to even relatively small, controversial points. To mention two specific instances, more than a dozen secondary authors have dealt learnedly with Roman legions and at least twenty have written of the Battle of Hastings.

Original records are not usually valuable in this study until fairly recent times; considerable reliance must be placed on the surveys by past historians, but it is difficult to include some and reject others, particularly when so many works contain varying amounts of the same basic material. With all this in mind, I have made up a short list of books (Part I below) dealing with the period ending about 1920. It is obviously incomplete, but the books shown are accurate, valuable and mostly available in the larger libraries.

A bibliography for the period from 1920 to date is even more complicated. A vast literature in connection with WW II, Korea and guerrilla war has sprung up; official and unofficial history is being written at a rate never approached before. But all these new books, and all those previously written about war since 1920, tell only a part of the story. Actual visits to the armies of the Free World have been collectively the most valuable single source of my information. Second in importance are the many military handbooks both current and from the recent past. These are not available, save for small selections in military libraries; a title can create confusion because some pages have been changed a dozen times before the entire manual was replaced by a new one which sometimes had the same name.

A third source of information has been U.S. Department of Defence unclassified intelligence information; I have relied heavily on Russian and Red Chinese reports. Similar long pamphlets were useful for Germany and Italy during WW II. But these have not, for the most part, ever gone on public sale and are rare outside

U.S. service libraries. The technical reports of the Historical Section of the U.S. Army in Germany following WW II, and written by German officers about their personal experiences of a professional nature in WW II, are also valuable, but hard to get. Not many copies were printed; they were classified until recently and were never offered to the public.

A fourth source for what is happening in armies today is the mass of official and semi-official military journals. I have listed a group which appear in English in Part II. No effort has been made to refer to individual articles, however, because of their transient nature and the narrow circulation of some of the periodicals.

Currently available books, as a group, ranks fifth in importance in my source material. I have relied more heavily on the other sources because of my preoccupation with small units. Not many books are produced which deal with low-level military matters. We are fortunate, however, in having the three most brilliant modern military historians writing in English still active. Captain B. H. Liddell Hart, Major General J. F. C. Fuller, and Brigadier General S. L. A. Marshall have written so much that is significant, and all are still producing. I have referred to only two or three titles for each, but the careful soldier cannot do better than to know all three thoroughly through serious reading of their works which apply to his field. I have added a few additional titles to the books by these three giants in Part III. I realize as I look at my own modest shelves of books on military history, weapons and tactics how many more titles I could justifiably add. I have listed, however, those to which I have referred most often and do not believe any useful purpose would be served by extending the list.

PART I:

BOOKS FOR THE PERIOD UP TO ABOUT 1920

Earle, Edward Mead and associates, MAKERS OF MODERN STRATEGY, Princeton, New Jersey, 1943.

Fortescue, John W., HISTORY OF THE BRITISH ARMY, 20 vols., London, 1899–1930.

Fuller, J. F. C., DECISIVE BATTLES OF THE WESTERN WORLD, 3 vols., London, 1957; ARMAMENT AND HISTORY, New York, 1945; and several other works in whole or in part about this era.

Hart, B. H. Liddell, STRATEGY: THE INDIRECT APPROACH, London and New York, 1954; A GREATER THAN NAPOLEON: SCIPIO AFRICANUS; and several other works.

Nickerson, Hoffman and associates, WARFARE, New York, 1925.

Oman, C. W. C., A HISTORY OF THE ART OF WAR IN THE MIDDLE AGES, London, 1898: 2 vols., New York, 1924; A HISTORY OF THE PENINSULAR WAR, Oxford, 1903–30; and several other works.

Palmer, R. R., ATLAS OF WORLD HISTORY, New York, 1957.

Yadin, Yigdel, THE ART OF WARFARE IN BIBLICAL LANDS, London, 1963.

PART II:
VALUABLE CURRENT MILITARY PERIODICALS

Armor	Washington, D.C.
Army	Washington, D.C.
Army Quarterly and Defence Journal, The . . .	London, N.W.1
Au Cosantoir	Dublin, Ireland
Globe and Laurel (Royal Marines)	Portsmouth
Infantry	Fort Benning, Georgia
Marine Corps Gazette . .	Quantico, Virginia
Military Engineer . . .	Washington, D.C.
Military Review . . .	Fort Leavenworth, Kansas
Ordnance	Washington, D.C.
Royal Engineers Journal . .	Chatham, Kent
Royal United Service Institution Journal	London, S.W.1

PART III:
BOOKS FOR THE PERIOD AFTER 1920

Cross, James Eliot, CONFLICT IN THE SHADOWS, New York, 1963: London, 1964. This short book is authoritative in itself and lists the best of other recently produced guerrilla war literature.

Eisenhower, Dwight D., CRUSADE IN EUROPE, New York, 1948.

Fuller, J. F. C., THE SECOND WORLD WAR, London, 1948; ARMOURED WARFARE, and many other works.

Greenfield, Kent Robert, R. R. Palmer, B. I. Wiley, THE ORGANIZATION OF GROUND COMBAT TROOPS, Washington, 1947. This is one of a series of many volumes about the U.S. Army in WW II produced by the Historical Division Department of the Army which continue to appear.

Hart, B. H. Liddell, THE ROMMEL PAPERS (Edited), London and New York 1953; THE GERMAN GENERALS TALK, New York, 1948; THE SOVIET ARMY, London, 1957; and many other books.

Iseley, Jeter A., and Philip A. Crowl, THE U.S. MARINES AND AMPHIBIOUS WAR, Princeton, New Jersey, 1951.

Joslen, H. F., ORDERS OF BATTLE SECOND WORLD WAR, 2 vols., London, 1960. This is one of many volumes in a series prepared for the Historical Section of the Cabinet Office which is not yet complete.

Manstein, Erich von, LOST VICTORIES, Chicago, 1958.

Marshall, S. L. A., BATTLE AT BEST, New York, 1963; MEN AGAINST FIRE; and many other studies.

Montgomery of Alamein, Viscount, MEMOIRS, London, 1958.

Montross, Lynn, and Nicholas A. Carzond, U.S. MARINE OPERATIONS IN KOREA, 4 vols., Washington, 1954-8 This is one of several Historical Branch, G3, HQ, U.S.M.C.

Patton, George S., Jr, WAR AS I KNEW IT, New York, 1947.

Smith, W. H. B., SMALL ARMS OF THE WORLD, Harrisburg, Pennsylvania, 1960 and 1964 editions.

Index

Index